Nigel Mansell was born in the Midlands in 1953 and broke into Formula One in 1980. Twice the BBC Sports Personality of the Year, he became world champion in 1992 and retired from the sport in 1995, having won a then British record of 31 grands prix. He lives with his wife Rosanne in Jersey, and they have three children.

STAYING ON TRACK
THE AUTOBIOGRAPHY

Nigel Mansell

**SIMON &
SCHUSTER**

London · New York · Sydney · Toronto · New Delhi

A CBS COMPANY

First published in Great Britain by Simon & Schuster UK Ltd, 2015
This paperback edition published by Simon & Schuster UK Ltd, 2016
A CBS COMPANY

3 5 7 9 10 8 6 4 2

Simon & Schuster UK Ltd
1st Floor
222 Gray's Inn Road
London WC1X 8HB

www.simonandschuster.co.uk

Simon & Schuster Australia, Sydney
Simon & Schuster India, New Delhi

The author and publishers have made all reasonable
efforts to contact copyright-holders for permission, and apologise
for any omissions or errors in the form of credits given.
Corrections may be made to future printings.

A CIP catalogue record for this book
is available from the British Library.

Paperback ISBN: 978-1-4711-5024-1
Ebook ISBN: 978-1-4711-5182-8

Typeset in Garamond by M Rules
Printed and bound by CPI Group (UK) Ltd, Croydon, CR0 4YY

I would like to dedicate this book to the team owners and sponsors who gave me the opportunity to live a dream, which modelled me into the person I am today.

It is also dedicated to all the sports fans around the world who give sportspeople the excitement and energy to be motivated to win and who, in my personal case, motivated me to deliver 100 per cent performances whatever the team or car I was driving at the time. The fans are the lifeblood of any sport and without them even the teams and sponsors would not exist.

I would also like to dedicate this to my family, especially my late mother and father, who sacrificed so much time and effort to give me the opportunity to try to be successful. Thanks to all my family and friends for their unparalleled support, understanding and love over all these years.

A big thank you to Simon & Schuster for giving me the opportunity to write this special book and to all their team, who have worked so hard.

Finally, thank you to Mart for the wonderful experience of writing a truly special, incredible book together. The cheque's in the post . . . but not signed! Ha ha!

Contents

Part II: Formula 1 – Then and Now

Part III: Isn't Life Wonderful?

FOREWORD

I am on the grid at Silverstone, my favourite racetrack. To my left is a beautiful red Ferrari. Nearby is a Williams, among a long line of other immensely powerful racing cars. Everywhere I look, race rivals are either sitting in their cars, chatting to their mechanics, or just taking some time alone to prepare themselves for the race. Me? I think I'll go and get a cup of tea.

I am at the British Grand Prix, July 2014, ostensibly in my role as an FIA steward, but, mostly – especially at this famous track – as an avid F1 fan. I've been chatting to Lewis Hamilton about his push for the world title, and have also spoken with a few of the other drivers. It's been absolutely fascinating to hear these very talented young men talk about their cars, yesterday's qualifying, the race strategies they may use, the team's plans and the rivalries. In that sense, nothing has changed; on the other hand, as I stand on the grid on this day in Northamptonshire, Formula 1 has altered immeasurably since the last time I put my foot to the floor with venom, two decades ago.

In the ensuing 20 years or so, I've had the most wonderful life and enjoyed some amazing experiences, which at times have been as dramatic as anything I ever went through in motor racing. I've also undertaken two endurance events that were more demanding and challenging than anything I ever faced on the grid. Poignantly, on occasion, my mortality, and that of precious people very dear to me, has been touched in the most profound ways.

So I got to thinking: wouldn't it be wonderful to revisit some of those incredible races I was lucky enough to be involved in, recall the battles on the track, the famous racers I sparred with for world titles and those amazingly physical, and at times brutish, cars that we had to wrestle with? I am endlessly enthralled by Formula 1, so the idea of looking at how my beloved sport has changed since my heyday was hugely appealing to me.

I started writing this book and, sure enough, as I began to recount the races, the overtaking manoeuvres and various moments of high drama from my career, so much of that era – which feels like a lifetime ago – came sharply back into focus. However, as I kept writing, so many events from *outside* my time in motor racing also sprang to mind: fun times, sad times and lessons in life that I had either learned through magnificent experiences or sometimes found out the hard way. We are all of us faced with challenges and situations in life that test us, but throughout my career and certainly ever since – as you will see – I have always bounced back. You have to. Life is too fantastic not to do that.

Having done a few previous books and thousands of interviews over the years, it's also been fascinating to see how my view of events has altered, mellowed and maybe in some cases stayed the same in the two decades that have passed since I last drove a Formula 1 car in the white heat of battle.

I may not be about to dust off Red 5 again, but in writing this book I have immersed my mind back in the pits, in the garages and at the test circuits, cast my thoughts back to the team owners as well as to those remarkable drivers from a racing era when serious injury or worse was ever-present, when some of the greatest drivers the sport has ever seen graced the grid and when, I'd like to think, a kid from near Birmingham tried to make his mark. The British fans always told me that I made them happy, and, let me tell you, they were certainly a very major part of my story. Now it's my time to retell a few of those tales.

I was blessed with an amazing career in motorsport and have certainly enjoyed the most wonderful life outside of that profession since I hung up my racing overalls for the last time. Hopefully, you will enjoy reliving those classic moments with me and also discover a few personal stories that, until now, no one has heard about. Either way, let's have some fun.

PART I:

THE RACING YEARS

CHAPTER 1

MY CHILDHOOD
AND KARTING

The overriding memory I have of my childhood is the tremendous love of my mother. She was a very warm, loving and caring mom who lived to give. She was always so supportive – I can never remember my mom pushing me to do anything; she was just there in the background, supporting whatever I wanted to do. My father worked extremely hard and long hours, so I remember him being absent for lengthy periods of time. He was a great dad, though, and soon, when my motor-racing career started in karting, we would have a fantastic relationship, crowding around engines. It was just a shame that he had to work such long hours. He was a senior engineer at Lucas Aerospace and used to get up early in the morning to go to work and not come back till late at night. They both worked very hard. Mom looked after the family home and a tea shop. In fact, it was above this tea shop in Baughton, near rural Upton-upon-Severn, that I was born on 8 August 1953. I was the third of four children, having an older brother and sister, Michael and Sandra, along with a younger sister, Gail. There was an eight-year difference between my older sister and me, with my brother 18 months younger than her.

We grew up in a very modest, semi-detached home and my family had to struggle and save for everything. Despite the relative lack of money, it was a very happy home. I can remember not really having enough room for us all to fit in and the garden being incredibly small. But we made do, like everyone did in those post-war years. They were good times. I loved my mom and dad, Joyce and Eric, very much; they were fantastic parents.

Before me, there was no motor racing in my family. It was actually my mother who was the fast driver, and I used to love sitting in the back with my siblings, speeding along, sometimes as quickly as 100mph. She only ever lost it once, as far as I recall, in the snow, but I just loved that sensation of speed. We didn't have any new cars, ever.

Unfortunately, life was not so comfortable at school. It's been well documented that I was badly bullied. My parents moved around a fair bit with Dad's work. For instance, when I was only three, we relocated to the southern suburb of Birmingham called Hall Green. The regular house moves caused complications because it meant I was always the new kid at school. I never seemed to start the first day of term at any school, which made me an easy target. I would often come in halfway through the year, so I was the perennial new boy to kick around.

Kids can be very cruel in terms of bullying. Fast-forward to my time spent helping the charity UK Youth (which I will come to later), I can relate to not being able to fit in. At times, I had the most horrendous experiences being bullied at school; it was diabolical. It wasn't just me they picked on; some of the schools were so rough that I even saw teachers getting beaten up. On one occasion, I saw a tutor pushed to the ground and actually knocked unconscious.

Aside from the bullying, I didn't enjoy school academically. I loved sports but little else. I wasn't particularly studious; quite honestly, I found a lot of the subjects not very interesting at all. Plus I was a very countrified person – I liked being out in big open spaces. I didn't like towns; I found them very claustrophobic. During my time at the all-boys Wellesbourne prep school, I found great solace in competing, so whether it was cricket, football, athletics, tennis, whatever, as long as it was against other schools I could lose myself in trying to beat them. At numerous times, I was the captain of the football and cricket teams. I was in one school's chess team for a while, but only because it meant I didn't have to study Latin. Then halfway through a term, I moved from Wellesbourne to a mixed school called Hall Green Bilateral, where the class sizes doubled to about 30 and the bullying stepped up a notch. Despite not always fitting in, I didn't roll over; I tended to stand up for myself but, of course, this often just made things worse.

I always tell people that I tried to put a positive spin on those difficult years at school. If you think about it, despite the bullying, having to regularly start from scratch with new friends and different schools, and being challenged in this way time and again, did at least make me very adaptable as a young kid. It certainly toughened me up. I just wish I could have been toughened up in a less violent way.

I decided at eight years of age that I was going be the Formula 1 world champion. As early as that. If you were to ask me how I came to that conclusion, the truthful answer is I haven't got a clue; it was just there, in my head. Like many children my age, I was a big fan of Formula 1. What I loved about the sport, apart from the racing, was the characters. I didn't have one specific hero on the track; there were several drivers who really fascinated me. The late, great Jimmy Clark was just astonishing; Stirling Moss too, also Sir Jackie Stewart, as well as the Argentinian legend, Juan Manuel Fangio. What can you say about drivers like that? If you push me to choose one, I would say Fangio is probably the driver who stood out the most for me back then because I just couldn't get over that he was racing without a helmet, without goggles, without seatbelts, without anything really, he was just ... wow! Later on in this book, I will talk at length about the very real dangers of racing in my era, but the risks he was facing were just on a whole other level. I also loved Jim Clark, who was the most stunning starter of grands prix and raced in a way that was so inspiring. I loved watching as well as reading and hearing about all these drivers and their amazing achievements on the track. Perhaps naturally, that was what I wanted to do, too.

My own motor-racing story starts, as it does with many drivers, in a kart. My dad was involved in the local karting scene and raced for a while, and I was captivated as a young boy by the speed, the sounds, the smell, the whole experience. I nagged my parents to let me have a go and they eventually relented, hoping it would be a novelty that I quickly became bored of. However, I loved everything about it. From the very first time I sat in a kart, I was totally hooked. Even at that tender age, I felt that this was my destiny – to be a motor-racing driver.

In the modern era, karting is a highly commercialised and very expensive sport. By contrast, back in those days it was certainly far less expensive, consisting mostly of families enjoying days out together, and there was a real community spirit. Of course, everyone still wanted to win, but if you were short of a part or needed some help, people would be only too willing to oblige. It was a great atmosphere.

My first kart was powered by a lawnmower engine bought

second-hand for £25. There was an allotment near where we lived and kids would race around that on a makeshift dirt track. I took part in my first properly organised race underage, at just eight – you were supposed to be older but I fibbed about my age. Some of the lads racing that day were a lot older. Isn't it funny that when you are younger you want to be older and when you are older you want to be younger! That karting debut at Edgehill near Banbury didn't go well. As I headed down one particular straight I suddenly lost all power. The reason? My engine had fallen off and was lying behind me on the track!

I also remember another race when I had no gloves and just a cloth racing suit, and the rain was so cold on my hands as they gripped the steering wheel that I was crying from the pain. Those early races were a big shock because I was used to winning around the allotment, but on a proper track I was finishing one or two laps behind most of the other boys. My initial karting struggles quickly made me realise that there was a whole world of things that needed to be done before I could be competitive, stuff I had never even contemplated. I can vividly recall saying to myself, *Well, this is a lot harder than I thought*. It was a sharp learning curve.

My father was on a limited budget, of course, but we were able to gradually upgrade my kart and get better equipment. My grandparents would often buy spare parts for the car or help out when it was Christmas or my birthday. I spent all of my spare time tinkering with my kart; I was obsessed straight away. My dad was fantastic. He used to take me everywhere racing and do all the engineering and mechanics on the kart. We used to have a blast, and through karting we shared a wonderful relationship. I have some great memories of coming home and eating a quick tea before going straight into the garage and working with him all evening.

As I improved, my father, my mother and I started to travel to races all over Britain. Places like Chasewater, Shenington, Little Rissington, Morecambe and Rye House. Quite quickly, I started winning races and being seriously successful. I was delighted when I was chosen to represent my country at junior level, and then we began racing in Europe and Scandinavia. It was all a big family adventure at times. My sisters would come along and we'd have great fun on all the ferry trips, enjoying the foreign travel. I remember driving all around England back when there was hardly any traffic on the roads. I also remember that when we braked too hard in the car it used to pull left or right because the braking was so dreadful, so maybe getting to the track was actually more dangerous than the race itself . . .

One time I was due to race for England abroad. The school announced the exciting news in assembly one morning that I would be going to Holland for two weeks to race for my country, and that I had been given a special two-week leave of absence. This did not go down well with the bullies. That afternoon, I was attacked viciously with a cricket bat in the playground, which put me on crutches for six weeks.

I think that attack probably finished me off in terms of self-esteem at that point. I never realised at the time but, as I sit here now looking back, I think I was probably in shock for some time afterwards. I just didn't understand what had happened; I wondered what I'd done wrong. I'd worked hard and been successful enough to be picked for the British karting team. I thought the other children would be proud of me. How wrong can you be?

Let me tell you about the time I told a priest to get lost. Yes, you'd think that's not one of my finest moments, not least

6

because I am not a fan of swearing and I have a lot of respect for the Church. However, I do have an excuse, of sorts.

I was nearly dead.

Karting was relatively safe, but at the higher levels you could find yourself travelling pretty fast, so there was always going to be risk involved. Fortunately, I didn't have too many crashes but my first biggie was quite severe. As I have said, I was a teenager busily working my way through the ranks of the junior British karting scene, when I had a terrible accident at Heysham near Morecambe. It was a great track on Heysham Head, which was even able to attract the Karting World Championship for many years.

On this particular day, I was doing really well in the race and found myself belting downhill at a fair rate. Unbeknown to me, the steering wheel column had a hairline crack in it and, as I came down this particular descent at approaching 100mph, the column snapped and I slammed into a kerb, the kart somersaulted and I ended up being thrown out of my seat and on to the track. Unfortunately, the bumper of a kart coming down the hill then struck me a glancing blow on the head. I was obviously knocked unconscious and, worse, the impact from the other kart compressed my helmet such that my scalp had been split into a large open wound. I woke up on the operating table at the Royal Lancaster hospital.

I'm pretty sure the ideal surgical routine is that you *don't* wake up on the operating table, but I did. Luckily they'd finished the surgery by then, but I could still sense the needle and stitches going into me. I was lying there confused, thinking:

What on earth is going on?

I wasn't really lucid; I was paralysed. And I later found out I'd been unconscious for a long time. I do remember distinctly how awful the feeling was. I wasn't in good shape. When I came to the next time, I was in bed in the ward and I had a weird taste in my mouth and my ears felt wet. I touched them and realised there was blood coming out. My nose was bleeding too. It turned out that I had haemorrhaged, so I was bleeding from my ears, nose and throat. In my fleeting moments of consciousness, I knew I wasn't in great shape but it was all rather hazy – I don't remember anyone visiting me or anything in detail. Now that's what I call a 'bad day at the office'!

Then, the next thing I knew, I was in this unbelievable deep black hole and there was a little spot of light at the end of this massive darkness, a tiny shard of light and a very small figure at the end of what I suppose was this enormous tunnel. It looked like a stick man in a very childish drawing.

Then I heard someone's voice, closer, much closer than the distant stick figure, saying, 'What else can I do for you, my son, besides pray . . .' This voice was really echoing around my head and it was actually quite abrasive and annoying. I could still see the little figure at the end of the tunnel and it seemed quite peaceful, but by contrast this nearby voice was so loud and irritating; it was starting to wind me up, yet I was powerless to move. The noise of this voice kept chiming back in, going on and on; it was really annoying me by now and I was thinking, *Please! Go away!* But it didn't.

Eventually, in this dream-like state, I had to say something. I found out later that I momentarily woke up and told the priest – who was praying for me – to get lost. Sorry about that!

Shortly after this, I sat up again, vomited blood then passed out. This is what severe concussion can do to you – it's not just a bump on the head. I was asleep for two days after that, but was gradually able to begin my recovery. I had scar tissue in my ears from the bleeding and suffered sporadic bouts of hearing loss for some time.

I learned a lot about racing that day in Morecambe, not least to always check four things before you go on any grid: steering, brakes, suspension and aerodynamic parts. If other parts fail you might be okay, but if any of those four elements fail, you will have a bad accident. With that crash, as indeed with any others I had during my career, I used to pore over what had happened: was it the kart, was it me, was it a rival making a mistake? I always had to find out why an accident had happened and how to avoid a repeat.

Obviously, I have thought about that incident with the priest a lot. Clearly, I am not in the habit of telling men of the cloth to get lost, but, comedy aside, I do believe that was a near-death experience. How else can I categorise it? I honestly think that I was drifting off, I was gone. I felt I was going somewhere I had never been before and I didn't like it. So I fought back to tell whoever it was I could hear talking to go away. Ironically, the priest's prayers sounding so annoying to me meant I fought back and came away from the light. Maybe that is not a coincidence, I don't know. It clearly wasn't my time, but I do believe that incident was me on the very cusp of going for good.

Eventually, I was well enough to think about kart racing again. You might wonder what makes racers get straight back into the same kart or car again, after a big accident or injury. It's a fair question. Part of the answer is that, in my opinion, most racing drivers are fatalists. During my whole career, I felt that if it was my time, then so be it. If it was not my time, then I would bounce back. That day in Morecambe I bounced back – it simply wasn't my time. I believe that everyone has a clock with their time preset and when that time is here ... I think you can accelerate that time – you can be negligent of yourself and have an earlier departure than you should have – but ultimately

I do feel that our own time is predetermined by a ticking clock, which eventually tells us when it is our time to go.

I should qualify my statement about most racers being fatalists. I must point out that it is a very private topic and I have never discussed this with any other drivers. So I cannot say for sure that they are fatalists. However, I would be very surprised if the majority on the grid did not share my view, especially in the earlier eras of the sport when life-threatening danger was ever-present. Otherwise, they would have needed an inordinate amount of courage to do the job – and I don't believe courage works like that.

In my opinion, if you believe you can do your job to a very high standard then, as long as Lady Luck is not totally against you, you might have an accident but you will recover. I think if you are not fatalistic and are in the slightest bit worried about hurting yourself going racing, then you shouldn't be doing it, because invariably those kind of drivers end up getting hurt. I wouldn't say fatalism is a comfort blanket, but if you feel like I do then it does dilute the potential for anxiety, which in itself can be very dangerous in a 200mph car.

Tragically, on two very black days in 1994, Ayrton Senna and Roland Ratzenberger found out to their cost that if Lady Luck, or destiny, is not with you on a racetrack, then there can be terrible consequences, something I will talk about elsewhere in this book. As painful as it is to use another more recent example, the terrible tragedy that happened at Brands Hatch when the fantastic young Henry Surtees was killed in 2009 was, again, a freak accident. For a loose wheel from a crash to come free of its tether then bounce across a track into a group of cars, then hit poor Henry on the head in precisely the place to kill him is *so* unlucky, so improbable, it is ridiculous. If you had to calculate a mathematical equation to work out the probability of that happening at all, it would be impossible, surely? You see an incident like that and think, *How on earth did that just happen?* What a lovely young man, a great talent and a terribly sad loss.

Luckily for me, that day in Morecambe wasn't my time. That feeling would return on several occasions in my career, when I suffered big accidents that might easily have proved fatal. This is how I viewed my job then and I still hold that view today. Of course, all drivers have their own approach, their own beliefs, and some of us are more religious than others. So I can't speak for anyone else with certainty. But speaking as a race-car driver and a competitor in dangerous sports, I really do believe in fatalism.

Anyway, I've digressed. Let's get back to my karting days. I had that big accident at Morecambe, but once I was fit and ready to go again, I was relentless. I was on a mission; I was not going to let anything stop me. Head injury and haemorrhaging? Yup, fix that, stitch me up, helmet back on, bounce back, go again.

It was a really exciting time. I kept karting, I kept winning, and by the end of my teenage years I had won seven Midlands championships, one Northern championship, a Short Circuit British championship as well as many other races. Inevitably, questions were starting to be raised about the next step, which traditionally was to go into single-seater racing cars. At the time, the proven strategy was to race in the British Formula Ford series, then graduate to the Formula 3 championship, with the ultimate goal, of course, being a Formula 1 drive.

My parents were not particularly happy about this new development. They had enjoyed encouraging me in karting, but they were less enthusiastic about single-seaters – primarily because of the safety fears (a parental instinct that I would come to

11

understand more when I later became a father myself and my own boys wanted to go racing). They also knew there was a severe cost implication of stepping up to the higher formulas. My father was wary, too, of the disappointment if I failed, fearing that – perhaps understandably if you look at my background and financial circumstances – the chances of me becoming a Formula 1 driver, let alone winning the world title, were probably slim to zero. Their preference was for me to pursue a career in engineering, keep karting and just enjoy racing as an amateur passion. By now, I was studying at Hall Green College and then I went to Solihull Technical College, later transferring to Matthew Boulton College in Birmingham to study engineering, all supported by a full apprenticeship at Lucas Aerospace. But by then, my racing career was up and running.

CHAPTER 2

LUCKY BREAKS IN A YOUNG LIFE

When I was 17 I met someone who would change my life back then and to this day, and who, thankfully, became my wife. I had seen this lovely young woman called Rosanne around and one day spotted her on my way to college, so I stopped and offered her a lift in my Mini van. She seemed pleased and climbed in, then after about 50 yards, she looked at me and said, 'I don't know you, do I? I thought you were someone else!' From that moment, realising she'd got in the car with a perfect stranger, to the time of writing, we have been together. We have just celebrated our 41st wedding anniversary and are still the best of friends, 46 years on.

When Rosanne and I first started dating, I really wanted to make an impression. My dad had a second-hand Rover coupé, which wasn't too old but had very high mileage, so he was able to get a good deal and afford it. This car was his pride and joy. Anyway, I really wanted to impress Rosanne, so one day I said, 'Dad, can I borrow your car?' I never asked him for anything as a rule but, amazingly, he relented so, after sorting out the insurance,

I headed off for a night out with my new girlfriend in his car.

I picked Rosanne up and we went to a country pub for a nice drink. When it was time to head home, I needed to reverse out of the car park. The Rover coupé back then had one of those gear levers with a button to press for reverse, so I did that and lifted it up and, to my horror, the entire gear lever came off in my hand! Worse still, a two-foot length of gear linkage also came up and out into the car. I was mortified. Here I was, trying to make a big impression on Rosanne, and I was sitting there trying to shove this linkage back in. She was just giggling and, to be fair, I was too, although all the time I was thinking, *My dad is going to kill me!*

We'd spent the evening with a friend of ours who was a mechanic, so I went back in, explained what had happened and he came out to help. I was hugely relieved when he appeared to have fixed the problem, so we eventually got back in the car and tried to drive off again. That's when I discovered that he'd turned first gear into reverse and reverse gear into first!

After a lot of lurching backwards and forwards, I eventually got the hang of it and we steadily made our way home in the dark. I really had to concentrate. Then, after a few miles, it started to rain. I put the windscreen wipers on and – I can still see it now – the driver's-side wiper went, 'Swish, swish, ping!' and just flew off into a hedgerow. It was so comical, all we could do was laugh. Then I heard a scratching sound and realised that the wiper arm was now gouging a big arc into Dad's windscreen. *Oh my word, this is getting worse!* I pulled over, swapped the passenger's wiper for mine so I could at least see to drive, and lifted Rosanne's wiper arm up and away from the windscreen. I dropped her off and got back to my home, backed the Rover coupé close to the garage and went to bed, relieved.

The next morning, I was up and out early, before Dad. Now,

let's just say Dad could be quite a formidable man when he was annoyed, so I was pleased to have avoided any mishap, and hopefully he wouldn't notice anything. I came home that night and my mom was waiting for me on the drive.

'Nigel, what on earth did you get up to last night?'

My first thought was, *What on earth has Rosanne said? We didn't get up to anything!* (Although not for a lack of trying, of course.)

'What do you mean, Mom?'

'Have you seen the garage, Nigel?'

I turned to look at the garage and then did a double take as an awful realisation dawned on me.

My dad had climbed into the Rover coupé that morning to go to work, he'd put the car in first and, of course, the broken gearbox had flung him backwards in reverse. Worse still, it had caught him off-guard, so he actually put his foot down on the accelerator, slamming the car – his pride and joy – through the garage doors.

He never let me borrow anything again.

Thankfully, Rosanne did not dump me after the Rover coupé debacle and what a lucky boy I am as a result. Without Rosanne's incredible support – then and throughout my career – I am sure things would have turned out very differently for me. She was simply amazing. We continued going out and soon became inseparable.

While I was studying at college, I was keen to make the step up to single-seater racing but, as I mentioned, my parents were less enthusiastic. I'd joined Lucas Aerospace as an apprentice, so my dad said that if I studied hard and passed all my exams then he would help finance my dream of single-seater racing. This was a real motivation to me and I really got stuck into my studies. I worked at Lucas part-time and did my classes too, with this goal constantly in the front of my mind. By the age of 21, I finally passed all my exams and qualified with ONC and HNC certificates in Engineering, which prompted a promotion at work too. Imagine my disappointment, then, when I told my dad and said I was now ready to start single-seaters, but he turned round and said he could not help me do that after all.

I have described in previous books how absolutely gutted I was at the time. I was angry with Dad and so demoralised that my dream was apparently going up in smoke. However, with the benefit of my years, and speaking as a dad myself, I have to say he did absolutely the right thing. He said and did whatever was necessary to get me educated; he helped me remain motivated, to stay the course. He knew I was a very gifted practical person but that I struggled with the theory. He knew I needed to really focus. Back then, of course, I was overwhelmingly disappointed and much less philosophical about his change of heart than I am now. So I asked him why. He simply said he could not afford to fund the next step, which to be fair was true. Nonetheless, it created quite a lot of tension at home.

By April 1975, Rosanne and I were very much in love and committed to each other, so on the 19th of that month we got married. Not long afterwards, we were very excited to buy our very first brand-new car, after our house had flooded and we had some money left over from an insurance payout. Up until that point, buying a new car was out of the question as money was so tight, so this lovely little yellow Mini Clubman felt very special to us.

One day we were driving to see my grandfather, who lived in the Malvern hills near Worcester. I was very tired from working late nights, so Rosanne was driving, and we were heading down a dual carriageway. I was snoozing on and off when, the next thing I knew, we'd screeched to an abrupt halt as Rosanne slammed on the brakes. Luckily, this car was also the first one we had with seatbelts, so we were both fine. I was startled and half-asleep, and asked, 'What's happened Rosanne?' As I did, there was a really loud banging and, when my eyes opened fully, I could see a man in plimsoles kicking the front of our car furiously. I squinted and shook my head to make sure I wasn't still asleep and dreaming, or imagining things.

I remember this guy's eyes were really dilated, much wider than normal, and he was really angry, furious. It was very frightening. Then, suddenly, he jumped up on the bonnet and started smashing the windscreen with his fists. At this point, because I'd been asleep, I didn't even know what had happened, whether we'd hit him or his vehicle and he was cross with us. I just knew that he was extremely angry and was attacking our car. He was going berserk on the bonnet. You can imagine Rosanne's terror and fright, so I said, 'Put it in reverse, put it in reverse, quick!'

However, as soon as we started to back up, he just ran off across the road. Rosanne said we hadn't hit him, and that he had just walked out into the road and started attacking cars. I got out and looked at the damage. I couldn't believe the amount of destruction that had been done: the grill was parted and smashed, one of the headlights was shattered, the bonnet was all buckled – our beautiful little Mini was wrecked. I jumped in the car to drive and just caught sight of the man turning up a lane ahead. I speeded up there and pulled off the main road to where he'd been heading, then got out of the car and started trying to track him down. When I finally found him he was attacking a parked car nearby, tearing a wing mirror off, which he then proceeded to throw over a hedge.

Then from behind me I heard these really strange groaning noises. I turned around and, about 30 yards away from me, there was another guy heading towards Rosanne (who by now had locked herself in the car). This second guy was walking slowly and looked very dazed, not right at all. I thought, *Oh my word, we are going to be attacked again!* So I ran back to the car and I stood in front of him and said, 'Don't you come any nearer ...'

He smiled at me and said, 'It's all right, mate,' pointing towards the first man who'd attacked our car. 'I used to be like him but I'm all right now.'

'Do you know him?'

'Yes, and I know where he lives.'

'Where? What on earth is going on here?'

'He lives in the mental hospital where I live, just up that entrance there.'

At this point I heard more noise from the other direction and I turned to see the first guy throwing a brick through a house window. I jumped back in the Mini and drove straight past him and towards the entrance of the hospital at about 50mph, then jumped out and raced into their reception. I was shouting and pointing and ranting myself by this stage – I just had to get the message over that this guy was out there causing all this damage. At first, they seemed doubtful about whether I was telling the truth, but I persisted and eventually they realised the situation was serious, and some nurses and security ran out with a strait-jacket to get hold of him. Thankfully, the situation was contained soon after that.

They'd tackled this man and taken him away, but when I said, 'I need to talk to you about the state of my new car, he's pretty much destroyed it,' I was amazed to hear them reply, 'Sorry, there's nothing we can do. He's not responsible for his own actions, he is ill.' We could only afford third party rather than fully comprehensive on our insurance policy so someone had to pay for the damage; we certainly couldn't afford it. They were not interested, though, so I said in that case I'd have to make a report to the police, which I did. To my alarm, the police told me it'd happened before: 'Usually they just run up the bonnet, over the roof and down the boot, so you were unlucky.' I couldn't believe what I was hearing! To be fair, the police were very good about it, but pointed out that they couldn't prosecute a man who was medically unwell and not considered capable.

The disagreement over the costs of damage to our car went on for months until, eventually, I found out that the house whose window the man had bricked was owned by a worker at the hospital and they had been recompensed for the damage. That set a precedent, which meant that I was then able to get the repairs to our car paid for.

It was just the most surreal experience. We'd witnessed a human being having a so-called 'brainstorm'. It was such an extreme thing to witness. It later transpired that the guy had actually broken his leg when he was kicking the vehicles. If you have never seen anything like that, it's pretty terrifying; it was certainly an unforgettable experience, although it's not one I'd like to go through again.

When people see sportsmen and women on the television, perhaps in a nice car, at some high-profile event, or in a big house with all the trimmings and maybe even their own plane, of course they think those people have made it and, to a degree, they have. However, in the early days of my career, we were completely and utterly skint. We had nothing, and I mean *nothing*. One story that Rosanne recounts about when I was going through the lower formulas really sums up how tight money was in those early days: she lined up a row of jars on a shelf, these amber-coloured glass storage jars that you could get free from the petrol station with so many gallons of fuel. There was one for the insurance money, one for petrol money, one for gas, electric, one for food and so on. They were often full of coins, just loose change, never many notes. It seems laughable now compared to the astronomical finances of some modern-day young racing drivers in their mid-teens. Bizarre almost, but that's how it was. We were virtually penniless.

We had to be so careful with money. We had no credit cards. We wouldn't take out anything on HP because we were worried about getting behind on our payments. We used to get a TV from Rediffusion on a free month's trial and then, at the end of the month, go and get another free trial TV from somewhere else. In one of my earlier books, I called this period of single-seater racing 'the hungry years', but perhaps, looking back, I was just talking about not being able to afford to eat much! It sounds rough when you read it back, and at the time it was, but if I am being honest, I see that now as character building. Easy to say, I know, but it was, and it also meant we valued having money when it eventually came to us. Even now, I can't go shopping and squander money – it's just how I am. Rosanne is the same. There are issues in most modern sports with very young and talented individuals being paid exorbitant sums of money, and then people are surprised when these youngsters go off the rails or struggle to cope with being paid in maybe one week the equivalent of what most people earn in a few years. We had no such problems!

Our chronic financial limitations were a potential threat to us even getting a start in single-seaters at all. With my father not wanting to fund the move, we decided to do so ourselves. Most people would go and book a week's course at a driving school, but we could only afford one lesson which bought me a half-day session at Mallory Park, so I excitedly went along to see what the transition from karting to single-seaters was like. I drove quite a few laps and was instantly hooked. I was also delighted to find that the car felt predictable and relatively reassuring to drive; I understood what it was doing and how to make it go faster. I felt comfortable with the experience and was excited to find out how I could go racing in one of these machines. Unfortunately, I was the only one who believed this, as all the instructors said I was useless and was doing it all incorrectly. Seems to be the story of my life . . .

So we took the plunge and bought a 1600cc single-seater race car. It was used, with several previous owners. It also ate up all our savings, about £1500. Necessarily, we also had to buy a trailer and all this cost meant we had to sell our nice Mini to fund it. Rosanne never hesitated when that became apparent, even though it was replaced by an old Maxi. Just in terms of the financial demands my aspiring career placed on us as a young couple, she was incredible. The costs of racing were always increasing, yet our incomes were very modest, mine more so than hers in fact, but she never moaned or doubted me for one second. What a lady. We parked the old race car in my parents' garage at nights, and Rosanne would sit with me into the small hours as I tinkered away on our pride and joy. The Formula Ford cars were pretty basic at the time, but with my engineering background I was able to do a lot of the work myself, preparing the car for my first season in Formula Ford.

Rosanne's brother had a picture-framing business and we used to make extra money helping him make the frames, then I would go out on to the late-night streets of Birmingham, trying to sell the pictures to clubs and hotels. Most nights I would work till around 3am, then I'd be back up and at work again at Lucas Aerospace by 7.30am.

During these hard years Rosanne was amazing. She worked as a British Gas home-service advisor in the day and took on evening jobs too, doing up to 80 hours a week to bring home money, virtually all of which was spent on my racing. It wasn't a case of not having very glamorous holidays during this period of our lives – there were simply no holidays at all! That was an easy decision for me: do you want to sun yourself on a beach somewhere or do you want to be Formula 1 world champion? Even at this very early stage, it was that simple, very black and white.

All this dedication from us both was worth it because on the track I was completely focused. My very first single-seater race was Formula Libre (an open formula line-up), but my very first Formula Ford race was at Mallory Park in 1976. I genuinely felt like I was on my way. At that time, Formula Ford was probably one of the best developmental series in the world. You could have as many as 140 people entering in the series, plus all sorts of heats to get through; it was very competitive. There was some very intense racing; it was like a mini Formula 1, a very good standard.

That first season in Formula Ford, I won six of the nine races I entered. However, in order to progress I knew I needed a better car. The following year, 1977, was a big milestone because I found that better car when a very colourful Irishman called Patrick let me run one of his single-seaters, which was brilliant. Although it wasn't the best car on the grid, it was a significant upgrade from what I was used to. We had a few reliability issues, including a driveshaft falling off after being on pole and a wheel coming off (imagine that, a wheel falling off – that would never happen in Formula 1!), but it was a great step forward, with quite a few wins in the season. I had recently been introduced to a man called John Thornburn, who was known to run good teams and had played a part in Keke Rosberg's rise to success. Thankfully, he took a gamble on me and helped us so much, he was a very pivotal supporter and a loyal friend in these early years. After I won one particular race, John later told me he was stunned by this win because he thought the car was 'a load of crap'. He also later said I had the 'most potential since Jimmy Clark'.

As my single-seater career developed, I became more and more focused. One of the choices I made to hone my fitness and help push things forward was to go teetotal. As a young man I used to enjoy seeing my mates down the pub occasionally, like most lads of that age. For me, if you want to focus on doing something really special, then you have to make sacrifices. At first, I found I had a cushion in that I was able to win most of the races. I obviously had a talent that I didn't fully appreciate in the early days, but I always wanted to be extremely fit and focused. I just wanted to win races and do whatever it took to be on the top of the podium. I was running several miles every day and going to the gym four or five times a week. I was *so* dedicated.

These days, I will have a small drink occasionally. I like to have a sip of champagne if we are christening a baby or celebrating something like a wedding, but it really is a sip because, sadly for me, I am pathetic with alcohol. I only have to have one glass of something and I am gone. Still, I am very cheap to take out and after a glass, or maybe two, I don't even know where I am!

On his deathbed, my grandfather told me something which I thought was strange and amusing at the same time: 'Nigel, stay away from the three evils: slow horses [gambling], fast women and too much drink.' And he added, 'If you go to a party don't talk about religion, sex or politics then you'll get on with everyone!' And he was absolutely right.

*

As well as John Thornburn, there were other influential people who helped me in my early career, in those formative years which are so important – men such as Mike Taylor and John Crosslé, who owned race teams bearing their names. In fact, John Crosslé asked John Thornburn how good I was and he replied, 'Well, from a Formula Ford point of view, he's the best there's ever been.' With a Crosslé car on board, I took the big leap of faith and decided to turn professional. We had no money, limited resources for racing and I was quitting a solid engineering job with a bright future. However, the weekend shifts at work were a major problem in terms of clashing with races, so I had a stark choice to make – engineering or racing. It was no competition. I handed in my notice at Lucas Aerospace. I was just 24. Exciting, yes, but financially very precarious, not least because three weeks later I broke my neck in my new Crosslé car.

We were racing at Brands Hatch and I had just received the new car. There was no headrest and no proper seat, but I was very excited and keen to use it at the forthcoming Brands Hatch race. On the day, the conditions were semi-damp and unfortunately I had the most shocking accident. Basically, a driver in front of me wasn't focusing on the slowing-down lap after qualifying, and when I came to overtake him, his position forced me straight off the circuit. As soon as I hit the wet grass the car accelerated, flew into the barriers backwards and the whiplash snapped my neck. The third, fourth and fifth vertebrae in my neck were crushed and one was split open, so I was very lucky to survive and not be paralysed for life. From a life-threatening point of view, although I have had several big accidents in my career, when you break your neck it is the most serious part of your body to damage. I was in hospital for some time and lost the use of my arms and legs for a period, which was terrifying. In the first few days, they told me the recovery time would be around six months. Then I was told I would never race again. Then they said I'd probably never walk again.

Well, I wasn't having that.

So I discharged myself.

Seven weeks later I was back on the grid in my racing car wearing an orthopaedic neck brace.

I had missed some races but by the end of the season I had regained the lost ground, and at the last race at Silverstone I was in touching distance of winning the Formula Ford title. John Thornburn was very motivational in my early days in the lower formulas and he became a very good friend and supporter who helped enormously. He had a wealth of experience and I learned a lot from him. For example, at the race before Silverstone, I was driving very hard but we were off the pace because my tyres were so old and had lost all their grip. At the time I didn't realise that, so I was sliding all over the place, nearly three seconds off the pace.

I said, 'I can't drive any harder, John.'

John just said, 'Look, you need a new set of tyres.'

'I can't afford any new tyres; I just don't have the money.'

'Well, give this guy a ring and get some new tyres. We'll worry about paying for them another time.'

So I got the new tyres, then at Silverstone I went nearly three seconds faster. In fact, we won the race that weekend, got pole position and fastest lap, and took the championship by one point. I'd won the 1977 Formula Ford FF1600 Championship. Across all my various races that season, I'd won 33 out of 42 starts. Despite the offer of a works car for the forthcoming Formula Ford season, I knew it was time for the next step on the ladder: Formula 3.

*

My experience of Formula 3 was initially very hard, not from the point of view of driver skills, but because of the financial cost. Finding sponsors was a nightmare. At one point, we wrote to over 400 companies without one single penny coming back. I'd started cleaning windows and doing administrative work to bring in extra cash. March Engineering had offered me a Formula 3 drive for 1978 provided I bring some money to start the season, so then we took the monumental decision to sell our home to fund the drive. We also sold pretty much all our worldly goods to raise cash. However, after just six weeks, when those funds ran out – every penny we had in the world, literally – they terminated the relationship, which I thought was dreadful. So now we had no money, no home; we were living in rented accommodation with seemingly no future. I can't deny that 1978 was very tough indeed – I had some drives in the BMW County Championship, but apart from the five Formula 3 races and a short-lived Formula 2 race, that was it. Very disappointing.

Then, in late January 1979, Rosanne's mother died of a heart attack. She was only 56. We were both devastated. She was a fabulous, wonderful woman, and for my part I felt like I had lost a second mother and a very dear friend. She'd been complaining of chest pains on New Year's Eve, but she was sent home from the doctor's with suspected indigestion. By the end of the month she was dead. That would never happen today, so we both feel tremendously resentful that she was taken away from us so young. We were devastated, numb, and felt like our world had come to an end. Seeing the total devastation continue through the eyes of Rosanne, her sister Sandy and her brother Malcolm was very sad.

Conversely, in my second year of Formula 3 things began to look up. I secured a paid seat with Unipart, which was a great opportunity – I got £25 a week and the occasional use of a

Triumph TR7 sports car. A man called Dave Price took me on and we maximised the opportunity, even though I wasn't the number one driver (not for the last time!). My team-mate Brett Riley and I got on very well and I have some great memories of certain races that year. However, we were using Dolomite engines which were, at best, unpredictable. You could actually have two apparently identical engines yet one would be three seconds a lap faster than the other.

That 1979 season in Formula 3 was okay; we only got one win at Silverstone and struggled with those engines, but it was all invaluable experience. The standard was very high and I was racing against people such as Nelson Piquet, so it was a fantastic apprenticeship. Off the track, one highlight was borrowing an old VW Dormobile that we drove down to Monaco, where I finished 11th, making me the only Unipart driver ever to qualify for a Monaco Formula 3 race. David Price very kindly let us use his hotel room for a shower! Most importantly, however, at the British Grand Prix in July that year, the Formula 3 grid was the supporting race, and that is when I met a man who would change my life: Colin Chapman.

I'd met a chap called Peter Collins on the Formula 3 circuit and he worked with Colin Chapman, founder of the Lotus Formula 1 team. At the British Grand Prix, Peter came over to me and said, 'Nigel, the Old Man would like to meet you.' He was with a gentleman called Peter Windsor who, like Peter Collins, would also prove to be instrumental in my career, and they are both very dear friends.

I went along to meet Colin and he shook my hand and started asking me a few questions. He asked me how I got on in the race, to which I replied, 'I did the best I could. I had fun but we were down on power.'

'Well,' replied Colin, 'I was impressed by the way you went through the chicane, your braking and the speed you carried through there. Very good.'

I was amazed that he had watched the Formula 3 race and even more stunned that he had been impressed by my performance. We chatted a brief while longer then he had to leave. I was so pleased to have met him. I knew Colin was an incredible engineer, inventor and taskmaster. Lotus had very charismatic, beautiful black and gold racing cars and was undisputedly one of the best teams in racing at the time. I knew there were a number of brilliant individuals in Formula 1 who ran their own teams – great names such as Ken Tyrrell, Frank Williams, Enzo Ferrari and, of course, Colin Chapman. These were all people who were renowned for spotting talent and then being able and willing to give that talent a chance. I had been keen to drive for Colin Chapman before that meeting, like many drivers of my age, but after meeting him I was more determined than ever.

Not long after I'd met Colin at the British Grand Prix, Peter Collins phoned me to say that Lotus needed someone to go round all their suppliers and check quality control and compliance, because the standard of work required to supply a Formula 1 team was exemplary. This was a fantastic opportunity to get close to an F1 team and – hopefully – get to know Colin. I jumped at the chance. So, for more than a year before I eventually drove for Colin, I was working for him as an inspector and engineer, outsourcing suppliers, effectively checking to see if they had the technical prowess to supply the parts to Lotus. I was given a Ford Escort 1300 and a basic salary plus fuel expenses. I didn't think twice because, although it involved a lot of driving to and from work and the various sites, it felt like my chance to get to know Colin. Plus the weekday hours allowed me to carry on with my weekend racing in Formula 3.

I would visit various suppliers' factories and report back with my opinion on whether a particular site was up to scratch. Despite his vast experience and my relative youth, Colin rarely questioned my assessment. He would obviously ask for facts and evidence to back up my judgement, and he expected that I had done my research and homework, but invariably he would listen to my presentation and accept my conclusions. Fantastically, it wouldn't be long before I would get the opportunity to show Colin what I could do behind the wheel of an F1 car, rather than a Ford Escort.

Before then, however, my 1979 Formula 3 season was about to get much worse: in mid-September, I broke my back in a very serious accident at Oulton Park, Cheshire. From my point of view, the incident was totally avoidable. Andrea de Cesaris (who only recently passed away, bless his soul) was coming up on the inside of me going down a hill, but there was no room. In those early days, he had something of a reputation for being erratic at times, and on this particular day his car touched mine and instantly flipped me over. My car somersaulted at about 165mph and landed upside down. It was a massive accident.

At the moment the car flipped, there was a serene quietness; all was silent as I flipped through the air. There was a slowness to the sensation; I felt like I had a lot of thinking time and I knew that this was going to be a biggie. By sharp and very painful contrast, the second my car impacted on the ground, everything went from quiet, calm and slow to a cacophony of noise, smells, violence and pain. I blanked out, my back was crushed and two vertebrae were badly broken.

When I came round the pain was excruciating. I knew my back was badly damaged. They took me to hospital and informed me that I had crushed my lumbar spine. Overnight,

I was half an inch shorter in height. I was angry about the crash because I felt it was avoidable. I was always far more at ease with accidents I had caused myself, through my own errors, but this had not been my fault. The recovery took many weeks and I would be left with painful sciatica in my mid-20s. However, just as with the head injuries at Morecambe and the neck fracture at Brands, I knew I was lucky to be alive.

I remember lying on a gurney outside the X-ray room later that day, when they were running tests on me. There was a young man next to me who didn't look in pain and was talking, but his head seemed somehow disconnected to his body, which wasn't moving. I asked him what had happened.

'I was playing rugby and I ran up behind someone in a maul and apparently it's snapped my neck. I can't feel or move my arms or my legs.'

You see what I mean about being lucky?

CHAPTER 3

TESTING FOR LOTUS AND SLOWING DOWN TIME

When you are operating at the very highest level in any sport, your reflexes, senses and reaction times are acutely honed. This is the result of combining pure talent with thousands of hours of practice. It is said in some sports psychology circles that, aside from natural ability, luck and sheer determination, to perform a chosen sport to the skill level of a world champion you have to have practised that particular discipline for a minimum of 10,000 hours.

For example, if a member of the public, rather than a professional tennis player, faced a serve from Roger Federer, the ball would fly past them virtually before they even realised he'd hit it. Yet his top-seeded rivals not only see that ball, they are usually able to return it with venom. The same amount of world-class skill applies to all sports at the highest levels, and Formula 1 is no exception. With this in mind, and given the context of my very first test in an F1 car, I want to talk to you about a racing driver's apparent ability to 'slow down time'. Let me explain.

In late 1979, I was delighted and very excited to be invited by the Lotus Formula 1 team to test with them at the Paul Ricard circuit in France, along with four other aspiring drivers (Peter Collins had kindly put my name forward). Among the names there was Elio de Angelis. He was a lovely guy and brilliant driver, and we had briefly been team-mates for a one-off Formula 2 race at Donington in 1978 (where I crashed out in second qualifying after hitting an oil patch left by another car). Elio had already raced a full year in F1 for the Shadow team. Two of the other drivers, Eddie Cheever and Jan Lammers, also had some F1 experience, and there was another Brit in contention – Stephen South, who was doing well in F2. So the competition was stiff, but this was potentially my big break so it was a *huge* day in my career. When David Phipps from Lotus had phoned to offer me the test, he asked if the accident at Oulton Park had injured me as badly as he'd heard. I was not going to let a broken back compromise this remarkable opportunity, so I simply told David I was fine, then phoned the doctors for more painkillers and packed my bag.

I had a long wait on the first day as all the other drivers went out on track before me, but eventually my turn came and I was strapped in for about 20 laps. I knew that if I blew this chance, my hopes of a Formula 1 seat might be gone forever.

You would think those first few laps in a Formula 1 car would've been the most exciting moment in my life, and that I would be stunned by the car's performance. Not so. I was actually hugely disappointed and incredibly frustrated, even unnerved. It was a massive anticlimax. I didn't understand what was happening. Everything seemed to come at me so fast – the corners, the decisions, it was all just too quick. For example, I was going down the main straight okay but then having absolutely no time to go into the corners; it was all a blur. At the end of my session I was five or six seconds a lap off the pace. *Five or six seconds* – in Formula 1, five or six *tenths* of a second is a lifetime!

The grip never felt right and the gearbox was a real struggle, too. It was so disappointing. I thought the car would handle much better, have more grip, be nicer to drive and corner, but it was just ugly. At one point, the great Gilles Villeneuve came up behind me in his Ferrari so, of course, I let him past. Then I vainly tried to follow him. For a couple of the slower corners I was keeping up with him. That momentarily buoyed my spirits, but then he went around a fast corner lightning quick and, when I tried to follow him in the same manner, I span off. I remember just thinking, *How the hell did he go around there that fast?*

I was really dejected when I finished my laps and rounded up my things at the end of the test. I trudged back to my hotel and phoned Rosanne, who instantly knew something was wrong. She asked me if I was okay and I said, 'Rosanne, I don't know if this Formula 1 game is for me.' I was so dejected; the experience just didn't work for me. I thought, *This is a step too far – it doesn't work.*

However, the next morning something amazing happened. For one, I was given a car that had fresh tyres. So immediately the levels of grip I could feel were completely different. I was naive and wet behind the ears, so I didn't fully realise the colossal influence worn tyres would have had on my performance the day before. We were talking five seconds! The gearbox was smoother too. So that was all massively encouraging in terms of performance. However, if the car on day one had been a struggle, then surely this faster, grippier car would be even worse in terms of being able to cope with its pace and computing the speed? Not so.

The human brain is an incredible piece of technology. What had happened is that during the night, while I was consciously thinking about the events of the first day and later during my sleep too, my brain had upscaled and processed what it had witnessed the day before. Remarkably, within two laps on the following day, *everything* was different. The car was going faster in terms of absolute speed and grip levels were far higher, but to me it all seemed so much slower and easier to process. I was hitting 200mph but I could see the trees going past, I could even pick out individual branches, as well as parts of the fencing and barriers. As the laps went by, it felt progressively 'slower' and more manageable, even though my lap times were getting quicker. My confidence soared; I started to feel the car instinctively, and within a few laps I was six seconds quicker than the day before. Then you think to yourself, *Well, that wasn't too hard after all!* It was such a huge relief.

Driving a Formula 1 car is all about having the time to make decisions. If you go into a corner and feel like you are doing 200mph on the approach, then it is very hard to make the right decisions at the right time. At that velocity you are covering approximately the length of an entire football pitch every second, so factor in maybe a rival trying to overtake you or oil on the track, bad weather, tyre wear, fuel worries and so on, and you have a lot for your brain to compute, all at a viciously fast speed.

However, on that second day it all felt so much more ... 'leisurely' is not the right word, but certainly more manageable. I could see my racing line miles ahead; I could feel the track, change gear smoothly when I needed to, and so on. Going from the night before, telling Rosanne that I wasn't sure if F1 was right for me, I suddenly knew I could do it. Once you get that feeling, you can work on making it better and better, each day, each week, each season. On that second day of testing, my brain had made all these adjustments.

Essentially, it means that F1 drivers are bending time. We are travelling at the same speed, the corners are coming up just as fast, but, in terms of our perception, time is moving slower than in reality. When you are really on top of your game, it is almost like racing flat out but in slow motion. You have more time to do the job. Your brain processes the information much quicker than the average person could do. Only then can you become at one with the car and the track. As I mentioned earlier, the ability to process speed and time in that way, plus how your brain teaches itself to adapt to the faster speeds, is partly a gift, but it is also certainly learned over the many thousands of laps that top drivers do.

I have been very lucky to meet some highly intelligent people in my time, and the neuroscience of this phenomenon is absolutely fascinating. If an ordinary person with no racing experience jumped in a Formula 1 car and was able to drive it (at all!) around a circuit, their brain would be concentrating on moving their arms, legs, eyes, head, just to get the car around the track once. Each decision would need to be consciously made. *Turn the wheel here; now the car is sliding so I need to correct that* . . . and so on. The problem is that the conscious part of the brain is very slow; it is a big overhead in terms of energy consumption, so therefore it is quite sluggish. The conscious circuits in the brain are not very precise; they are coarse and quite laborious, which, when you are driving a car at 200mph, is not very helpful.

This is where practice comes in. Clinically, it has been proven that if you practise something often enough, that process does an amazing thing – it switches from conscious to unconscious. There is a section at the back of the brain called the cerebellum, and when you practise the same activity or action thousands of times, this part of the brain recognises that repetitive activity. Then, rather than consciously making a decision every time, it assumes that it would be far faster and more efficient to react *subconsciously*. When it makes that switch – from conscious to subconscious – the signals transmitted from your brain via your spinal cord to your arm to turn the steering wheel become an instantaneous, subconscious movement. You don't need to work out what to do every time. That is when you get *really* fast. When a champion is driving a car, their brain subconsciously knows what to do – *Here's a certain type of oversteer I have seen 6000 times before – this is how to correct that.* But this is all done instantaneously. A driver in the zone doesn't even think about it.

What this means is that the conscious part of the driver's brain is free and untaxed; it has lots of spare processing power because the subconscious part is doing the majority of the work. Therefore it can process the trees flying past; it can see faces in the crowd; it can see the pit lane as if it is going past at only 40mph. The brain has room to spare. It can make decisions in a race in a millisecond, yet almost leisurely. This is why champion drivers can seem to slow down time. To use an analogy: if you are walking along the street and you wave at a friend, you don't need to think about what is involved – lifting your hand, saying hello and not falling over – because it is something your subconscious brain is processing. However, take that same situation but put you on a tightrope ... Try waving then!

The role of sleep in processing the events of the day is tied into this as well. Sleep is when the transfer from conscious to unconscious occurs; this is when the brain decides to switch. That is why some days when you wake up it feels, as if by magic, that you have learned something when you were asleep, but this progression is actually because of the practice you've done when you were awake.

This is the known, recognised neuroscience of what I was doing that day at Paul Ricard. I have observed this conscious-to-subconscious transfer happen in myself and seen it in others many times, and it is truly fascinating.

Back to the reality of my ambition to be Formula 1 world champion: the impact of that process in terms of my future career in F1, my belief in my ability and my performance in front of the Lotus team during that second day testing at Paul Ricard was *huge*.

CHAPTER 4

THE LOTUS YEARS AND COLIN CHAPMAN

I must have made the right impression at the Paul Ricard test because, shortly afterwards, I was offered the role of test driver for the Lotus Formula 1 team. Stephen South had queried some details of a deal that was put to him, so Colin Chapman went with me instead. Elio de Angelis, who would become a close friend, got the F1 seat alongside the existing number one, former world champion Mario Andretti. There was even talk of me starting three grands prix in the forthcoming season.

I was on top of the world.

As it turned out, 1980 was a rather unsuccessful year for Lotus but, even so, my role as a test driver allowed me to learn so much. Just being around people like Colin and Mario was a massive learning curve. I felt very privileged. I knew I had worked extremely hard to get there, and I was determined to seize any tiny opportunity that came my way. I gradually got to know Colin and bided my time for a chance to show him what I could do. He had already given me such a massive confidence boost just by taking me on – I wasn't exactly well funded, so I felt he had picked me purely because of his faith in my ability. In the first year of working with Colin, I found out that he'd said I was 'the best natural talent' he'd seen since Jim Clark, and he also told a television interviewer that I was 'a future world champion'. Well, in my eyes, there were no higher compliments.

So, when it came to my first official track day as a Lotus test driver, I was totally focused on performing to my maximum – I had to justify Colin's faith in me. It was at Silverstone and the other two drivers weren't available, so it was just me and the mechanics, a few of whom were (perhaps understandably) unsure how this young F3 driver would cope with the spotlight of being the sole test driver of their F1 car. The conditions were beautiful but, even so, I took the first few laps cautiously, and only then started to find my rhythm before blasting out a few laps that I felt were pretty strong. There was no indication from the pit board about the times so I was unsure, nervous even, of how well I had done when I came back into the pits. So imagine my delight when the team told me I had lapped in 1 minute 12.5 seconds – the fastest time ever in a Lotus around Silverstone. That would have put me on the second row of the grid for the previous year's British Grand Prix.

I swapped fastest lap times with Elio in testing over the coming weeks and my efforts were rewarded when Colin announced I might get an actual race drive at the forthcoming Austrian Grand Prix in August 1980, shortly after my 27th birthday. That race weekend couldn't come soon enough.

You do come across some strange people sometimes. A few weeks after I had just broken the track record for a Lotus at Silverstone, I'd been playing a round of golf in the most awful weather – it was more like an extreme sport, with gale-force winds and lashing rain. A group of us used to play together and, on this particular day, at the end of the round, we headed to a local pub for a hot toddy – a little bit of brandy, sugar and hot water – to warm us up after such bracing conditions.

We walked into the pub and I could immediately hear this guy inside talking rather loudly to a group of people, holding court. He was saying, 'Yes, I am the outright track record holder at Silverstone,' and he was really giving it some, going on and on about it very brashly. 'It was fantastic. I couldn't believe I broke the track record at Silverstone – what a brilliant day, I couldn't have driven any better ...', this, that and the other. Everyone was listening so intently to this guy. I sat down and was thinking, *Wow, I should know him*, and I actually felt a bit silly for not recognising him. I was still very green in terms of Formula 1, so I chastised myself for not having done enough research to instantly recognise this fellow.

I listened some more and then, eventually, I went over and congratulated him. He didn't recognise me, which wasn't surprising as I was, after all, still in my early days at Lotus. I asked him what car he had been driving. I was thinking, *I am a numpty, I should know this guy*. Everything I was asking him was with the intention of triggering my brain, because I was really embarrassed that I didn't know him. I could see he was getting a little bit agitated with my line of questioning when I asked how much horsepower his car had. Another couple of questions later and he snapped, 'Well, who the hell are you anyway?'

I said, 'I'm nobody. I'm just really interested – that is a big achievement. I know that it is really tough to beat the track record around there.' I was polite and I decided to leave it there, so he turned away and resumed regaling people over and over again with his story. Eventually, I had to say something so I nudged him politely and said, 'I'm sorry, I feel like I should know you ... Would you mind telling me what time you did around Silverstone, please?'

'I did a 1:24. Why?' He was getting quite rude by now.

'Oh, okay, that's a very good time. Congratulations.'

'Yes, it's the outright track record. Why do you want to know? Who the hell are you?'

'Well, since you asked, I am Nigel Mansell and I am the Formula 1 test driver for Lotus and Colin Chapman, and a few weeks ago I smashed the outright track record for a Lotus at Silverstone with a 1:12.5.' He just looked completely stunned, got up and walked off. Everyone in the pub momentarily paused then clapped me. I had actually been reproaching myself for not knowing this guy, thinking I was not on top of my game because I thought I had the track record and yet here was a driver who said he was the record holder, and I didn't know him. Isn't it strange what people say sometimes?

I also had a few races in Formula 2 that year, with mixed results, but the most exciting development was clearly the potential opening into Formula 1. Flying out to Austria ahead of my first grand prix start was just so exciting. This was everything I had ever dreamed of – all those years of hard work, the struggles, it was finally coming together. The grid was rammed with talent: there were four world champions in the field and 13 grand prix winners, names such as Jones, Villeneuve, Laffite, Pironi, Fittipaldi, Scheckter, Reutemann – all amazing drivers. Add to that the fact that the beautifully located Österreichring was the fastest circuit of the season (averaging around 140mph), and the cars were running the fantastic but at times highly unpredictable so-called 'ground effect' aerodynamic technology (more of which shortly), it felt like a real baptism of fire.

I was in the team's third car, which was seven inches longer than the two standard cars of Elio and Mario. Consequently, it was very lethargic when changing direction because the wheelbase was longer, plus it was heavier, but the team wanted to try it out. Unfortunately, there was no way I was going to qualify in that car, but luckily for me, with just a few laps to go, they squeezed me into Elio's car and I managed to put in a good enough lap to scrape in at the very back of the grid. I would be back in the longer car for the race, but I didn't care. I was about to start my first grand prix. It was a sensational feeling.

However, that excitement soon started to fade on the grid when I began to sense a fair bit of pain in my buttocks. At first I thought, *Wow, it's hot in here*, but then I realised it was actually a burning sensation. I called my engineer over and he put his hand down into the cockpit, where he found a pool of fuel was leaking around the top of my legs.

'Nigel, you might have to put up with it.'

'What's the alternative?' I asked.

'Get out of the car and miss the race.'

'I will put up with it.'

Apart from being very dangerous, it was becoming really painful, so the mechanic went and got a bucket of cold water, which he threw into my cockpit to dilute the fuel I was sitting in. So the start of my first ever grand prix was coloured by physical discomfort and an all-pervading smell of racing fuel. Even so, I was mightily excited.

At first, it wasn't too bad, but after ten or so laps the water evaporated and the fuel started to burn me again. After about 40 laps the engine blew and my race was over. I can't pretend I wasn't relieved, to be honest, because by that point the pain was really quite unbearable. I'd sat in fuel for over an hour, causing second- and third-degree burns to my buttocks. Also, when I got out of the car, the fuel had shrunk my hamstrings so I couldn't walk properly. I just hobbled back to the garage.

My backside was raw and blistered; I felt really ill. The blisters were the size of my fist, huge. I'd thought I might be sitting with Rosanne in the hotel that evening, celebrating my first ever grand prix race, but as it turned out I spent the night at Birmingham Accident Hospital. At one point, a kindly nurse came in and said, 'Mr Mansell, now we have to de-roof your blisters.'

'What on earth does that mean?'

I didn't like the sound of that. Painfully, a few moments later I found out that what 'de-roofing' meant was bursting the pocket of fluid inside the blister then slicing off the dead skin. It was agony. Then I had to be dressed with heavy gauze for nearly a month before new skin formed. I didn't complain to Colin – who had said he was impressed by my drive – and just took it on the chin. Besides, I was so keen to get back in a Formula 1 car and try again.

Notwithstanding burning your bum, I will try to describe the cockpit of a Formula 1 car from early on in the era in which I raced, if only to attempt to illustrate how incredibly hostile and unwelcoming the environment could be at times. First of all, depending on the size of frame you were, you'd have a difficult job getting in the car and getting comfortable. In the very early cars, there were no special seats, maybe just a piece of foam, so your backside would effectively be on the bottom of a metal tub, your hips would be squashing into the sides so you'd be very uncomfortable, and you'd have instant backache in about two minutes. The cramped dimensions meant that your shoulders would also be hunched up around your neck because the cockpit was too narrow. Your knees would be bashing the dashboard because there was not enough leg room and your shins would be hitting the exposed steering column. This was just getting in.

Once settled into the cockpit, you would get yourself as comfortable as possible, relatively speaking. You'd make sure the pedals were correctly aligned, so you could confidently and accurately slide your foot from the accelerator to the brake and vice versa. You had to be absolutely sure that your foot didn't catch as it travelled across – the pedals had to be flush. Then you'd check that the clutch pedal had enough play in it to disengage the clutch properly. You also had a foot rest, which was absolutely vital because, when pulling the G-forces that F1 cars face, your foot needed to be on the foot rest and not the clutch, otherwise you risked riding the clutch and wearing it out. As you came to a corner that created a lot of G, you'd have to use the foot rest wisely because, when the G-forces hit, if you didn't have your leg in the right place you could wear yourself out in a matter of minutes. This is because you can only support your leg and body under G-force for so long.

When you were sitting in the car and ready to go, things didn't get any easier. If you tried immediately to turn the steering wheel when the car wasn't moving, you could hardly turn the wheels at all, because the steering was just so heavy. Back then, there was no power assist. It was all incredibly physical. When I'd got the Lotus test contract, I installed a mini-gym in my garage at home because I felt I needed to be in peak condition at all times. This was an approach I tried to carry with me throughout my career.

Once you pulled away in the car, the reality of the claustrophobic environment was multiplied many times, because now you were in a very dynamic racing situation and nothing was static inside that cockpit for the best part of two hours. As soon as you turned the steering wheel, your knuckles might hit the sides of the cockpit. There wasn't enough room to change gear freely because your elbow was restricted – you had to change gear with just your fingers. Don't forget, in the early part of my career these were fully manual cars, so no semi-automatic gear-shift. It was a very physical operation each time you changed gear – there was no assistance; it was all mechanical. However, all the cars were very similar; there wasn't any one that was particularly more roomy than the next. So, we all had to devise our own methods of working in an incredibly cramped cockpit.

Obviously, bear in mind that you would be wearing a helmet, so your visibility was limited by the size of the visor, the weather conditions, perhaps by smoke on the track or oil being picked up by cars in front and thrown into the air and on to your helmet.

Inside that cockpit, for me the rev counter was the most important dial. Nowadays, of course, the gear-shifting is all electronic, assisted by LED lights to pinpoint the optimum time to change gear (along with an audio bleep through the driver's earpiece), but back then it was purely mechanical, we had none of that. We used to have to judge when to change gear, so we felt the torque of the engine and where the top of the power curve was.

In the early cars, I would always look at how awkward it would be to get my finger round to try to reset the rev limiter, because if you over-revved the engine you'd get a bollocking. However, as it was a mechanical rev meter, you could sometimes reach down and reset it to save a telling-off. Of course, the teams quickly figured this out and so they'd always place it somewhere that was virtually impossible to get to, so you couldn't actually cheat the system. Sometimes I'd be doubled up inside the already super-cramped cockpit, banging my head and straining to reach the rev meter, all the while usually chuckling to myself at the absurdity – and pain! – of the situation.

You would have all your temperature gauges, your oil, water and various other pressure gauges that had greater or lesser importance. The pressure of the fuel pump was vitally important because, quite simply, if you starve the engine of fuel it can essentially detonate and blow up. That tended to be a bad thing! There would also be a dial or lever that allowed you to alter the bias on the brakes.

Essentially, the cockpit of those cars carried the absolute minimum required to run an F1 car of the day. What's more, if anything did start to feel wrong with the car, maybe there was a definite problem or you just had a bad feeling, then of course there was no two-way radio to the pit lane in the earlier cars. There were radios once you were in the pits, so when you came in during a race they'd plug you in to talk, but for large parts of my career, once you left the pits, that was it, you were on your own.

Just a quick digression here, about my wonderful and dearly missed friend Colin Chapman. We had these radios that could be plugged into the cars in the pits and sometimes the cables were really quite long. Coming into the pits as we did at very high speed it could all get a bit messy! At my first race, I'd just come off the back of a good lap and I drove into the pits to talk to Colin and my engineer. I was very pleased with the lap and my engineer put his thumb up to gesture his satisfaction. Colin was standing next to the car but not really looking around, and the next thing I knew he'd grabbed the engineer's thumb – thinking it was the radio plug – and was desperately trying to ram it into the radio socket, all the while talking to someone and clearly unable to work out why the plug wouldn't slot into his belt controller properly. I was shouting through my visor, 'Colin, that's his thumb!' But I was mostly just laughing out loud, it was so funny. He was so focused on the car and the race that he simply didn't notice he was effectively about to amputate this guy's thumb instead of talking to me on the radio. Fortunately, most radio hook-ups went to plan rather better but, nonetheless, the reality of driving F1 cars during that era was that once you left the pits, you were on your own.

I hope you can see from this description that an F1 car in the early 1980s was a very uncomfortable and at times extremely lonely place to be. There is really only one word to describe a Formula 1 driver's cockpit: hostile. If you are driving an ugly car, then of course it is more hostile; it is not a nice place to be. However, if you are driving a good car that is balanced, has good suspension and great grip, then it is an *excitingly* hostile car. On those occasions, despite all of the discomfort, the claustrophobia, the heat, the extreme demands on your body … there is no better place in the world.

I was due to race twice more in my first grand prix season. In Holland, I had some mechanical failures and ended up doing a qualifying lap in Elio's car, complete with his personal seat, but I was still good for 16th on the grid. A brake failure retired me on lap 16, which was obviously disappointing, but my lap times had been a few tenths behind the two main drivers and it was another grand prix under my belt. The final race of the season for me was supposed to be the European Grand Prix at Imola, but I slid off in first qualifying and was unable to start the race.

There was another opportunity to race at the forthcoming United States Grand Prix, so I was still buoyant, despite the frustration of Imola. I was *so* focused. I'm not going to reel off the usual lap times and stories of how much testing I was doing, but I do have another barometer of how hungry I was at this point.

In Formula 1, you need focus to succeed and climb up the grid towards a world title. However, you also need focus to stay alive; more so in those yesteryear races when safety standards were not what they are today. It's stating the obvious, I know, but if you didn't concentrate in an F1 car from the late 1970s and early 1980s, you could end up dead. It's as simple as that. In elite sportsmen and women, the level of focus they have is often way beyond what non-professional people *think* is focus. Sometimes I am focused to such an extent that I shut out all distractions and am pretty much in my own world. Let me give you a funny example from those early times with Lotus.

As I mentioned, I was supposed to be travelling to Watkins Glen for the final race of the 1980 season, the United States Grand Prix. Rosanne and I were all geared up to go; we were both very excited about the prospect as we had never been to the States before. Unfortunately, shortly before, my team-mate Mario had a big accident in his car in Canada and the monocoque was written off. Then I got a phone call from Colin and he said, 'Nigel, I'm really sorry, you won't be able to race in America because we have lost a car and there is no way we can get it repaired in time. We need to use your spare car, so I'm afraid you don't have a drive. I'm sorry to say that the USA race is off, for you.'

He could obviously tell how devastated I was, so he said, 'Look, I know it's no compensation, but when was the last time you and Rosanne had a nice holiday?'

'I can't remember the last time we had a proper holiday, Colin.'

'Well, how about you both come out to the States anyway and visit all the tourist spots? You will absolutely love it out there.'

It might sound odd but, as much as I was flattered that he'd offered, I was actually still really disappointed not to be racing. I wanted to be at the coalface, so to speak, to be racing, not lying on a beach or at a theme park. I'd have been far happier if he'd said, 'Come at our expense to Watkins Glen and just watch.' That would've been much better for me. I'd rather be in the mix, learning, consuming information and knowledge, not soaking up the sun.

Anyway, that wasn't going to happen and Colin, being a total gentleman, made his generous offer, so off we went to America. However, the whole time we were there my mind was basically in the pit lane. As beautiful as some of the local scenery was, I was constantly thinking about what was happening at Watkins Glen. Funnily enough, Rosanne's mind wasn't stuck in the oily pit lane like mine!

One particular day, we were due to go on an organised coach trip to see the sights. I wasn't really interested, but Rosanne was keen so I agreed to go on the escorted tour. We got on the coach with a crowd of other holidaymakers and off we went. I have to be honest, this wasn't really my cup of tea at all. I prefer my own company with Rosanne, just us two; being stuck on a coach with a load of strangers would never be my idea of a fun holiday.

We visited various spots and the guide told us all about the area, but after a couple of hours, I'd kind of had enough. Then we stopped for a break at a vineyard, by which time I'd decided I needed a bit of peace and quiet. We all started to file off the coach and, with my back to Rosanne, I took her hand and said, 'I need a bit of separation from all this. Let's just have a wander off for a bit.'

I could feel a bit of resistance in her hand, and I noticed she wasn't particularly taking mine that eagerly, but I was determined – focused! – on getting away for a little while. I didn't look at her; I just held her hand tightly and walked off the coach. 'Come on, Rosanne. Let's go, please.'

I was talking to her as we walked away from the coach and when we got up to a viewing area I said, 'Isn't this nice? Look at that beautiful scenery.'

Silence.

I thought, *Oh dear, maybe I've overstepped the mark?* So I started to say, 'Look, we haven't fallen out have we ...?' But when I turned to speak, I actually ending up saying, 'Who the hell are you?'

It turned out I'd grabbed some complete stranger's hand, marched her off the coach and there I was, a hundred yards away from the group, talking to this poor woman, while Rosanne was still standing by the bus! My wife was with the woman's husband and they were both killing themselves laughing.

I said to the woman, 'I am so sorry. Why didn't you say something?'

She just smiled and said, 'Well, you were very persuasive so I just went with it.'

You see – the power of focus.

It was at the end of the 1980 season that I found out that Mario Andretti was leaving to join Alfa Romeo and that Colin Chapman wanted me as his number two driver, alongside Elio. Colin was keen to have a British driver in his team and, despite some initial resistance from sponsors, he was adamant and eventually announced that I had been given a full contract to drive the 1981 season. This was incredible news: I was going to be a full-time Formula 1 driver. Not a test driver. The real deal. I was to be paid $25,000 for the year, but would have to cover my own travel expenses, which were to be considerable. I didn't care. Frankly, I would have walked barefoot to the races if that's what it took. This was it: Colin had given me my big chance.

Colin Chapman was just the most fantastic person, who basically became my second father, my mentor and the most inspirational man in my life until the day he died. As I write this book, I still find myself getting emotional when I remember him. His premature death is still devastating to me to this day. He was truly unique.

He was an incredible character and an unbelievable talent. The history books tell us that he was a pivotal figure in the world of motorsport and, trust me, from personal experience, every word of that is true. I would say he was both a maverick and a genius. Perhaps you can't be one without the other, I'm not sure, but I do know that Colin was an inspirational figure with a brilliant mind. He had the ability to go off at a tangent when he was facing a problem or a particularly difficult challenge. He was surrounded by many hugely talented people and sometimes he would have an idea that might raise a few eyebrows or be considered almost bizarre. However, he would investigate that idea nonetheless and, most times, he would be proved right. I think certainly in motorsport, and also to a degree in life in general, you have to be a maverick to be brave enough to do something that most others don't believe in, and then to have the vision to follow through on your idea. Maybe a better word than maverick would be cavalier. Certainly a genius, without a shadow of a doubt.

Long before I finally got my chance of an F1 drive with Lotus, I was so focused on driving for Colin that I tried to think of every possible way to set myself apart from other prospective drivers. Perhaps the most extreme example of this is that I learned to fly. I am lucky enough and very proud to have held my pilot's licence for many years, during which time I have owned and flown some wonderful planes. The truth is that I deliberately learned to fly to have synergy with Colin Chapman. I knew Colin loved his planes and helicopters, and I was convinced that if I could fly, too, we would have a great interest in common. I would be able to 'speak the lingo', if you like. So, even though money was extremely tight, I started flying lessons. This meant holding down three jobs and Rosanne working incredibly hard as well. Without her support at home, I simply couldn't have afforded it. She was brilliant.

When you are young, you can do that, you can burn the candle at both ends and still somehow get up the next morning and feel okay. Tired, maybe, but off we'd go again. I was completely dedicated to and energised by my career, and I saw Colin Chapman as the perfect team owner to drive for.

Paying for flying lessons was exhausting for both of us. The cost was so high compared to our income that I had to have lessons spread out over many months, because we simply couldn't afford to have one big block of tuition. It took some time but eventually I was delighted to pass the exams and earn my licence, in 1979 (I also have a helicopter pilot's licence). Sure enough, I enjoyed many fascinating chats with Colin about flying and it was something that we definitely bonded over.

That said, I do remember vividly one occasion when he nearly scared the living daylights out of me with a plane. One night he flew to the Lotus headquarters in Hethel, Norfolk, but unbeknown to us at the time, he'd had a little engine trouble. By which I mean one of his two engines wasn't actually working! That's how good a pilot he was. The team was due to fly out to Paul Ricard the next day, so the plan was for me to co-pilot with Colin and head off early the following morning. Shortly after dawn, we all piled into the plane but, as we were taxiing,

I noticed I couldn't hear one of the engines, so I politely said, 'Er, Colin, you haven't started the other engine yet … are you trying to save on fuel?' In fact, despite Colin's best efforts, the engine wouldn't start so he wisely got us out of the plane and we all ended up going to Paul Ricard on a commercial flight.

With Colin there was never anything other than complete and total dedication to developing the best cars and winning races. He was focused on getting one step ahead of his competitors and designing something that was totally incredible, utterly innovative. If you look at just two of his innovations in the time I was racing with him, they will tell you all you need to know about the mind of the man. Firstly, he developed the so-called 'ground effect' car, which revolutionised the grip that F1 cars were able to create and in turn sent all the other teams scurrying to their design departments to play catch-up (I will expand on this shortly). Secondly, he also developed the amazing twin-chassis car, which was so revolutionary that it was banned before it had even raced! He was always so ahead of the game.

Mind you, when you have someone who is such a visionary, you do occasionally get a piece of new technology that scares the bejesus out of you. The most terrifying technical advance we tested was a bendable steering column. The steering column went through the dashboard and then bent 90 degrees and into the actual steering rack, so you had two bends in it, all made from woven wire mesh. The problem was that when we were out there testing it at very high speeds, we found – much to our horror – that, under load and G-force, this steering column would steer the car itself in the corners. Under extreme load the car would do really funny things, then, when you took the load off the steering, it would move unpredictably again. I have never been so scared in my life! I went round a few totally terrifying laps at Snetterton to try it and, when I came back in, probably white as a sheet, Colin smiled, laughed and said, 'Well, it was a tongue-in-cheek job! At least we tried it!' Frightened the hell out of me, that did, Colin.

Colin would draw his ideas old school, as a draughtsman. This is a great point to make in terms of new technology and how the sport has changed since its early days. In the modern era, the teams and designers have so much computer-processing power that they can come up with new ideas and, before anyone even sits in a car at a test, the experts back at team head-quarters can tell if it will work or not. From that point of view, modern-day drivers have a much easier ride, because they are not physical guinea pigs, at least not to the same degree we were. Of course, sometimes the calibration between systems such as computational fluid dynamics and the real-world track is not quite perfect and there may still be an issue. However, generally speaking, real-world driving and testing are now more of a validation that an idea or upgrade will work as per the computer prediction. It is the final tick in the box. When we were testing the new ideas, there wasn't even a box! Sometimes, maybe only one in ten new ideas would work; they'd all be handmade and, if they failed in testing, they'd be taken off the car and scrapped. Literally, back then, the engineers would build a part, stick it on the car and send you off round the track at 200mph to see if it worked. I tell you what, though, it was great fun.

As a man, in private, Colin was totally inspiring. He would walk into a room with his white hair and big smile and everyone would be captivated by his massive charisma. He was lively and full of mischief. He loved playing pranks. One example of his fun side was when he threw the most fabulous end-of-season party one year in Nottingham. We were enjoying strawberries and cream and I asked Colin if I could play a little trick on one of the sponsors. Colin was all for it, so I duly pressed a whole plate of cream on this guy's head. There was laughter all round and then the most enormous food fight erupted, with cakes, fruit, cream, food everywhere. I was laughing so much it hurt. Colin was left with a little extra on his hotel bill for having so much fun. Incredibly fond memories.

He made me laugh so many times. My first grand prix in Austria was, of course, in the days before electronic timing. I was in the pits while they were working on my car when Colin came over to me and said, 'Mario is flying today!' He held up his stopwatch in preparation for a fast lap time then he said, 'Look, I think he's about to do the fastest lap ...' Then I watched as Colin proceeded to walk quite slowly towards the first corner 50 yards away and *only then* did he stop his watch, at which point he turned to me and said, 'Told you!' In reality, he'd gained Mario a few tenths of a second by shortening the lap for him just by walking down there! It made me laugh so much.

Another time I will never forget was when a particular person was really agitating Colin one day. Don't get me wrong, this person certainly wasn't being objectionable, quite the opposite in fact. This was a fairly important individual who was going on and on. 'Colin, if I can do anything for you, anything at all, just say the word ...' I could see Colin getting a little bit rattled and eventually, when the guy repeated himself yet again, 'Is there anything I can do at all?', Colin replied, 'Yes – piss off!' It was so funny. To be fair to the guy, he took it in good spirits; he realised he'd been a little intense and he backed off, and we all had a giggle. Plus, Colin just had a way with words – even words like that! – which meant he was able to say things and not necessarily cause offence. Moments like that you just sit back and go, 'Wow!'

I have so many happy memories of being with Colin and also his lovely wife Hazel. In fact, I would like to take this opportunity to personally thank them both, as well as the whole family, for their generous and unwavering support. Colin taught me so much. Obviously, just to sit down and listen to that man talk about engines, aerodynamics, chassis design, the intricate mechanics of what we were doing, was just a joy every single day. However, he also became a mentor to me outside of racing. I was still a young man and finding my way in life as well as motorsport, and Colin never missed an opportunity to offer me a piece of advice; he was so generous in guiding me at that time. Mind you, sometimes his guidance was delivered fairly brutally.

I lived nearly four hours away from Hethel (on a good run), so my time at Lotus involved a lot of driving off the track as well as on the circuit. I hate being late (still to this day) and ever since I was a young man I would always leave what I call a 'fudge factor' – by which I mean I would allow plenty of extra time to get to meetings. This one particular morning, not long after I'd started as a test driver, we had a 9am meeting with Colin, so I set off before 5am to make sure I would be there on time. Unfortunately, the weather was not on my side, with a thick fog enveloping the motorways. Worse still, about halfway along my journey there was a fatal car accident which completely blocked my planned route, forcing me to take all sorts of diversions. Despite these various obstacles in my way, I arrived at Hethel just two minutes after nine o'clock.

I walked into the meeting room and Colin absolutely launched into me. He bluntly berated me for being late. He said it was completely unacceptable and that if I ever did it again he would sack me. I was disappointed to have been late, but I really felt I had done my very best in exceptionally difficult circumstances, so I started to explain. 'I sincerely apologise,

Colin, but can I just explain? The fog was appalling and the motorway was closed for hours due to this big accident. It's been dreadful out there.'

'Nigel, frankly, I don't care,' he said. 'If we have a meeting at 9am then you have to be here at 9am. No discussions. You should've come up the night before.'

I said, 'Again, sorry, Colin, I am not complaining but I can't actually afford to come up . . .'

He wasn't interested.

About two weeks later, there was another meeting scheduled for 9am and I wasn't going to make the same mistake again. I drove to Hethel the night before and I slept in my car. I've got to be honest, it wasn't the best night's sleep I've ever had but at least I knew I was going to be there on time. The next morning, I was still dozing under a blanket in the car when I saw Colin park up nearby (he always came into work very early). He started to walk to the factory doors, but then out of the corner of his eye caught sight of me stretching in my car. He walked over, looking slightly puzzled, tapped on the window and said, 'Nigel, what on earth are you doing?'

'You said I was never to be late for a meeting with you again. I can't afford a hotel, so here I am . . . There's no way I'm going to be late for you again, sir!'

He shook his head and then walked away, saying as he turned, 'Nigel, you're a funny bugger.' I watched him walk to the factory doors and, as he pulled the handle to go in, I could just see him smiling.

He could be extremely generous, too. I want to retell a story that sums up how incredibly and spontaneously magnanimous Colin could be. In my first full F1 season, Rosanne had to stay at home for many races because I couldn't really afford to pay for both of us to fly around the world. We couldn't stand being away from one another. In Monaco I qualified very well (third in fact), which Colin was delighted with, but I was still unhappy because I missed Rosanne. Colin quickly picked up on this and asked me what the problem was.

'I am delighted about the grid position, of course, Colin, but I miss my wife and she's still at home working so hard. I want her to be here, sharing the journey with me.'

That night at dinner, Colin announced in front of the whole team that he was doubling my retainer so that Rosanne could leave work and accompany me to the races. That is the mark of the man.

Colin only ever treated me with great respect. Back when I had been just a young lad driving round in that little Ford Escort checking up on suppliers, Colin had never questioned my opinions. Fast-forward to being his actual F1 driver and that trust continued. If I said something to Colin about a car's set-up, balance, handling, whatever element we were testing or racing, he never queried it. He genuinely valued my opinion. He was fantastic; you could talk to him about anything, cars, engines, planes or indeed just life. Perhaps he and I hit it off so well because we were both strange and similar in a number of ways.

Not long before Christmas week in 1982, the world of motorsport was rocked by the news that Colin had died suddenly of a heart attack. After Colin's tragic death, my time at Lotus was not entirely enjoyable. There were some very difficult relationships which have been well documented, so I won't repeat myself here, but suffice to say the moment Colin passed away my world altered almost completely. My relationship with Colin was so special, so rewarding, and I am so grateful for the chance to have known and worked with him. I firmly believe that had Colin not passed away, I could have been world champion a lot sooner. By that I don't mean for one second to denigrate the incredible job that Sir Frank and Patrick Head did for me at Williams with that amazing championship car; nor, indeed, everything that Ferrari also did for me – that goes without saying. I am just suggesting that perhaps, if destiny had allowed Colin to stay with us longer, we could have won the World Championship together.

There was nothing I wouldn't have done for that man. According to some motorsport mythology, Colin Chapman has apparently been spotted in some far-flung town in the depths of Argentina. I'm not usually one for stories like that but, in this case, were it to be true then I hope he is having the most wonderful time, and I have to say the world would be a much more beautiful place if Colin were still here. I still miss him, very much.

CHAPTER 5

WHAT IS GOING TO HAPPEN NEXT?

This was a very exciting time for me, debuting my first full season in the sport I loved. However, conversely, 1981 was a very turbulent year for Formula 1. There was a power struggle for control of the sport and there were also issues and concerns about the safety of the cars – in particular, the astonishing speeds that cars were generating due to the ever-improving so-called 'ground effect' technology. Sadly, there were also some horrific deaths and injuries, very distressing reminders of a driver's mortality.

In my first full season, I had eight retirements, one failure to qualify, my first ever podium finish, and ultimately finished 14th in the championship with eight points. Back in March 1981, the start of the new season was dominated in some ways by the controversy surrounding Colin's amazing so-called twin-chassis car, the Lotus 88. At the first grand prix of the season, in America, the twin-chassis car Elio was driving was thrown out of the race, and this led to very protracted arguments, legal battles and debate. The car would, eventually, be banned and Colin was absolutely gutted. The politics of that situation aside, the car itself was an astounding piece of technology – yet another genius idea from the Colin Chapman team! Two chassis and two suspension systems – very complex, very clever, and a remarkable car.

After qualifying a pleasing seventh at the first official grand prix of the season, I retired after clipping a wall, which was obviously disappointing. The second race at Rio was more fruitful, with an 11th-place finish for me, which was a solid improvement. That Rio trip was quite memorable, as we were there for six weeks because we couldn't afford to fly home and then back out to Argentina a few weeks later. However, we had nowhere to stay – I think modern-day drivers would laugh if they knew what it was like back then. We ended up sleeping in the house of a friend of a friend in the back of the hills, which was pretty rough. I was feeling, *Where on earth are we, Rosanne?* We had no choice because of the money situation, but it was all very scary. We could even hear gunshots from the favelas at night. (Another year we went down there when the police and fire brigade were on strike and that night there were something like 80 murders. Several F1 people were attacked in those areas.)

Money was still tight and we couldn't afford to spend a lot on meals, so, for example, we would often budget for one hamburger each per day. We always liked Wendy's; we pretty much survived on those for some time. Not exactly your modern-day professional sportsman's diet, I admit, so maybe I won't mention that next time I bump into an F1 sports nutritionist. When you are an F1 driver battling it out on the track, admitting to being fuelled by Wendy's is not something you like to own up to!

However, I will remember Rio in 1981 for an altogether

more dramatic event. People say I was a courageous driver, and in my era the drivers had to have nerves of steel to go out lap after lap after they had seen a friend or colleague seriously injured or even killed. There is a very interesting philosophical debate about bravery in motorsport. There is an implied bravery in being able to do our job. People have often said to me, 'Oh, racing drivers are really courageous.' I am not sure I would class myself or any other racing drivers as brave. We as racing drivers have programmed our minds to go out there and try to win, even if someone has been injured or killed. I'm not sure that is bravery or courage; it's just what we do for our jobs. I'm not denying you have to have nerves of steel, you have to be very competitive, you have to push yourself more than many people would be prepared to, you have to get back in the saddle at times when you don't want to, you have to dig deep, all of those things ... But courageous?

Courage for me is an outstanding act of valour, when someone goes way over the normal call of duty and in fact puts their own life at risk to save others. Courage is more spontaneous, instinctive; less premeditated. If someone steps out with a knife pointed at you, do you dive for cover or grab the knife? I feel like I have only been *truly* courageous once in my life and that was in Rio in 1981. This incident has been documented briefly before, but I want to revisit the afternoon in more detail because it summarises my belief about, and philosophy on, courage. The only time I have shown unconditional, utterly selfless courage in my life is when I had to pull my very good friend Peter Collins out of the sea in Rio and save him from drowning, in March 1981.

As you know, Peter had played a pivotal role in bringing me to the attention of Colin Chapman and, since then, we had become firm friends. He is a lovely man who I will always be very grateful to for his part in helping my career. In Rio that day, we were relaxing on a typical Brazilian beach, surrounded by bronzed bodies. Rosanne went in the sea initially, but she didn't like the strength of the undercurrent and soon got out. I jumped about in the shallows for a while then we both went back to our towels to lie down. We were chatting and having a lovely time when we both noticed Peter was still out in the sea; in fact, quite a long way out and, at first, we thought he was waving at us.

Then I said, 'He's not waving hello – he's in trouble.' I shouted to Rosanne to go and get some help and then sprinted to the water, jumped in and started swimming towards him. By the time I got to him, he was in big trouble, gasping for air as the undercurrent tugged away at him. Then our lovely friend and my team-mate Elio swam in to help too, but he got pulled away by the fierce current and started swimming in the wrong direction. I couldn't believe it. It was getting really scary and by now Peter was pretty blue. It was terrifying. I realised that we didn't have much time, but I couldn't swim strongly enough to fight against this vicious riptide – it was so violent. That's when I realised that I was probably about to drown, too.

Meanwhile, Rosanne was running up and down the beach looking for a buoy or a safety ring, but there was nothing. She was getting frantic, shouting, 'Somebody help!', but they all just sat or stood there and watched. Nobody could speak English, although it was pretty obvious there was a problem. She was desperately trying to get help, but to no avail.

I just fought and fought, while holding Peter and treading water. By now his eyes were bulging. I will never forget his face, his eyes. I just kept thinking, *Oh dear me, we are in trouble here*. Luckily, destiny was on our side that day: by the grace of the good Lord we momentarily found a sandbank out of nowhere and that very brief – but crucial – moment of sanctuary meant that we could just touch our toes on the bottom for a matter of a few seconds and breathe and gasp for air. Then the waves started crashing over us again and we were fighting against drowning once more. I later found out that many people died every year on that strip of beach and, let me tell you, I thought we were next as I tried to save Peter's – and now my own – life.

We were so lucky. Eventually, I managed to drag him nearer to the shore and pull him up, then we caught one of the waves and I sort of surfed him in. He was almost unconscious by this point. It felt like we had been out there an eternity, yet there were hundreds of people on the beach just watching – no one came. I later found out that Rosanne was on the beach literally begging people to help us and nobody would. It transpired that people were so frightened of the tide that they were fearful they would die in any rescue attempt. Peter was from Australia and perhaps understandably saw the surf and thought this would be fun to swim in. It was just an innocent, and almost fatal, mistake.

Eventually, Rosanne found some guys who were willing to help. They waded into the shallows and made a chain with their linked arms, then grabbed our arms and passed us up to the beach and safety. We were both lying on the floor, exhausted, and they began to perform CPR on Peter. They tried to start doing the same to me, but I pushed them away. I was fine – shocked, spent, traumatised, but fine. Peter was taken to hospital, as was Elio, but luckily both were okay.

Later, the enormity of how close I came to losing my own life with that act of friendship really hit me. Peter has very graciously told many people that he wouldn't be here now if it wasn't for what I did that day. Had I not been at the height of my fitness, then this particular part of the story could have been very different, because I simply wouldn't have had the physical endurance to keep us afloat for such a long time.

I have raced inches from concrete walls that would take my life if I lost control of a car. I have tested parts on cars at 200mph that are completely unknown in terms of performance and safety, effectively being a human guinea pig for what are essentially untested, ground-based missiles. However, that day in Rio is the only time I would suggest that I could use that very special word for my actions: courage.

Back on the track, my debut full season in F1 was marred by tragedy, with incidents that tested even the most experienced and resolute drivers. In May, the F1 circus rolled into Zolder, Belgium, which was to be a weekend of extreme opposites for me. On the one hand, I would secure my first ever podium, but, in dark contrast, one mechanic was killed and another seriously injured.

In the pit lane, a mechanic suffered severe head injuries when he fell between the wheels of a car and, terribly, he died the next day. The tragic accident sent shock waves around the paddock. Then, at the start of the race, Riccardo Patrese's Arrows stalled, so a mechanic jumped over the wall to restart the car. I was sitting behind Riccardo's car and therefore witnessed what happened. Patrese's team-mate Siegfried Stohr saw the green light, started his grand prix and slammed into the back of his colleague's car, smashing into the legs of this poor, trapped mechanic.

It was so graphic, so shocking and, coming just a few hours after the mechanic had been fatally injured, it felt horrendous. Carnage. At that specific moment, I was strapped into my car, a few feet away from where this guy had been crushed. At the time, I was certain he would die from his injuries, but thankfully, although his legs were broken, he did survive. However, seeing that terrible accident had an instantly destructive impact on my psyche. I have spoken about this before, but I sat in the car and I couldn't move my arms or legs. I don't mean I was strapped in tightly; I mean, *I literally couldn't move*. I was paralysed with shock. I was crying behind my visor. The team wanted to get me out of the car but I wouldn't, or rather I couldn't. In retrospect, it was a blessing that I couldn't move because I honestly think if I had got out of that car at that moment, I would never have got back in again. It was that shocking. I was so distressed that they even fetched Rosanne to the grid to talk to me and calm me down. There seemed to be an all-pervading sense of tragedy on the grid that weekend. This was only my seventh official grand prix. I just felt, *What is going to happen next?*

When the race finally got under way, I managed to put the distress out of my mind and drive very well. I had no choice, it was my job. After a thrilling tussle with the great Gilles Villeneuve, I managed to grab third in a rain-shortened race. Zolder was a very challenging, twisting, undulating circuit. I got the car reasonably hooked up and, despite everything that had happened, I was very focused. Villeneuve was pushing me hard in his Ferrari – he was known for his unbelievable car control and his fiery style of trying to overtake, so to have the pressure of his Ferrari behind me and still succeed in beating him to the podium was a very proud moment.

Stepping away from the injury and death of that weekend, that first podium was a fantastic milestone for me personally. I had beaten a well-established team-mate. I had held off one of the sport's greats for third place. I actually felt like I had won the race. I would even say that first podium, given the extreme circumstances and the standard of drivers around me, is on a par with my first win. Part of the reason for my delight was that I felt I had consolidated my position within F1. When you break through into the top level of any sport, it is a great achievement. However, some people relax and forget that they have to then consolidate that position. They have to validate their membership. In Formula 1, validation is gaining a podium. For me personally, it meant the world. There were so many other drivers who were waiting in the wings all the time, lots of teams; injury was a constant threat, from testing to racing and accidents, so drivers came and went really quickly. Your window of opportunity could be frighteningly small. I felt Zolder had validated me as a Formula 1 driver and it gave me a huge boost of confidence.

The twin-chassis controversy rumbled on to Monaco, where I was very proud to qualify in third, but in the race itself I retired with rear suspension problems (a disappointment that was mitigated a little after Colin had doubled my retainer, as I mentioned before). Then, after that, the 1981 season was pretty patchy, with three top-seven finishes and five more retirements, four through reliability issues, one through driver error. Lotus performed only modestly well for the rest of the season, but, despite the many difficult moments that year, I was aware that I was gaining experience all the time. I also heard that a few other team owners had been talking about me and asking questions.

The most disappointing race of the year was at Silverstone, my first British Grand Prix. Naturally, I was very excited at the prospect of racing in front of the home fans. Unfortunately, the twin-chassis controversy overshadowed my weekend because when that car was stopped from racing, Lotus didn't have enough time to prepare a replacement for me, so I wasn't able to qualify and therefore didn't race. How did Colin Chapman

react to my obvious devastation, on a weekend when his technological tour de force of a car – which had cost him a fortune
to develop – had been prohibited from racing? Well, he'd heard
that Rosanne and I were having difficulty getting a mortgage
and so he stepped in and helped us so that we could afford to
get our own home. What a man.

CHAPTER 6

GROUND EFFECT AND THE PSYCHOLOGY OF FEAR

A s I was trying to establish myself as a top driver, one of the most exhilarating aspects of the amazing technology on these cars that I had to learn was the so-called ground effect. This was perhaps the most brutal, dangerous and yet hugely exciting technical development to appear during my career, and it was Colin Chapman who first introduced the concept in Formula 1, with devastating performance effects.

To be there at the time when this technology was evolving in Formula 1 was a great privilege and a real thrill. As savage and unpredictable as the cars with full ground effect could be, I loved the challenge and the adrenaline rush, but at the same time it could occasionally be genuinely frightening. Proper frightening. For those of you who do not spend hours poring over the history books of motorsport engineering and evolution, here is a basic explanation of how ground effect worked. It is well known that designers use wings and aerofoils on the top of cars to control the flow of air and therefore the amount of drag and downforce. Formula 1 cars had utilised wings on the car's body for many years by the time I was racing, of course. What ground effect did was to exploit the fact that *the ground itself* was a part of that equation. By that, I mean the air between the underbody of the car and the ground plays a crucial part in the amount of downforce that the car generates. When the genius minds of people like Colin Chapman and his team dug further into this principle, it became apparent that by forming tunnels – known as venturis – along the underside of the body (and later the introduction of side brushes then skirts), the ground effect could be controlled, thus generating massive downforce, which in turn allowed cars to take corners far quicker. By using skirts and venturis, the gap could be controlled – like a very precise wind tunnel under the car – and therefore the air underneath could be manipulated to accelerate. Consequently, the pressure in that space would drop, while the pressure on the top of the car was unaffected, thus creating a downforce pushing the car on to the track. If you take an airplane, the principle is that the air pressure under the wing is greater than the air pressure above the wing, which creates lift and forces the plane into the air. Put very simply, ground effect is the opposite of that. Essentially, the presence of ground effect sucks a car down on to the track. The amazing thing was that the faster you went, the more the car was sucked down! In some cases, it was thought the massive ground effect was estimated to be as much as ten times more powerful than the downforce created by the wings on top of the car. Easily enough to drive the car upside down along a tunnel.

This all sounds extremely clever, and it was. Speaking as someone who helped test the principle at high speed on many hundreds of breathtakingly fast laps, I can also say that in terms of grip and downforce, when ground effect worked correctly it was *absolutely astonishing*. You could head towards a corner at 200mph, then brake no more than about 50 metres away from the entrance and still carry an incredible amount of speed through that corner. For a very fast corner, you could fly in at a staggeringly high speed and yet maintain that velocity, it was that stunning. The cars were glued to the track and you were just doing these ridiculous speeds. It was so violent, so staggeringly incredible, so amazing.

The science of ground effect kept evolving, too. The people developing the system were so brilliant they were quickly able to tweak and tune the way ground effect worked depending on which circuit you were at and the demands on the car. For example, they were able to alter the angle of the tunnels underneath. They used what were called 'shims', which helped to move the centre of pressure backwards or forwards along the bottom of the car. If you were on a slow circuit and wanted better turn into the corners, you'd move the centre of pressure to the front of the car by altering the tunnels, or by altering the rake of the car, which also adjusts the angle. On very fast circuits, where you wanted a stable rear end, you could move the centre of pressure backwards a little bit and carry more front wing to get the car to turn in and then to keep the stability so that you could go round the corners flat out. You could tweak it; you could move the main centre of pressure of the car depending on how you set the ride height and the angle of the wings, so it was a very complex science indeed, tuning these cars in a completely different way. To complicate matters, every time a car compressed – namely, when it braked and the underbody tilted, even minutely – the centre of pressure moved up and down the length of the car. So the challenge of regulating ground effect was a constantly moving target. Some of the brains behind the science were just legendary and they were able to manipulate where that centre of pressure was located, and in so doing they could make the car more driveable.

Of course, there was a price to pay for ground effect, on a number of levels. Firstly and perhaps most obviously, the sheer savagery of the cornering speed massively increased the amount of lateral G experienced by the drivers. Lateral G is the most toxic kind of G-force. You could be pulling around 5G through corners and it was just totally brutal on the body. There were corners on some tracks that drivers were used to going around at a speed they were familiar with from the days before ground effect. Now we were heading into and through these same corners at substantially quicker speeds. On certain tracks, it was almost like having to relearn the entire circuit. I have to say I always enjoyed that part; in my opinion, I was one of the fastest learners on the grid, so I personally felt I could quickly absorb the changes that ground effect created in terms of driving lines and the altered subtleties of each track.

The perfect ground effect set-up led to such colossal G-force that it was rumoured that some drivers were blacking out. The problem with G-force is that it is rarely constant. It changes from one moment to another. Also, linear G and lateral G are two very different experiences. The linear G-force in a straight line was massive; when you are loading up into a corner, heading straight towards the bend under deceleration, you just have acceleration or deceleration G. That is pretty immense at times.

However, the really vicious manifestation of this phenomenon is so-called lateral G – that is, the G you experience when you are cornering. This is the most dangerous G-force in the world. We were experiencing more G-forces than an astronaut might be faced with and yet we were not even wearing G-suits. Even fighter pilots who experience considerable positive and negative G do not experience the lateral G that an F1 driver does. To give you real-world context to that statistic: if you corner at 5G then you are experiencing the equivalent of five people of your own body weight pushing against your head.

It gets worse, much worse. It has been shown that when an F1 car bottoms out in the middle of a corner, for that split second the G-force shoots up to somewhere in the region of pulling 25 positive G. That's 25 people pressing down on your body, all while you are driving at very high speed and trying to race other drivers, think about lap times, track position, strategy and so on. If that sounds extreme, that's because it is. So when you see a car fly round a corner and sparks briefly fly up from underneath the body as the car bottoms out, you probably think that looks rather dramatic. Let me tell you, it's absolutely dramatic for the driver!

Dealing with G is an absolutely pivotal part of being a great F1 driver. Understanding when the G will hit you, in what direction, how severe, how that will affect your driving and so on are crucial parts of the jigsaw. G-force is *such* a massive force, so powerful, that you have to find a way to cope with it. The best way in my opinion is actually counterintuitive, in that you have to learn to relax into the G, otherwise your own body's tension works against you. Easier said than done when you are cornering at 150mph and your body is being battered and smashed inside the cockpit. The downside of relaxing into G-force is that when you learn to do that successfully, your muscle and skin and bone are literally forced into every tiny crevice and corner of the steel cockpit, and that can be really painful. That is when you feel every corner of the car, especially if you have got no foam or seat in the cockpit. Yet if you tense up in anticipation of that pain, you will negatively affect your performance. So it is quite an acquired skill, absolutely mind over matter, and really quite hard to do successfully for long periods of time.

Another crucial development that ground effect created was the need for far harder suspensions. The reason for this was simple: given that ground effect worked by precisely controlling the gap and airflow under a car, you could no longer have nice, soft suspensions that absorbed all the bumps and lumps in a track, cushioning you as you drove. That movement up and down would, of course, dramatically alter the air pressure under the car and either dilute or possibly completely destroy the ground effect. Therefore, the optimum aim was to maintain a specific ride height where ground effect could operate consistently. Consequently, the ground-effect cars were fitted with much harder suspensions. In terms of ride quality, you went from the soft springs that provided a not unpleasant ride to what was essentially a rock-hard, super-powerful go-kart travelling at lunatic speeds around corners. In terms of your day-to-day experience out on the track, the enormous change in ride quality was really quite dramatic. And I can tell you from very painful experience over thousands and thousands of laps of having my arse and pretty much every bone in my body completely battered that ground-effect suspensions were *much harder*.

There were many cost implications of ground effect, too. For example, the soft springs on cars cost several hundred pounds, but the much firmer and more precise ground-effect springs cost thousands of pounds. For other teams playing catch-up with Lotus, it was far worse, because the cost of developing ground effect from scratch was potentially enormous.

As a driver, you could learn to live with the severe lateral G created. You could train your body to absorb those new extreme forces. You could relearn tracks and understand where the ground effect worked and where it was less powerful. You could get used to the harsher ride. However, the most chronic downside of ground effect was the fact that at times it was *inconsistent*. When you are travelling into a corner at speeds in the region of 200mph, inconsistency can be lethal. Literally. This was the ultimate price you risked having to pay for using ground effect – if a car bottomed out for some reason and that crucial ride height altered, the ground-effect system could fail and if that happened then you were nothing more than a helpless passenger in the lap of a monster.

Why was ground effect inconsistent and therefore at times highly dangerous? Well, let me explain. If you were able to maintain a consistent ride height and the skirts at the side of the car stayed in their correct position, with the predicted airflow under the car precisely as expected, then it was just the most beautifully powerful, savagely exhilarating system. There was a perfect window of ride height whereby the car was amazingly driveable, *incredibly* so. The tremendous downforce was just a joy when it was there. But then suddenly ... BOOM! ... it could be gone. At that instant, if you are halfway through a corner at 160mph, then you are in big, big trouble.

Usable ground effect could literally disappear in an instant. This could happen if one or both of the side skirts moved or became stuck, and also if the ride height altered for some reason. In those situations, the positive air pressure you had generated would stall and that incredible suction would dissipate instantly. You could go from having several thousand pounds of downforce to almost nothing in a heartbeat. To use the technical terms, the ground effect could 'attach' and 'detach' at times very unpredictably.

When ground effect disappears, the car becomes almost undriveable. If you were in the middle of a corner when that happened, there would be absolutely nothing you could do to save the car, and more than likely you would fly straight off and have a massive accident because, by definition, you are cornering at high speed. If that happened ... you'd better hold on tight. Certain corners you would enter and be thinking, *I might not actually come out of this corner at all, finito.*

The scariest part of ground effect was that you didn't know *when* it was going to fail. That's not strictly true; there were times when the car would start to do what was termed 'porpoising' – that is, bouncing up and down. This happened when the ground effect was detaching, reattaching, detaching, reattaching and so on. Maybe the skirt was partially stuck; there were a number of other possibilities, too, but the manifestation of the problem was this porpoising – which, I can tell you from personal experience, when it happens at nearly 200mph is very unsettling indeed.

The window of operation was so small, and the consequences of failure so vast. Ground effect was such a poisoned chalice. If you can imagine a car's performance is like the tip of a needle, and balancing perfectly on that tip is the optimum performance. The danger of going off line even a tiny fraction spells disaster. The aim was to make a ground-effect car's optimum performance more akin to an oblique curve, so that in the event of a failure you would still have a bigger window of working opportunity for that car before it flew off the track. However, at times, ground effect was all or nothing. It was very hard to harness the incredible energy and downforce and maintain it in a stable fashion. Everybody could get massive downforce using this idea; the trick was creating *usable* massive downforce.

The engineers, aerodynamicists and brains behind the system worked tirelessly for months and indeed years on end to try to solve the problem. They battled to try to regulate the ground effect, to make it 'solid' so that it did not compress – this prevented the centre of pressure under the car moving about unpredictably and therefore made the system consistent. They tried fixed skirts and other ideas to try to control the beast.

Ground effect suited my driving style. It suited a strong racer, a driver who would go into a corner and hang on for dear life. You almost had to have a suicidal trait, where you were willing to risk everything to try to do the job. Ultimately, the limitation of ground-effect technology (if it was working perfectly) was the human being driving the car. It was a case of how brave, how stupid, how talented are you? And how prepared are you to put it out there and risk everything? Literally *everything*.

Tragically, there were fatalities that some experts speculated ground effect may have contributed to. Patrick Depailler lost his life testing in Hockenheim in 1980. To be absolutely accurate, it was never actually certain if ground effect contributed to his fatal accident, which was attributed to a suspension failure. He went into a corner and the car appeared to simply fly off the track. Even if that fatality was not related to ground effect, there was much conjecture that the system could be very dangerous.

Ground effect was used between 1977 and 1982. As I mentioned, there were efforts to tame the idea to a degree, but it remained an essentially risky science. The F1 authorities eventually banned ground effect due to very justifiable safety concerns. I think if it had been left to continue and evolve unfettered, it could easily have killed many drivers. So they banned it, for all the correct reasons.

Despite all the negatives I have detailed, from a purely technical point of view ground effect was a truly phenomenal invention, and it was simply amazing to be involved right at the point when it was introduced into Formula 1 with Colin and then to see the evolution of that dark art.

From a driver's perspective, perhaps the single most damaging consequence of ground effect was the shattering of your confidence if it failed in a corner and you flew off the track. As a wider topic, this is the most crucial element of a driver's psyche. Specifically, during the era when I raced, the issue of how much you pushed your car was not just a question of how many race wins or podiums you might or might not get – it was potentially a matter of life or death. I am not being overly dramatic here. The harsh reality was that you had to have an abundance of confidence to win races at the top level at a time when serious injury and death were regularly witnessed. However, if that confidence started to crumble, you were in big trouble. Let me explain.

Formula 1 cars can be very unpredictable. Some are extremely quick in fast corners, but terrible in medium corners and vice versa. Part of the challenge of being a top driver is to understand your car's idiosyncrasies, learn to accommodate them, work with them. I called it the window of operation and you needed to learn to apply what you knew at the right moment.

The correct word to describe the best Formula 1 car is 'consistent'. That is what you crave in a racing car. Those cars are easier to set up and easier to drive. The more consistency, the greater the trust you could have in the car. A lack of trust in a car is the biggest problem that racing drivers face in the cockpit. Certainly for me it was anyway. Having the belief that you can go into a corner as fast as possible and still come out the other end alive. As much as Formula 1 drivers are very determined individuals, at the same time we are not fools, and in my era we were all petrified that we might go barrelling into a corner on some of the circuits knowing that if something happened it would most likely result in a massive accident. At times, the potential for injury was so severe you knew you could lose your life. Remember, there were certain corners, deathtraps essentially, that we knew had already taken people's lives.

Those corners were ready to bite you and it wasn't going to be a small accident if they did. So you respected that corner, you had to. I will never forget going round the Bosch Curve in the early 1980s Austrian Grand Prix, where you'd go in flat out and you'd come out flat out. If you had a car set out really well then you were flat out all the way round. In the middle of the corner you would be doing in the region of 180–190mph, so you knew if something broke in the middle or the exit of that corner, the chances of your survival were very remote. Factor in the necessity of lapping over 50 times and you were potentially facing death four or five dozen times in two hours. 'Petrified' seems like an extreme word, but actually I think it is the right term. We were all acutely conscious of that threat.

In my experience, this made the psychology of racing Formula 1 cars in my era very complex. When you were in a high-speed corner, the biggest fight was never with your rivals, nor your reliability or tyre wear or strategy – it was with *yourself*. I know that maybe I have a reputation for being very sure of myself on the track, confident, certain, determined. That is true, I felt like that, but let me tell you I also had never-ending battles with self-doubt, which at times were chronic. However, it was how I – and all the other drivers – dealt with that self-doubt that made the difference between a mid-grid finish and the fastest lap or even a win.

So if you would like to sit with me in my ground-effect Lotus and head into a super-fast corner, this is what would have been in my head at that exact moment: an intense battle raging in microseconds each time. You go into the corner, you know you are doing perhaps 180mph or more, you know there are no run-offs nearby; in fact, there might be a barrier or in the earlier days even mesh catch fencing. Remember, it's not how fast you go in a Formula 1 car that injures or kills you – it is how quickly you *stop*. So you drive through the corner on this knife edge, trying to feel and sense if you are absolutely as fast as that corner allows, then you come out of the other side and that fear is gone, but then instantly you think, *Damn! I can go through there faster!*

So when that corner arrives again a couple of minutes later, you go in faster, you take a greater risk, you push the boundaries again, but all the time you know you are playing Russian roulette with your own safety. The mental fight never ends: *Push harder, go deeper, carry more speed, you can go faster through this corner*, while also thinking, *If this goes wrong I am in big trouble – you can't go that fast through here*. Fear versus performance. Self-preservation versus aggressive competitiveness. Of course, throw into the mix the fact that a rival driver might be on your tail or there might be backmarkers cluttering your path or oil on the track or maybe tyre degradation, and it can get pretty hair-raising. The mental battle is so tough, it's exhausting.

The solution is more complex than just 'thinking confidently'. There is a physicality to this battle. When you are racing at that extreme edge, the correlation between your brain and your body's reactions is absolutely fascinating. If you move your right foot off the pedal even a tiny amount, the performance of F1 cars is so staggering that your rivals will fly past as if you don't exist. The physical precision in the foot pedal is very exact. So when you are having this battle, the risk that your fear will lift your foot off the accelerator – almost involuntarily – is very real. You almost have to think very deliberately to make that foot stay on the throttle and hang on, yet just as you go into that corner your foot comes off – you don't want it to come off but it still comes off! There is a constant struggle between the brain and the body's motor system. If the self-doubt wins, your foot will lift ever so slightly – we call it feathering – and, although it might only be a tiny shift, it can equate to a tenth of a second. In Formula 1, that can be a lifetime.

It is the most amazing dynamic. If you have never fought with your own body and brain like that it is perhaps hard to imagine, but it is a fascinating exercise. It is like playing a really crazy game. I suppose the nearest thing to actually driving a Formula 1 car yourself would be – and don't try this at home! – to put your hand on a table, spread your fingers out and then take a very sharp knife and try to quickly stab the gaps between your fingers, over and over again, for two hours.

I think you can directly relate the movement of a driver's foot to the level of confidence in their psyche. If you could draw a graph that registered their confidence around a circuit's corners, it would largely correlate to the movement of their foot on the pedal. Some people call it a lack of confidence, some call it fear, some call it things like the 'heebie-jeebies'. Call it what you will. Inside a Formula 1 cockpit, whatever name you give it, that feeling is toxic and highly destructive. Without confidence, a Formula 1 driver is ruined.

CHAPTER 7

CHALLENGES ON AND OFF THE CIRCUIT

My confidence going into the 1982 season was pretty strong. My first full year in F1 had been a relative success in my opinion, although I knew there was plenty of room for improvement and I was very hungry to make those strides. In fact, if anything, I was more hungry than ever. However, by the end of the year Colin would be dead and my time at Lotus heading towards an end.

The season started brilliantly, with Colin offering me a new three-year deal. In essence, after all the years of financial hardship, this contract would effectively make me a millionaire overnight. It was the most incredible offer from one of motorsport's true legends.

I couldn't sign it.

There was some wording in there which I felt made me sound like a commodity; it seemed very dehumanising and made me feel uncomfortable. I went to Colin and told him that I couldn't sign the contract and, to be honest, he went ballistic. He was absolutely astounded, telling me that I was

The tea shop in Baughton, near Upton-upon-Severn, where I was born in 1953.

Sitting in a kart in the local park with my younger sister Gail.

With Rosanne at Cadwell Park in 1972 – note racing number 44, long before Lewis Hamilton was born.

Rosanne shows off our lovely new Mini Clubman that we bought soon after we got married in 1975.

Karting in the rain at Little Rissington.

Formula Ford was very popular, as this picture taken in 1977 shows. It was my first full season at this level, and I took a big step forward in my career that year.

Racing in Formula Ford was exciting, but I wasn't yet at the stage of having any sponsors on my car.

My Unipart car on its way to ending upside down in 1979. This was my first full season in Formula 3, and it ended up being a good one.

Celebrating a win at Silverstone in 1979 – my performances that year caught the eye of Colin Chapman.

Nigel Mansell

With Colin Chapman of Lotus, the man who not only gave me the opportunity to race in Formula 1, but taught me so many other lessons about life.

Elio de Angelis was my first team-mate in grand prix racing – a lovely guy and a brilliant driver.

John Townsend

Unsurprisingly, the twin-chassis Lotus that Colin developed attracted lots of attention – and was banned before it could ever race.

Resting on the pit wall with Rosanne during the Detroit Grand Prix.

Walking away from the 1982 Canadian Grand Prix with a broken arm. Sadly, Riccardo Paletti wasn't so lucky that day – along with Gilles Villeneuve, he was one of two drivers to be killed in horrific accidents that season.

On the podium at Brands Hatch after coming third in the European Grand Prix of 1983, my best finish of a difficult season.

I led the Monaco Grand Prix in 1984 – the first race after Mom's funeral. Many drivers crashed that day and the race was stopped shortly after I went off.

Everyone shelters from the scorching sun in Dallas, 1984. After two hours between concrete walls on a track that was breaking up, there was little left to push the car, but we did it anyway, resulting in my lights going out.

Keke Rosberg and me, along with the rest of our new Williams team-mates in 1985.

Celebrating my first ever grand prix victory, at Brands Hatch in 1985 – an amazing achievement to join the winners' circle of F1 racing, something that many drivers sadly never get to do.

Rosanne, Leo, me, Greg and Chloe together. It was hard to maintain a normal family life with being constantly on the Formula 1 circuit, and Rosanne had to sacrifice so much to support my career.

Happy times on the Isle of Man, albeit a little windy.

saying no to the most incredible deal, a fabulous pay packet, amazing opportunities – he was fuming. He said if I didn't sign then I would never make it in Formula 1.

I said, 'Yes, Colin, I have to agree, you are absolutely right. One hundred per cent correct.'

He just looked at me in shock, and said, 'Well, what's your problem then, Nigel?'

I explained that some of the wording would paralyse me as a human being, that it described my role as a commodity and not as a person, which was very disconcerting. He just stared at me, bemused.

'So, Nigel, is that the only thing you are upset with?'

'Yes, the rest of it is fantastic, wonderful.'

'So, if I alter that wording as you say, will you then sign the contract?'

'Yes, everything else is absolutely fine.'

He raised his eyebrows a little, 'Well, in that case, I will change the wording,' then, as he walked away with the hint of a smile on his face, he said, 'You are a funny bugger, aren't you?'

We signed the contract shortly after and Colin very kindly bought some champagne to celebrate the deal together.

That season saw me finish 14th in the championship again, with one less point at seven, but I still felt I was progressing as a driver. I'd secured my second career podium at the race in Brazil and enjoyed five other top-ten finishes. Again, there were reliability issues, causing five retirements, and I crashed twice (what a contrast to the modern era, when reliability is so good). Due to an internal F1 dispute I didn't race at Imola at all (two organisations, FISA and FOCA, were arguing about the direction of F1). The reliability issues were in part a result of the fact that the team had focused on the twin-chassis car and now had to abandon that set-up, so they were playing catch-up on the new Lotus. They worked so incredibly hard but it was always a struggle.

However, despite my own battles and the challenges faced by the team, 1982 was far worse for other people: we lost both Gilles Villeneuve and Riccardo Paletti in horrific fatal accidents, as well as seeing Didier Pironi suffer career-ending injuries in a very nasty smash in his Ferrari during a wet practice for the German Grand Prix when visibility was severely restricted. By December, Colin Chapman would be taken from us too.

I raced cars in an era when, tragically, many people lost their lives. Of course, the generations before me saw even more fatalities, so I have to acknowledge that huge leaps in terms of safety had been made by the time I sat in an F1 car, and we raced on circuits that, at that point in time, were utilising the best safety measures the sport was aware of. Unfortunately, it was still an incredibly dangerous way to make a living. Between 1980 and 1994, for example, six drivers were killed and many more suffered serious injury. Across motorsport as a whole the figure was much higher. I am incredibly blessed to have survived and, although I have sustained many serious injuries that are now manifesting themselves on an almost daily basis as I get older, I am still here.

We all had to find a way to process and work through our psychological wellbeing when there was a serious or fatal accident. All the drivers had to do this – we couldn't just say, 'Oh, I am really upset by what's happened. I will take this week off and not race.' It was our job; we had to go racing. That said, we are all human and seeing your friends and colleagues badly injured or even killed doing the same job, then having to go out and perform at the highest level – or even at all – is a big challenge. Let me take the terrible loss of the great Gilles Villeneuve as a case in point.

Gilles was a dear friend of mine; I loved Gilles, what a guy. He befriended me as soon as we met and I loved his company. We always ended up talking to one another for whatever reason, in the pits and away from the track. Gilles was always an excellent source of wisdom and friendship. He was the epitome of a great racer, a proper racing driver, everything that any driver should aspire to be. He was full of energy, full of life and mischievous behaviour at times, and not slow at coming forward and making himself heard if he had a view on something. For me, at that age, when Gilles came into my world of F1, he was a total breath of fresh air. I don't know why he took a liking to me but I certainly took a liking to him. We sat and chatted for hours and just got on really well. I admired the way he drove and I loved his passion for driving and for life. He was a real fun guy.

Gilles was killed in qualifying for the Belgian Grand Prix, again at Zolder. Seeing Gilles die is just the most awful memory. I was following him and therefore right behind the accident; I saw the whole incident play out before me. Gilles struck the rear of a slower car, an impact that launched his own car into the air for approximately ten metres before slamming nose-first into the floor and somersaulting along the edge of the track. The subsequent impact threw Gilles out of his car and into the catch fencing, a full 50 metres away from his car. Seeing a close friend smash into fencing like that, knowing inside that there was no way he could possibly survive the impact, was the most sickening, dreadful feeling. I drove past and returned to the pits in a daze; I was just numb. Total disbelief, shock, horror, all of the above.

The first doctor arrived within half a minute of the incident, but there was nothing anyone could do. We were all in the pits waiting on news when it was relayed to us that there was no hope at all, his injuries were too severe. When I heard that, I felt sick, physically sick. In my distress, I somehow found myself between the pits and the medical centre. I was adrift in my own mind and body. I didn't know where I was or what I was doing, to be perfectly frank with you. I eventually found my way back to the pit entrance, but as I went to enter the garages an official stopped me and said, 'I need to see your pass, please.'

'What do you mean?'

'I need to see your pass. You can't come through into the pits without showing a pass.'

'My pass is in the pits!'

I simply couldn't believe what I was hearing. I was wearing my racing overalls and had obviously been on track. I was sweating and dirty, plus I would imagine I looked pretty distressed and troubled. I tried to explain what had happened, but he insisted on seeing some ID. In my shocked and distressed state, I got very confused and in my mind, which clearly wasn't operating correctly, I thought maybe he was trying to grab me by the neck to throw me out. I educated him very quickly in the strength and power of a Formula 1 driver, and he got out of my way at 200mph!

When I arrived back at my garage, I do remember feeling very strange. I think on reflection that is when the shock had really started to kick in. I didn't know at the time that I was suffering from shock, but that's clearly what it was. I have had this situation a number of times in my life, and each time is different but equally difficult. Shock is an extremely toxic condition; it does very strange things to people. You are able to function in terms of walking, talking, being around your daily life or job, but at the same time you are not really there. Everything is a haze. It is the most peculiar experience. Nothing registers. You hear what people are saying but it doesn't compute. You observe things with your own eyes, but then somehow you haven't really seen them. You are just disassociated from the world around you, even though you are engaging with it. It is essentially an out-of-body experience, where the vessel of your body is there and your mind is obviously in that body, but it's not functioning. Your mind is paralysed; it has seen something that it doesn't understand, that it didn't want to see, and it spirals into a crisis mode. In my opinion, that's why your memory can be lost after a trauma, because your brain just doesn't know how to function normally. It's almost like there's a self-preservation chip in every human being which, when events are too painful, has to react. I don't think it distorts the truth, but sometimes when it is so bad the brain will not accept the visual input it is seeing and it shuts down. Shock is a known clinical condition, of course, with recognised symptoms of numbness, detachment from your surroundings, episodic amnesia and chronic anxiety. Medics will tell you that clinical shock lasts a minimum of 48 hours, but can actually linger as long as a month or so after a traumatic event. Well, in Formula 1, you have to get straight back in the car either that day or the next.

For me, Zolder in Belgium was ill-fated. I'd had that fabulous battle at the last (also tragically tainted) race at Zolder – and remember who I had been very proud to have beaten to third place and my first podium? Gilles. Now he was on life-support at the edge of death.

I was all over the place, absolutely bereft. I don't remember a thing for the rest of the day, absolutely nothing. I put that down to the stress of what I had seen and who had been so seriously injured.

Colin Chapman, wonderful man that he was, understood the destructive power of shock and how it could affect drivers and the people around them very badly. I will never forget when Riccardo Paletti was killed in a terrible accident in Montreal just two months later, after smashing into the back of a stalled Ferrari on the grid. There was smoke pluming up from the circuit and we all knew it was bad. I wanted to go to see the incident, to see if I could help, to see what had happened. However, Colin wouldn't let me. I was distressed and tried to push past him, but he actually got me in a headlock and wrestled me away, all the time saying, 'Nigel, you are not seeing this, I will not let you see this.' He manhandled me away and would not let me look because he knew that, if I did, my mind would be plagued by what my eyes had seen. I'd like to take this opportunity to thank Colin all these years later for saving me from the emotional turmoil of remembering something that I didn't have to see. I knew the outcome for that lovely young man Paletti, but I didn't have to see it in graphic detail. Colin was being a dad to me; he was being caring and loving, 'You cannot see this, Nigel!' I knew instantly that if I saw it, it would affect me. So he said enough and did enough to prevent that. Thank you, Colin.

After Riccardo Paletti had been killed at the start line in Canada, we restarted the race. His best friend had qualified just in front of me and, unbeknown to me, was crying in the cockpit, for obvious reasons following the devastating loss of his friend. On the second lap he decided halfway down the straight to lift off at 185mph at the precise moment I was slipstreaming him, then I smashed into the back of his car. As my car went airborne my hand was jolted through the steering wheel, then when the car landed the wheel rotated sharply, taking my hand with it, fracturing the wrist and arm. I missed the next race and then at Brands Hatch I did my best to race in extreme pain, but ultimately I had to retire when it became too much to bear. At least I had tried.

Back at Zolder, that day when Gilles crashed was one of the worst in my life. I eventually fell asleep very late at night through total and utter exhaustion. What I have found over the years of racing, and life in general, is that when you do finally sleep – which is not always easy, of course – your mind at least starts to try to compute and process what it has witnessed. The body is at rest but the mind is busy trying to reprogramme itself and come to terms with the new situation. This applies to good events as well as bad ones: your mind reassesses your injury, reassesses the damage, reassesses the joy, the victory, and so on. This all happens in your subconscious, you can't encourage or control it, and for some people this process is easier than for others. Some people who are not used to any kind of stress or traumatic situations can, in an instant, have their world rocked to such a degree that they never recover. Of course, it may take several days, weeks, months and sometimes years, to fully come to terms with your loss emotionally, but in the case of the brain, it sets to work immediately trying to process what has happened. As for Formula 1 drivers, we have to recover and we have to do so very quickly.

Having said that, for me the entire weekend at Zolder was a haze. Knowing what I now know about the effects of shock, I find it all the more remarkable when racing drivers experience something like I did that weekend in Belgium, and then go out either later that day or the next and race, and often race very well. Which is some feat when you consider the complexity of a Formula 1 car, the skill required to race at the top level and the guts to throw that car into every corner, and all this after having been in shock. You function in a very sombre disposition, but you do find a way.

In part it's because you know as a racer that you have a job to do, and that discipline kicks in. Also you know that if you don't do that job then someone else will. Being injured or even killed comes with the territory, especially so in years gone by, so you can't complain – you knew what the parameters were before you joined up. So you just have to get on with it.

Whenever there was a big incident, I would find a quiet corner to sit alone and try to gather my thoughts. I would never talk to other drivers and rarely spoke to anyone else either. I wasn't alone in that. The entire pit lane, from drivers to team owners to mechanics to tea ladies to cleaners to engineers, everyone is shell-shocked after an incident like Gilles's, the whole mood is sombre. Unfortunately, during my era we did see a lot of injury and, sadly, death; we all lived through that happening many times. The weird thing was, it never got any easier. It never got any better. You almost think, *Next time there is an injury or a big crash, I will be able to cope better*. I never found that to be the case. The circumstances of each crash are always unique, different, so there are always new questions in your mind. It is always horrendous. And you don't want to be the next person it happens to. Year on year, that was the reality.

I tried to mitigate the psychological and emotional stress and trauma of a big accident by trying to be logical and meticulous. I would always try to find out what had happened, to see if I could learn anything from that and take it with me going forward. You had to try to take positives from these very sad situations, otherwise the distress would simply overwhelm you. I always wanted to know why the accident happened, what caused it; I needed to know. The easiest thing for me to hear was that it was driver error. If that was the case, then you could look at the error, make sure you never did the same and learn from it. It was a quantifiable incident. If you know what mistake has been made then you can log it, programme it into your brain and say to yourself, *In those circumstances be very wary, don't repeat this mistake because last time it happened this mistake was fatal. There will be no second chances.*

However, if it was mechanical failure, some random part causing the incident which could never have been foreseen, that was harder to compute. I would try to find out why the part failed, where it failed – was it faulty, what stresses on that part might have caused the failure? Sometimes the information was very sketchy and often, if a car had been almost completely destroyed, there was very little left to examine. In the modern era, they are able to analyse the minutes, seconds and even microseconds leading up to a failure, it's all there in the telemetry, but back then we didn't have data-logging technology. If a car was destroyed, it was often exceptionally difficult to figure out for certain which part had failed.

This meant that at times you were going back out on the circuit knowing that the failure could, in theory, be repeated. A failure is a failure and it often seems to happen at the worst possible time. I always found great reassurance in the meticulous nature of the team and their engineers. Certainly in the 1980s it was a bit 'finger in the air' at times, not from any lack of expertise or diligence, but because we simply didn't have the technology at our disposal that the teams do today. However, we had some very ingenious people in our teams and they were able to gather an amazing amount of information from a damaged car – their forensic skill was incredible to witness. This is why I have been very fortunate racing for great teams like Lotus, Williams and Ferrari; they have systems in place for these eventualities. They can crack test their suspension after every race; they change the rose joints on a regular basis, because they can be damaged almost imperceptibly; these things cost money but they do everything they can within the realms of possibility to eliminate the chances of a failure being repeated. They basically exercise the best possible prevention strategy they can.

The teams are there to race, that is why they exist. I have seen teams after a big crash putting the new race numbers of the next driver on a spare car within a few hours. That can make you feel pretty dispensable, and I know it sounds brutal but that's just the reality of motor racing. The teams are there to win and to go racing. You come to realise that life continues and you have a job to do. However, these big crashes were always a painful reminder that motor racing can be very dangerous and is potentially lethal.

Gilles was kept alive on life-support in the hospital until his wife could get there to see him. He died just after 9pm that evening. That was my dear, dear friend, taken right in front of my eyes. He was just the most wonderful man and an astonishing racer. And with Colin Chapman's passing in December, a very dark year ended in the most terrible way.

My last two years at Lotus were extremely difficult. With Colin no longer there, tensions surfaced with certain individuals in the team management and my sense of self-confidence was eroded. Looking back, I have said I 'overdrove' during this period and that is a fair comment. I was very much the number two driver to my great friend Elio in terms of engines, technology, developments, everything, so the entire time was a struggle. The 1983 season was very difficult; I had a poor car and no points until the seventh race in Detroit. A newly designed turbo Lotus was encouraging and stunned me with the power advantage this type of engine offered (I will come back to this topic later, during my time at Williams, a team that produced just the most sublime turbo cars). I would end the season with another podium (at Brands Hatch for the European Grand Prix); four other top-ten finishes, including a very pleasing fourth place at Silverstone; too many reliability failures to detail, but ironically my best points tally thus far – ten – finishing 12th in the championship. I stayed at Lotus for one more year, the final one of that three-year contract Colin had given me, but the writing was on the wall. The 1984 season would be my last with his team.

Just before I flew out to Dijon for the 1984 French Grand Prix, my mom died of cancer. She had been ill for some years and had had to go through some lengthy and traumatic radiation therapy and other treatments. Sadly, she could not beat the disease and eventually the illness took her at the age of just 60.

I was completely devastated. This was compounded by the fact that I knew nothing of her illness, as she'd hidden it from me for two years. So from finding out that she was so ill to her actually dying was a very short period of time.

If I am being completely honest with you, as I write this book sitting in my study in Florida 31 years later, I still am devastated.

As a racing driver, you face many challenges every week – that might be on the track, in testing, after or during an accident, the politics, the relationships with teams, sponsors, other drivers, the media. It is a very demanding environment. However, by far the biggest and hardest challenge I have ever had in my life was when my mother died.

Within 24 hours of seeing my mom in the hospital mortuary, I had to fly off to race at Dijon. I was in pieces inside, but I didn't show anything outside. That was incredibly difficult. I programmed myself to have a quiet weekend. I spoke to the team and said, 'Look, I don't feel great this weekend.' I didn't tell them why; no one knew that my mom had died the night before. I hardly spoke to anybody; they just thought I was being a bit moody and insular. I didn't speak to anyone because, if I had, I would've fallen apart.

I decided it was best to really focus on my racing, but my appetite for doing the job and being there that weekend … Well, I honestly don't know how I found the concentration levels to drive at all. In hindsight, I suppose when you are on a mission you just do your job but, boy, that was a tough weekend. I didn't sleep properly, I barely ate. I was wandering around in my own little world. I actually have very few memories of being there.

I've touched on the effects of shock on a racing driver, but the worst experience of shock I have suffered is when I lost my mother. I went through the whole weekend as a zombie, functioning but not functioning. I needed to do a job and somehow – don't ask me how – I came away with a podium finish and was handed a trophy and the traditional garland. I often look back on that time and ask myself, *What can I remember of that whole weekend?*

Honestly?

I can't remember anything.

I can't remember how I got to the track, I can't recall qualifying, I have no recollection of practice. Nothing. I include the actual race itself in that statement. I have no recall whatsoever of what went on during the grand prix. I know I got a podium and I can read the history books or watch footage to tell me how I raced and against who, but I don't remember any of it myself. And I don't remember leaving the circuit and travelling home. Given my fractured mental state, it's almost bizarre to think that I actually had a good race.

In the back of my mind – to be honest, it was almost the *only* thing on my mind, even as I was racing – I knew that the next day after the grand prix I was heading home to go to my mother's funeral. However, unlike my memory loss of the actual race weekend, from the moment I woke up on the Monday, the day of her funeral, I can remember *everything* in acute, vivid detail. The race weekend is lost to me, but the day of the funeral is embedded in my mind forever.

I flew home on the Sunday night and barely slept, then went to my parents' house the next morning. It was still traditional back then to have the coffin in the family home before it went to the church, and sure enough my mom was there. It was very hard and things got worse because, when it came to taking her, my dad, bless him, had a meltdown. He wouldn't let the hearse leave the street unless I was driving it. This created a problem because the funeral director patiently explained that I wasn't insured and that they would not be able to allow it. However, Dad was adamant, so I said I would underwrite any problems that arose if there was a bump of some kind. I understand they were just doing their job and I was pleased they were able to help. I placed the garland I had won the day before in Dijon on Mom's coffin and we began the journey to the churchyard. Even now, I feel very sombre writing this. I still grieve for my mom; it's been over 30 years and I still feel the pain. I've never really been able to talk to anyone in depth about it, to share what I was thinking, it's simply too painful. Writing these words seems like a good moment to tell people. I miss her terribly. Maybe that's not the tough thing to say, but I am just being very honest with you.

The first race after Mom's funeral was in Monaco and it remains one of the wettest grands prix ever seen there – indeed, one of the wettest races in history. Alain Prost led, but I was able to overtake him on lap 11 and therefore take the lead of a grand prix for the very first time. Mostly, all I could think was,

Mom isn't here to see this. She only ever really saw me struggle. She was delighted when I got my drive with Lotus, but I dearly wish she and my father had seen more of the good times. I was thinking this inside my helmet as I led that Monaco Grand Prix. The brief moment in the sun didn't last long, as five laps later I put my tyres on the slippery white lines going up the hill towards Casino Square, lost the car and hit the barriers. I was absolutely gutted. What can I say? I was probably going just a little bit too fast and I slid out on a different line, and every-body knows as soon as you put your wheel on one of those white lines, it's like ice, so I crashed from the lead.

I have realised that I never really grieved properly for my mother. I never fully understood the magnitude of the loss because that didn't go with the job. I was worried that to show signs of emotion and grieving could be construed as a weakness. The thing is, in later life you realise that you never get that time with them back. Only now do I think I can finally grieve properly.

That moment when I was told my mother had died changed my life forever and the repercussions are still with me to this day, and probably always will be. Taking that hearse to the funeral for my mom was the hardest drive of my life.

There were some highlights in the rest of 1984. I earned my first pole position at Dallas in July, with Elio completing Lotus's first front-row lock-out since 1978, a proud moment for us both. However, that race is probably best remembered for me pushing my car over the line in 100-degree heat. It was the most crazy weekend – we had qualifying at six in the morning (Jacques Laffite came to the drivers' briefing in his pyjamas) and the temperature was so high the track was burning up. In the race itself, I struggled with handling and then deteriorating tyres, and, after a great tussle with Keke Rosberg, halfway through the last lap my transmission broke and I lost all drive. The speed I already had coasted me to the last corner, where I could see the start/finish line just up ahead. There was no way I was going to stop where I was, so I jumped out and started pushing the car. The heat was intense and I felt very light-headed, but I wanted that finish position – for the points and also because I was paid finishing money at the time. I remember pushing and pushing and pushing, and then all I remember is the lights going out, as I fainted on to the track next to my car.

Then I remember coming to and I was instantly very concerned because I was lying stark naked on a bed of ice. I could see all this silver paper around and over me and I was surrounded by all these mysterious figures in white clothes and masks. I honestly thought I had been abducted by aliens! I thought I'd been taken and was being examined and compromised. The reality was a little less Area 51 . . . They'd had to put me there to reduce my core temperature because it was so high. The headaches were incredible, so painful, but, hey, I got sixth place.

Six reliability retirements and four accidents meant that on track my last season at Lotus was only modestly successful. My highest points tally, 13, and a top-ten finish in the championship helped. I never finished higher than that year's ninth place in the World Championship for Lotus and, I'm not going to lie, it was often a struggle with the cars. However, those formative years in my F1 career were at times completely wonderful. I'd had the absolute privilege of working with, and getting to know, the legendary Colin Chapman. I had made my start in Formula 1 and thereafter progressed to a point where I was becoming a serious force to be reckoned with. Yes, towards the end, when Colin was sadly no longer with us, it wasn't so nice, but my main memories are of being around Colin and the fantastic people in the Lotus team. What a privilege.

By August, it was announced that Ayrton Senna was coming to Lotus and my time with Colin's team was drawing to a close. If I hadn't found a competitive drive I think I would have retired; right from the early days I felt there was no point in making up the numbers. Happily, there were some interesting offers on the table for me and, despite some frustrating delays when I had to tell Frank Williams that I was walking away because I was tired of waiting for his decision, it was eventually announced that I had signed a contract to race for his Williams team from 1985. I felt very optimistic about driving for Frank's brilliant team, which had won the World Championship twice in the last four years, although their more recent win ratio per season was relatively modest. Nonetheless, Frank and his chief designer, Patrick Head, were exemplary and proven winners. My good friends Peter Collins and Peter Windsor were also at the team and it felt very exciting indeed. My mission to win the Formula 1 world title was still on.

CHAPTER 8

1985 SEASON, WILLIAMS AND THE TURBO YEARS

My first few days at Williams were extremely exciting. Frank and Patrick made it clear they were looking forward to working with someone with my engineering background; the car I would be driving appeared to be a significant improvement on the previous season's Williams; and the team was in its second year of a very encouraging partnership with Honda, so I sensed I would have an impressively powerful engine behind me.

My team-mate at Williams was the 1982 world champion Keke Rosberg. We had a stuttering start but soon became good friends, and I admire the man hugely. Before I arrived, he had heard some negative stories about me from various people in the pit lane, including one particular person at Lotus, so he came to his relationship with me at Williams with a good deal of trepidation. In fact, that is something of an understatement, because he'd actually threatened to leave the team if I was signed. Frank had been unmoved and signed me anyway. However, after a couple of races and some tests, Keke came up to me and said, 'I am really sorry I believed the bullshit they said about you – you are fantastic to work with.' I really admired him for that.

I am extremely fond of Keke. He was an old-school racer, a man's man, a thoroughbred. He'd have a drink and a cigarette, he spoke his mind, he was a straight shooter. He was really funny and entertaining too, plus he didn't suffer fools easily and we got on really well. There wasn't anything that rankled with me and Keke.

I would also say I learned a fair amount from driving with Keke, which sadly only lasted that one year, my first season with Williams in 1985, after which Keke joined McLaren. In racing terms, he was a thoroughbred, a true champion with dignity and talent. In my opinion, he was an understated world champion because he had great car control and pure, unbridled ability. I thoroughly enjoyed my all-too-brief time with him as my team-mate at Williams.

One time racing for Williams in Monaco I came out of the tunnel backwards – never a good racing line – and then went on to complete a very quick practice time. Afterwards, Keke came up to me and said, 'Are you okay, Nigel?'

'Yeah, fine, Keke. Why do you ask?'

'Don't you remember what happened?'

'What?'

'You spun in the tunnel . . .'

'Oh, that, yeah . . .'

'I was behind you! I was waiting for bits to come off the car. You frightened the shit out of me!'

Keke used to give some fantastic backhanded compliments too! Another time, I'd done a really fast lap when, back in the pits, Keke approached me and said, 'I know now how you managed to do that lap time.'

'Really?' I was intrigued to know this former world champion's expert opinion: had he seen something about my racing lines, my braking points, my cornering, what? 'Why's that then, Keke?'

'It's because you're effing mad!'

I've mentioned the astonishing performance benefit of the turbo car when I first tried the new Lotus in 1983, but my fondest memories of the turbo era are at Williams. A modern Formula 1 car produces in the region of 750–800bhp. In a car that typically might only weigh around 550kg, that is staggering and the subsequent performance is savage. Back between 1977 and 1988, Formula 1 enjoyed its first turbo era. For me personally, this was my favourite period in which to race. We had cars in qualifying that were producing over 1350bhp! That's about 500bhp more than current F1 cars. Five hundred! That's like adding the might of a Ferrari F40 engine on top of what you already have (one BMW qualifying engine even hit 1500bhp). I loved those cars and consider them to be the grand stallions in the history of F1.

The golden years of that turbo era for me were the mid-1980s, particularly 1986 and 1987. My favourite turbo car was FW11B in 1987. The rate of development of this technology and these cars at Williams was simply astounding; they just kept relentlessly pushing forward. The work rate was unbelievable to watch.

For example, in 1985 we had so many different engine evolutions, you almost lost track. They experimented with different size turbos – big turbos for fast circuits with the long straights, smaller turbos, quicker response turbos, they were all over it. Williams and Honda together was such a dynamic team. It was mesmerising how the engineers and the team developed the turbos from virtually nothing into these astonishing power units in such short periods of time.

For us drivers it was just so exciting. You could get wheel spin in sixth gear with no traction control and a fully manual gearbox – you certainly had to drive the car! The surge of power when the turbos kicked in was breathtaking, I absolutely loved it. Mind you, learning how turbos operated was a bit of a knife-edge way to make a living, let me tell you, because those very early examples were utilising technology that was in its infancy, and that meant there were issues. Most obviously and crucially, the turbo lag – the time between putting your foot on the throttle and the response of the turbos in terms of injecting more power into the engine – was unpredictable and really quite slow at first. Then, after this uncertain delay, when the turbo did finally kick in, you had to hang on pretty tight! It was exciting because you never knew when the power was going to come in.

You would go like stink down a straight, then when you got to a corner you'd have to put the throttle down one or two seconds before you actually wanted the power to be available, to allow for the turbo lag. You had to learn to gauge that delay, but to be honest in those early engines it was essentially guesswork. An educated guess based on testing and race experience, of course, but guesswork nonetheless.

In 1985, we started off at the beginning of the year with a turbo that might just as well have been an on-off switch, it was all or nothing. When the turbo was off, the car wouldn't turn into the corner and when it was on the car was viciously trying to spin. We almost had to go to psychiatric units for tranquillisers the day before we'd have to drive the car . . . and that was in the dry! If it was in the wet, it was suicidal. We had so much power that we had to have barn doors on the back of the cars;

we couldn't get big enough wings on them to try to restrain the power. If anyone had done the aerodynamics perfectly, I think we'd have been doing 300mph down the straights. It is insane the amount of power we had.

One of the worst and in some ways most embarrassing accidents I've ever had in Formula 1 happened in Estoril in 1985 on the parade lap. I'd already ended up in a guardrail through no fault of mine in first qualifying, when Eddie Cheever's car bounced off Riccardo Patrese's Alfa Romeo and into me. Thanks to the amazing efforts of my mechanics and team, the car was repaired in time and so I was looking forward to the race.

On race day, it was raining but conditions were fair. I developed a misfire and then when I called for the power from the turbo nothing happened, so I took my foot off. However, as I did, the power suddenly came in for a few seconds, put me into a huge spin and I smashed into the barriers. Basically I didn't have any control over the car at all. When that happened, you really weren't driving; you were just sitting in the car watching what was going to happen. I limped into the pits and, not surprisingly, the whole front geometry and wishbone had to be changed, which was a huge amount of work to be done in a very short space of time. Consequently, I had to start from the pit lane. It was my first year with Williams and only my second race, so this was not a great way to impress your team bosses. I was actually really concerned that I was going to lose my drive. This was coming off the back of two years of a very negative atmosphere at Lotus. However, in very sharp contrast, after I span off in Portugal, Frank, Patrick and all the team were fantastically supportive and it all felt so very energising, inspiring even.

I'd had to start from the pit lane but I managed to haul

myself up to fifth, which was a great recovery. Ayrton won, his first ever grand prix victory. During the race, Keke was coming out of a fast right-hander in fifth gear when the car did the same to him – the turbos slammed in unexpectedly, put him into a spin and threw him into the guardrail, breaking a bone in his hand in the process. He was so upset and cross. I have to admit, I was gutted for Keke but, from a self-preservation point of view, at least it made the point that if this hugely talented former world champion could be thrown off track in that way, then at least it wasn't just me. When I saw Keke in the pits afterwards he was really frustrated, as were the team of course, so I tried to cheer him up by saying, 'At least you came off in the race!'

I will say it again, I *loved* the turbo era. As a racer, it held my attention all the time; it was very demanding and at times dangerous, but always hugely exhilarating. The turbo cars were what I would call an old-school man's car. A boy could not drive these cars, especially with the lack of driver aids and electronics, heavy manual gears and so on. This was about as physical as you could get in terms of driving an F1 car.

It wasn't just the physicality of the turbo cars that demanded you were on top of your game. There were so many subtleties too. If you called for power and changed gear at the wrong time, you'd basically blow the gearbox up! If you changed down too much, you'd mechanically over-rev and blow the engine up! Each driver's hands-on management of the engine and gearbox was so crucial to a turbo car's health, and by definition its performance and therefore likely success in the race. There were no wheel sensors, nothing like that, so the individual drivers had to do everything right. They had to have a real skill and understanding of how to drive those cars, and that's what I found so utterly fascinating.

There were other less obvious downsides to these turbo monsters. For example, in my days using a Renault V10, if those engines were only slightly out of balance, the vibrations used to make me cough almost uncontrollably. The vibration of the car was at a very specific frequency that coincidentally made me cough constantly. This was not a phenomenon exclusive to me, but when you are doing 200mph in a 1350bhp car and competing against the best drivers in the world, constantly coughing isn't an ideal ticket. One particular V10 was so bad they had to change the engine. I said, 'I can't drive it, really sorry.'

During that classic turbo era, there were three or four seasons when it was just sensational. Evolutions came along seemingly every week; cars that had 1350bhp melted your brain with their ferocity and power, and the races were so physical, so draining, yet so fabulously exciting to be a part of. It was exhausting and yet life-affirming, astonishing and frightening all at the same time.

Turbos were eventually banned in 1989 because of new regulations. Fast-forward to 2014 and turbos were reintroduced, but there isn't really any obvious comparison. The motivation back then was to go faster, to wring more performance and brutal speed out of the cars. However, in the new millennium, priorities have changed, on a global scale as well as within the context of Formula 1. The sport is quite rightly trying to reflect that change of emphasis and remain current or, indeed, strive to be pioneering. So the new turbo era is mostly driven by a need for efficiency and fuel economy.

I am fortunate enough to have seen some of this new generation of turbo engines up close and personal and they really are incredible works of art – compact, beautifully designed; the whole package is so clever, on a whole different level. I take my hat off to the engineers and designers. There's hardly any turbo lag at all now and there are all sorts of clever bits of engineering to keep the turbo spinning and operating at optimum performance. It's very clever stuff. The most astonishing thing is that in the space of a single season's regulation change, engines were developed that are capable of the same performance as the year before but on a third less fuel. That is amazing. There is no point criticising the new turbos; you have to embrace the technology and go forward, while all the time doffing your cap to the brains behind these remarkable engines.

I recognise that the sound of these new turbo engines isn't to everyone's taste. It's not to mine, if I am being honest. However, this is the way the sport needs to go at this moment in time. For me, the best noise – and it is personal taste – was the DFV or the flat V12 Ferrari going past at high speed in the 1980s – just wonderful! The good old DFV singing at the top of its voice was the most beautifully savage sound. The V10 Renault was pretty impressive as well. We are never going to hear the likes of that again, but times move on. We all have to move on, too, fans, drivers, teams alike. The different sound is not necessarily a bad development either. You might be interested to know that I sometimes struggle with my hearing, to the point where it can be quite hard for me to follow day-to-day conversations in a noisy room. This could have been caused in part by years of having these massive monster engines screaming at the top of their lungs inches from the back of my head.

There will no doubt be endless evolutions of the turbo engine and it will change again, that is for sure. I personally find it all very fascinating watching what will happen next. That is part of Formula 1's uniqueness, the constant and incredible evolution of technology, so there's no point denigrating the sport for that – just embrace it.

Rather excitingly, as I write this chapter there are rumours that increased horsepower might be something that could make a comeback. I don't know how true that is, but I would be thrilled to see a return to the days when cars had between 1000bhp and up to 1350bhp. Obviously, not at the expense of drivers' safety, of course, but just in terms of the pure spectacle. Let's get back to having wheel spin coming out of corners at 150mph – then the tyre manufacturers really will have a challenge on their hands!

That first season racing at Williams alongside Keke Rosberg in 1985 was exhilarating, with some fantastic successes, including my first grand prix win, and some disappointments too. Although I was clearly a number two driver, I had no problem with that status, given Keke's experience and the fact he was such a lovely team-mate. Besides, as a team, Williams had a very proud philosophy of always allowing their drivers to race; therefore, their cars were always produced to be as equal as possible, and if I was able to overhaul Keke, then so be it. I managed to out-qualify Keke seven times, which made me very proud as he was such an outstanding racer.

The season didn't begin well, though. After some awkward testing with the old FW09, I qualified fifth at the season opener in Brazil, but then was clipped by Michele Alboreto, which sent me off the track. Not a great start to the first lap of my first race with a new team. Although I was able to rejoin, exhaust problems eventually forced me to retire on only the eighth lap. It was a hugely disappointing start to my time with Williams, but just as they would be when I spun off on the parade lap in Estoril two weeks later, Frank and the team were hugely supportive.

Keke had proved the car could be a winner after taking the chequered flag in Detroit (after I crashed out with brake problems, suffering concussion and a jarred thumb). Nonetheless, all the signs were promising. I had not yet won a grand prix, but I felt like my moment might be approaching. However, when we got to Paul Ricard for the French Grand Prix I suffered a massive accident on the Mistral Straight. The turbo cars were just so fast, and by this point speeds in excess of 200mph were commonplace. I have previously said that at Paul Ricard in a turbo car the speeds were 'more like a land-speed record attempt than a motor race' and I think that sums up the sheer insane velocity of these machines.

I was travelling at over 200mph down the Mistral Straight when my left rear tyre exploded, ripped up the suspension on that side and the rear wing disintegrated too. When I hit the guardrail, the front left tyre exploded then the wheel snapped back and hit me on the head, instantly switching my lights out with a massive concussion. Thankfully, the brilliant but sadly late Professor Sid Watkins was on hand to care for me, and I was shipped unconscious by helicopter to hospital (in 1968, Mike Spence had been killed by a similar crash at Indianapolis). I actually woke up on the gurney attached to the outside of the helicopter and for a fleeting moment, as I headed through the sky, I thought I was on my way to heaven. That was a terrifying experience to have, semi-conscious and confused, so I was very grateful to pass out again quickly afterwards. A few days later I was able to go home and recuperate for the forthcoming British Grand Prix.

I made it to Silverstone and the team brilliantly built me a new car, but I wasn't fully fit in my opinion. I qualified well, but the real star of the show was Keke, who did an astonishing qualifying lap which proved to be the fastest average speed ever by a Formula 1 car, clocking in at *an average* of over 160mph (a record that stood for 17 years). Astonishing. What's more, my team-mate personally found me in my motorhome to congratulate me on my qualifying efforts, and then proceeded to tell the press how brave and skilful I had been. To prove the point about my concussion, I have no recollection of that motorhome conversation with Keke; I only found out about it when he told me a few days later. I retired from the actual race in third with clutch problems, and there was a sense of relief, to be honest.

The most obvious highlight of the 1985 season was my first ever grand prix win, which came in the European Grand Prix at Brands Hatch in early October. When we got to Brands Hatch I was still having to take painkillers for my wrist but, with improvements having been made on the car's suspension and transmission, I felt we could be very strong. Patrick Head had designed a new rear suspension with his team, which was fabulous. For me, Patrick is a fantastic engineer, designer and entrepreneur. I like Patrick, I love his manner; he is robust and he doesn't suffer fools gladly so we were quite like-minded, but he is great. He knew that he never needed to ask me to push; I would always give my best for him, and he liked that and embraced it, and I liked that too.

Anyway, before Brands that year, he put a new suspension on the car and in testing I went straight out and drove three-quarters of a second quicker. It was immense. He'd altered elements of the suspension, which allowed us to get more of that brutal turbo power down on the track. When anybody designs something that makes a car easier to drive, it is an absolute godsend, because a thoroughbred race car is always on its tippy-toes. If a designer can add something to the car that makes it quicker and yet consistent, then as a driver you are elated. The Williams team and Patrick were especially good at being able to do this.

So I went to Brands with a bigger comfort zone than usual, knowing we were going to be competitive. I made a good start and had a tussle with Ayrton, Nelson Piquet and Keke along the way. After Keke and Nelson had a coming together, the latter retired and I was up to second behind Senna. When Keke came out of the pits, I managed to get past Ayrton in the ensuing battle and into the lead. I stretched that lead and it was then just a case of nursing the car home, keeping a safe distance between me and the chasing pack and getting that first grand prix win. The 75,000 fans whooped with joy as I crossed to take the chequered flag, and in the car I was crying with elation and wonder. I had won my first grand prix. I was 32 and this was my 72nd race in Formula 1. When I got out of the car I was spent, totally spent. I remember almost passing out on the podium, I could hardly stand. I was shaking, I was excited. It was definitely a 'pinch yourself' moment. *Have I really just done that?* In a post-race interview I said, 'If anybody has won the race for me today, it's the people out there . . . the best feeling I have ever had in my life.' The British fans are just unbelievable, still to this day.

We stayed overnight at a hotel nearby and the morning after a helicopter picked us up. I remember one particular driver, who'd had, how can I put it, a late night with a female friend, wasn't particularly happy about being woken up so early by this helicopter!

That first win gave me such an injection of confidence. I trusted my car and now I was a grand prix winner; I knew what needed to be done. That win is still one of my favourites. Sometimes I get confused and say I have won five British Grands Prix, but that is because Brands Hatch that day felt like a home race, the fans were so incredible – it was a massive moment in my life (to be precise, I have won four British

Grands Prix, and once in England at this, the European Grand Prix).

In the quiet calmness back at home, I started to understand and appreciate that maybe all the sacrifice had been worth it. You do question sometimes what you have missed in life. For instance, I have found out now, through having grandchildren, that some of the quality time I can spend with them, I never had with my own children. That's not to say they didn't have a wonderful upbringing or that we didn't share some incredible quality time because we did, but you do realise that there was a price to pay to achieve what we did. Brands Hatch that day was the first win and it really felt like it had all been worthwhile.

I won the next race at Kyalami in South Africa too, making me the only driver to win back-to-back that year. In that 1985 season I also had a front-row start in Monaco, some fastest laps along the way and ultimately picked up a solid 31 points (Prost won the title), taking me to sixth in the World Championship. Yes, we had some reliability problems, but aside from that and the accidents, it just felt like the team were building us both very fast cars, their work ethic was wonderful, my perfor-mances, experience and points-scoring were inexorably gathering momentum and I sensed real, genuine potential.

Away from the track and all the intense demands on my time and energy that my F1 career entailed, the mid-1980s was a very special time for Rosanne and me because we became par-ents to three wonderful children. We were in our late twenties when Chloe was first to arrive in 1982, then Leo nearly three years later, followed by Greg in 1987. So at one point we had three children under the age of five. And some people say driv-ing an F1 car is demanding!

It was just wonderful to become a parent and I feel very

blessed to have had three fabulous children. In terms of my career, I found the arrival of the children to be mostly a hugely positive development. Their presence felt like a stabilising influence in my hectic life. It's nobody's fault but doing a job like I had, it is all too easy to get carried away; you can lose yourself very easily. You can get carried away with the fans, the whole superstar treatment, the money, the VIP status – it is a very rarefied lifestyle even though you are working very hard.

So, for me, after having a good day or, conversely, a really bad day at work, coming home to the children was very grounding. They were always the same to me; I was their dad first and foremost. Being so young, they didn't even comprehend my job, so I was either at home or I was away working. I might come in through the door with my head full of a car's problems, or maybe some frustrating politics, an argument perhaps, whatever, and there'd be Chloe wanting to play or the boys tumbling around the room. It instantly brought me down to earth and allowed me to recharge my batteries every night. Last or first on the grid? To my children when they were toddlers it didn't matter and that rubbed off on me, which I found very soothing.

Of course, the practicalities of touring the world on the F1 circuit as a father of three were not always the easiest. For starters, we had no parents of our own to help out (although Rosanne's father was still alive he didn't travel around the world with us). This meant that when I was away with work, Rosanne was all on her own, which was very hard for her. When we moved to the Isle of Man, we didn't know anyone at first, so Rosanne was alone in the house with three very young children. We eventually employed nannies to help out, but it was still a lot of work for Rosanne.

For my part, I missed the children very much. We calculated that during the 12 years we lived on the Isle of Man, I was travelling for nine and a half of those. For a young family, that is a pretty massive amount of time for a dad to be away from home. It was heart-rending to be away for so much time. We tried to alleviate this separation by taking the children to as many races as was practical. In fact, we were one of the driver families who did that as often as possible. I would hardly ever have seen them if we hadn't made the effort to take them with us.

Sometimes, taking the children with me worked really well; other times, you'd get home and think, *That was really much more hassle than it was worth*. Occasionally, the cost and energy that we put into taking the children to races was counterproductive to the end result. I remember flying to Australia with Leo when he was just ten months old in my first year at Williams, but that flight wiped us out – that was a mistake. We went to stay with my sister in Adelaide; it was an opportunity for us to be together, so we took the nanny as well as the children, but it was an expensive trip and very difficult from a practical point of view.

Plus I was always conscious of having to do my job properly, too. I was there to win races, so it was an incredible balancing act. For example, I couldn't afford to risk having the children keep me awake, so, to make sure I got a good night's sleep before a race, it was planned very carefully that they would always be in a separate room from me. In truth, Rosanne was very good because she cherry-picked which races to go to. I have to say that if we hadn't been privileged to have our own jet plane at times, we wouldn't have been able to experience some of the things we did as a family.

When my children arrived, it did make me reassess my relationship with my own father a little bit. It has been well documented in a previous book that after my mother died he remarried quite quickly, and I wasn't entirely comfortable with the situation. My father obviously needed some support and help, which I tried to give. I told him that, in my opinion, he was moving a bit faster than I thought was sensible to remarry, and to someone much younger. One time I was racing at Monaco, he called me the night before the grand prix, out of the blue, to wish me luck with the race and to say he was getting married in the morning. I just said, 'Well, who to?' because I had never met the person and didn't know her. That was a shock. Three years later, he passed away. That was very sad. However, he did what he felt he wanted to do, which was his prerogative.

Our children have fond memories of the races they did go to and, for the most part, I am glad we made the effort. In Austria one time, Bernie Ecclestone paid for a crèche for the drivers' children, which was really nice. In some ways people think Bernie is very hard and tough which, of course, he is when he needs to be, but there is a very human side to him which that gesture illustrates very well. One year we took them to Hungary. They didn't go to the track, but as a family we jumped on the tram to the city and went to the zoo, which was enjoyable. If you were to ask the children, the moments they would always remember would be playing with Frank and Ginny Williams' children, who were similar ages. They loved that.

We would always go to Monaco as a family. When we could afford to, we stayed at the Plaza hotel and walked along the promenade, and there was a little merry-go-round nearby that the children loved. Every year in Monaco, we would take a picture of them sitting on the same wall, so now we have a lovely photographic record of them getting bigger and bigger. They always remembered Monaco; Estoril too, which they adored because we stayed in a log cabin there.

Nora Tyrrell tells a classic story about Chloe when she was a baby. We had a function to attend one evening and we took our baby daughter with us. We never had anyone available to look after her, so we would just take her along. We got her ready for bed, put her in the pushchair and wheeled her along to the do. She was asleep, happy as Larry in the corner of the room, not making a sound. Then, when the event was over, we went back to the hotel, lifted her out, put her in the cot and she went straight back to sleep. Very rare, I know, but this wasn't unusual for Chloe – she was a very good little girl. Nora found this unbelievable and very kindly used to say, 'What an amazing baby!' Mind you, it wasn't like that when the boys came along ...

The craziest trip I did during that time was coming back from Japan to the Isle of Man, which as you can imagine is not a straightforward journey. At that time, I had to travel economy everywhere but I wanted to get home for the birth of Leo. I made lots of flight connections and managed to get there in time, but I was only in the Isle of Man for 17 hours before I had to get back on a flight to Australia. I really didn't want to miss the birth – I am very proud, and not a little amazed given the transient nature of my job, to say that I was actually present at the birth of all three of my children.

That particular trip was a bit much, to be fair. By the time I landed in Australia, the jetlag and tiredness were overwhelming and I didn't really know where I was, who I was or what I was supposed to be doing. In less than three days I'd spent over 50 hours in the air. It's funny looking back (although I don't remember laughing at the time), but I recall getting in the car after a number of days in Australia and I really didn't want to drive. I just wasn't with it. That has happened to me twice – that time in Australia and also once in Japan. The latter was more to do with the food and the time zones.

Like I've said, it helped that we often had our own plane. I have very much enjoyed being a pilot for over three decades and I'm glad to say I've had very few near misses. I've generally been lucky with incidents – I am meticulous with the preparation and safety of any flight – but there was one very hair-raising near miss one time we were flying transatlantic. I've always been very safety conscious and I don't like flying in severe weather unless I really have to – you shouldn't push the limits. On this particular occasion, we could've lost our lives when we were ferrying one of our new planes across the Atlantic. However, this wasn't due to being reckless or unprepared. We'd done our homework; the weather forecast was pretty good, rain or even just drizzle at worst; the plane was in perfect condition, everything was working beautifully. However, what I learned that day was that your life can change on a sixpence – one minute everything is fine and you have done all your home-work, you've done your weather reports and so on, but if Mother Nature wants to turn your life on its head, she can.

There is a moment called a 'wet footprint' when you are flying across a large expanse of water, which means you get to a certain point in the crossing where you have insufficient fuel to turn back and make it to land. So you have to carry on regard-less of the weather or the plane's status; there is literally no turning back. The point of no return, so to speak.

On the flight in question, we didn't have enough endurance to get straight to England so we had to refuel in Iceland. The weather was acceptable and perfectly safe for flying so that was the plan. We called in before the wet footprint, and that was all okay, but then about 20 minutes after the point of no return, the weather just went down the toilet in the matter of a few minutes.

In a heartbeat, we were in the middle of freezing, blizzard

conditions, a freak storm whipped up, the temperatures changed and the barometer suddenly dropped; the forecasted drizzle and then heavy rain instead became a thick blanket of snow. Almost instantly, visibility was reduced to near-zero, a complete white-out, and conditions were deteriorating to a very serious level. The air-traffic controllers were absolutely fantastic because the airport had to be closed, but because we had nowhere to go and couldn't ditch the plane, they let us land there. The plane was really being battered by this winter storm; it was terrifying for all of us. We came into the approach for the runway over the sea but couldn't see a thing; it was just a wall of white. I was thinking, *We could easily get this wrong and ditch in the sea, then we'd all be dead*. Then, at just 70 feet, we managed to make out the runway, thick in snow, but at least we could at last see the ground. There was a vicious crosswind and the plane was lurching from side to side. It was just awful.

Bill and I were both captains of the plane, but on that leg of the journey, I was in the left-hand seat. When Bill finally saw the lights of the runway, which was totally snow-covered tarmac, we were about 70 degrees to the runway because of the crosswind, so I could see nothing out of my side. I knew at that moment that unless the plane worked to perfection in every way, we'd be in the poo. Thankfully, by the grace of the Lord, we somehow managed to land the plane on the snow. I don't mind saying it was excellent teamwork; we did a great job. That's not to say we both didn't experience a little of the 'pilot's shuffle' in our seats, but we got down safely.

The snow was so thick by now that it took us a full 20 minutes to taxi through the drifts towards the main building. We finally parked up, and were preparing ourselves to disembark so that we could catch our breath, refuel and wait for the storm to lift. My dear friend Dr George Morris said that he would go out first and see what was going on. We were all mostly wearing flip-flops and shorts as we had been in Florida, so we weren't exactly dressed for the conditions. George, on the other hand, was perfectly ready; he'd got all the gear. 'I will sort it out,' he said valiantly. 'I will go and find somebody.'

We were just happy to be on the ground and delighted that George had volunteered to go out into the blizzard. We watched him zip up his thick winter clothing, get himself ready, unlock the plane's door like a conquering hero about to go forth and bring us salvation. Then he stepped off the plane … and promptly disappeared from sight into the deepest snowdrift I've ever seen. It's a bit naughty, but we did laugh. It was hilarious.

At least it was hilarious right up to the point we realised we had to go out there in temperatures of minus 25 and a blizzard to dig him out.

Fast-forward a little to my time racing in America and it's fair to say that the children enjoyed being around IndyCar perhaps more than F1. They were a little bit older and those races were, in my opinion, more family orientated. Loads of drivers brought their children to races; there was a real family atmosphere. One time in Cleveland, Ohio, I had a great race with Emerson Fittipaldi and afterwards all our respective children clambered up on the podium with us. Lovely! My children really had fun with IndyCar.

Sometimes having the children with me wasn't quite as soothing as I might suggest. I remember once we were going to the track so we packed up all Leo's baby stuff, but then almost as soon as we'd set out, we realised we'd left all his bottles in the fridge in the hotel, so we had to turn round and go back. It was quite comical in a way. By my mid-thirties I had three young children and was racing at the sharp end of Formula 1. Never mind having 26 cars on the grid, having three children under five at the same time is what I call busy.

One element you can't prepare for is how your children will react to your job as they grow older. Specifically, you know they are becoming increasingly aware of the risks involved in Daddy being a racing driver. A very significant moment in my life came in 1987, when I was paralysed from the waist down for six weeks after suffering spinal concussion and swelling on the lower part of my spine, following an accident at Suzuka (I will come to the accident and its consequences later).

The reason I remember this period very clearly is that Chloe, who was just a toddler at the time, was really upset that I couldn't play with her. I couldn't even get out of bed, so Rosanne had to explain that Daddy was poorly and his legs didn't work properly. We weren't sure how Chloe would take it, but she was devastated, really upset. Bless her; she got me to promise that I would never hurt myself again. That incident *really* made me realise for the first time the impact that my chosen career had on my family.

I was able to keep that promise until I had another biggie, in IndyCar at Phoenix in 1993, which was ugly. Fortunately, this time Chloe was older and seemed able to process the situation a little more easily. She was still bothered, but not as horrified as the first time. I could at least walk and, although I wasn't about to go down the park on the swings with her anytime soon, she was brilliant. So, yes, although as a family we were used to the risks of my job to a degree, young children can be affected very deeply by worrying about the dangers and their parents' welfare. I was ultra-conscious of that. Of course, years later, when it came to my own two sons going racing themselves, the tables would be turned.

Some of our travels around the world were really fun, some

tiring and some just downright hilarious. Once, we were coming back on a long flight with all the children in tow and, at the time, I'd employed a guy to manage a lot of my affairs; to look after the practicalities and generally lift a weight from my shoulders by taking care of the logistics. He was a good guy and very helpful, so this one time we had arranged ahead that he would be there to pick us all up at the airport. We landed on time and then disembarked, collected our luggage and made our way through customs. With three children, loads of suitcases and just the general chaos of a family of five after a long-haul flight, we were keen to get home. We walked out of Arrivals and spotted the newsagent's where we had agreed to meet.

There was no sign of him.

We waited for ten then 15 minutes, but he still wasn't there. So I phoned him up.

'Hey, it's Nigel. I'm waiting outside the newsagent's. Where are you?'

'I'm waiting outside the newsagent's, too! Where are you?'

It was really baffling.

'I'm next to the newsagent's, just down from the coffee shop, opposite Arrivals, like we said.'

'Well, this is weird, Nigel, but so am I. I can't see you at all. I wouldn't mind but East Midlands airport isn't exactly that big . . .'

'Hang on . . . did you say East Midlands airport? We're at Birmingham!'

CHAPTER 9

1986: A BIG YEAR

This was a big year. In 1986, I had a brilliant car and a fantastic team. Okay, it's fair to say that I didn't exactly see eye to eye with my new team-mate, the double world champion Nelson Piquet – let's just say he is an 'indifferent' person, to put it politely. He was the team's number one driver and being paid much more than me, but I had no problem with that, or racing against someone with his track record, just as I didn't with Keke previously. Frank always let us race to win, so it was up to me to show what I could do.

However, the difference between Keke and Piquet was that Nelson was never going to win any 'Nigel Mansell's Favourite Team-mate Award', which I don't mind mentioning. He played a lot of psychological games; he criticised me on many occasions, but he would also go on to say the most insulting things, and was even once very nasty about my wife. That's out of order. He was trying to psychologically rattle me, but it was never going to work. I learned that in order to rise above it and still perform to the very best of my ability, I had to pigeonhole comments like that – you take them and put them away, then get on with your job. In fact, I would go further and say that I used to try to breathe in the negative energy of people like that and turn it into positive energy. That way, for every hurtful word they said, it felt as if they were fuelling me, making me go faster and faster.

More importantly, however, the Williams FW11 car that year was wonderfully quick. Nelson was perceived as the pre-season favourite, but I knew I could make an impact so I let him do all the talking. I trained hard in the off season and enjoyed testing a brilliant car. Frank stood by me, too, when he was under pressure from Honda, and once again we were allowed to race freely and for wins. Horribly, in final testing, Frank Williams had a dreadful car crash on the way to the airport. I was one of several people on the scene shortly afterwards and it was a really terrible incident. I went in the ambulance to the hospital. The accident shook everyone to their very core, obviously, but Frank had instilled such a culture of determination in his garage and factory – the same determination that saw him bounce back from his own dreadful injuries – that his Williams team displayed the most incredible resolve and will to win. That year Williams would take the Constructors' Championship; given the circumstances, that is pretty special.

This was also the year when Ayrton and I took part in the closest ever finish in a Formula 1 race, in Spain, when he beat me (damn!) by 0.014 seconds, which equated to a distance of approximately 93 centimetres over a race of over 200 miles. There had been tension at the preceding race, the season opener in Rio, when Ayrton pulled what I felt was a sudden move on me as I was overtaking him, hitting my front right wheel and sending me off and out of the race. The close finish in Spain was just more of the same attempt to intimidate me, but I refused to be unnerved by these tactics. I'd overhauled Piquet and had to manage my fuel levels, but I was in the lead when I suffered a slow puncture and some diffuser problems with only ten laps to go. Eventually, I had to pit and it was a massive effort to reel Ayrton in after I rejoined the race. With one lap left, I was still 1.5 seconds behind, but we came out of the last corner with me all over the back of him and then it was just a straight fight to the line. It is true that I later said maybe we should have had 7.5 points each, which I thought was a very fair and excellent idea, but sadly the suggestion fell on deaf ears!

I was accumulating points all year. I managed to get five wins for the season, my best ever string of results, and the car was just flying, helping me on my way to a bagful of front-row starts and fastest laps. However, as well as Frank's dreadful accident, the entire year was also overshadowed by the death of my dear friend Elio de Angelis.

Sometimes in life you get a sense that something bad is about to happen. It has happened to me on a number of occasions; some people put it down to coincidence, others to a developed sense of anticipation, call it what you will. It is a very personal thing, but I do know that I have had this feeling several times.

You've no doubt heard stories of people who won't catch a plane on a particular day, or they won't get on a bus or train that they normally get every morning, for whatever reason. They can't explain why, but they decide they will stay at home or catch the next one. Then, they find out there's been a catastrophic failure and terrible accident that morning. How do you explain that? I'm not quite sure, to be honest, but I do believe it is something within us all and that we are sometimes guilty of not listening to ourselves.

In May 1986, I was testing at Paul Ricard in France before the Belgian Grand Prix. Elio was there with Brabham, the team he had switched to from Lotus. Strangely, the night before the test I just felt awful; I knew something was wrong. I didn't understand why, but I was really upset and had this overwhelming sense of dread about the next day. The feeling got worse when I drove into the circuit the next morning – I knew instantly it was going to be a bad day. It turned out to be among the hardest few hours of my life.

That was the day that my ex-team-mate Elio was killed in a terrible accident.

Elio's car suffered rear-wing failure and cartwheeled over a barrier at high speed, before catching fire. He was in the car for a long time. The accident was compounded by a series of unfortunate problems; nothing worked, nothing went in his favour. He was eventually helicoptered to hospital but died later.

I remember sitting on the kerbing in the pit lane after Elio had been taken to hospital and I knew he was dead. I was stunned, shocked, tearful. We'd been team-mates for a long time. One of my best friends in the paddock was dead. During the 1982 drivers' protest, Elio had entertained the drivers in a hotel with his beautiful piano playing – he was a concert-standard pianist. At the end of 1986, Keke Rosberg retired from Formula 1 and it is said that Elio's death was a major contributing factor in that decision. Elio was an enormously popular figure in the paddock.

Now he was gone. Sitting there on the kerb, I just said to myself, *If I am going to stay in this game, I have got to make it successful. I have got to win and make it pay, otherwise I am going to get out. This is not fun anymore.* Elio's accident was one of many I witnessed in my career, but it was the one that changed my life from that day on. I will come back to that unsettling sense of foreboding I felt the night before Elio's death. For now, I just want to say that he was a wonderful human being; he was much loved, a dear friend and I was absolutely shattered by his death, as were so many other people who knew him.

After that terrible day, I sat myself down and resolved to continue in Formula 1 only if I had a genuine chance to compete. The risks were too great to simply make up the numbers. It was a life-changing moment.

The race after Elio's death was in Belgium and I won. I dedicated the victory to Elio. With Patrick Head as my race engineer, we also scooped some very clever strategic wins, such as the next race in Canada. When the grand prix show rolled into France at the same Paul Ricard circuit where Elio had been killed just a couple of months earlier, it was tough. But I managed to win again.

The 1986 British Grand Prix at Brands Hatch is one of my favourite victories. Emotions were running high as, remarkably, Frank had recovered enough to return to the circuit for the race and he got a standing ovation from the assembled journalists at his press conference. The team was delighted by all this and I was also super-excited about the massive British crowd of 115,000. I was desperate to win in front of them.

In my opinion, the win that day was pretty much textbook. I got pole position, was happy with my car, and when the lights changed I had an incredible burnout off the grid, which is what you are supposed to do. Then suddenly a driveshaft let go, so I had no drive at all. Crap! Sadly, because I was stranded, I contributed to people having to go around me, and then the middle of the field had a coming together which was an almighty accident. This was a great shame particularly for Jacques Laffite, who broke both his legs in the accident, which ended his career (regulations introduced shortly afterwards ensured drivers' feet were behind the front axle line; before this race, our feet were sometimes only about nine inches away from the nose of the car).

The race was immediately red-flagged because we hadn't completed one lap, so technically the grand prix hadn't officially started. I went back to the pits to find out what was wrong with my car, but it was impossible to repair it in the time. There was only one option: use Nelson's spare car. This car was set up for the team's number one driver, with his settings, his seat, his pedals, gearbox, springs and so on. They only had time to put my seat in the car and adjust the seatbelts, nothing else. Although I knew it would be exceptionally difficult to drive competitively, I couldn't jump in the car quickly enough. I was back in the race.

I got off to a shaky start because on the warm-up lap the car stepped out on me a couple of times, which was hairy because there were no run-off areas at Brands Hatch. It is a super circuit but it was horrendously dangerous back then, in my opinion. So I was very wary of the car, and at the restart I dropped down a few places within the first laps. I was behind Gerhard Berger, but then I managed to overtake him. Then I overtook Prost as well and realised I was staying pace with Nelson, who was winning the race. Eventually, I got more trusting and confident with his spare car. I had to adapt my aggressive driving style to a more 'softer-entry' style on the corners. I like to go into a corner really aggressively and hustle the car round, and try to carry the speed through, but if I'd hustled Piquet's car it would have definitely stepped out on me. It is a fact that as soon as you are opposite locking a car, you are not going forward, you are going sideways. That might look great on TV but in reality it means you are slow. Also, your anxiety level jumps up through the roof because you think you're going to have an accident.

So I adjusted my style. I understood that by braking softly I would be able to manipulate the centre of pressure on the car. His springs were a little bit different to mine, so consequently the centre of pressure wasn't changing in the same way as it did on my car. His car was really good in places mine wasn't and vice versa. I mentioned earlier that the brain is a personal computer, and it took me quite a few laps to compute and programme my own brain to be at one with this car.

To be accurate, I wouldn't say I was ever 'at one' with Nelson's car, not in the way I could be with my own, but eventually I was beginning to drive it very fast indeed. I had to smile because he was driving absolutely beautifully that day, and I was thinking, *Crap – he has not made one mistake.* As you know, Nelson and I weren't exactly best friends, but I will quite happily say that he was driving brilliantly.

His superb driving just fuelled the impetus to give him a hard time. Then it happened. He made one tiny mistake. He actually missed one gear in the whole race, second to third on to the back straight, and that was enough for me to slice through, because I was close enough to have the momentum to get past him. With difficulty, but I did. That is how I won the race. He made one mistake. A single minuscule error that enabled me to beat him. That was a really hard race for him to lose and a brilliant race for me to win, in Nelson's own spare car. Nelson's second place also made it Williams' first one-two of the season, topping off a pretty triumphant weekend for the team all round.

I was now leading the World Championship by four points, and I stayed out in front until the final race. The only real blip was in Mexico in mid-October. It was Murray Walker's birthday party the night before and, unfortunately, I must have eaten something bad because I went down with Montezuma's revenge. Before the race, I was in the loo every five minutes and my constitution didn't improve as I headed for the start line.

Oh, my goodness me, driving the car that day was pitiful, terrible. When you are sitting in a car basically having accidents in your racing suit down every straight, it's not where you wanna be. To make matters worse, first gear wouldn't engage at the start and I was frightened that someone might shunt into the back of me, like I had seen with several bad accidents before. That's not a good feeling when you are already in the state I was! I laugh about it now, but it is the one race out of my entire grand prix career that was the most horrendous time of my life. Not great. It wasn't funny to me but a lot of other people found it hilarious. The mechanics even painted a line from the pit lane to the toilet. Sods! Still, I managed to finish fifth.

Arriving in Adelaide for that season finale, I was six points in front of Prost, so my task was pretty simple: finish third or higher and the title was mine. I was relaxed and focused. I played golf with Greg Norman beforehand, and Rosanne was at the race with me. Initially, the race went reasonably well, especially after Prost pitted with a puncture. Keke also had tyre trouble and sadly retired from what would be his last ever grand prix, a big loss to the paddock. Murray Walker, commentating at the time, said, 'Nigel Mansell is using every ounce of his considerable intelligence, acumen and experience', going on to say that if I went on to win, 'how richly it will have been deserved'.

Then, as I was consolidating my third position, with a very comfortable gap between myself and Stefan Johansson in fourth, and the world title in sight a few laps away, my left rear tyre exploded savagely at 196mph, leaving me to wrestle the car to safety as it twitched violently and shuddered along the straight to a gradual, dejected halt. All hopes of a title win disintegrated with the shredded rubber scattered across the tarmac. The footage of my tyre exploding so dramatically in a shower of sparks is one of the most famous snapshots of Formula 1 in any era. Murray Walker even called it 'the most memorable shot of all time'. The world title was gone.

That blow-out – what it meant for my title hopes – was obviously personally devastating. I think the most heartbreaking thing for me was that I could've been driving a lot faster. My overall lap times were relatively modest, but I'd made up my mind that third place was fine, it was enough to win the world title, so I resolved to stroke the car home on to the podium and ultimately the title. I felt as if I had everything under control. Prost was not far in front of me and Nelson was leading, but I wasn't trying to overhaul either of them; I was just following Alain at a sensible distance. If I'd been pushing hard and driving beyond the limits of the car, then maybe I could've accepted the blow-out more easily, but as it was, I felt very harshly treated by Lady Luck.

I did radio in to the pits to ask about coming in for tyres, but I was told that it was not necessary. I do not blame the team. Let me be very clear – the team were only acting on the information they had been given by Goodyear, which was that there were no issues with undue wear, so I absolutely do not hold anything against my garage, not at all. Also, you need to bear in mind that as far as Goodyear were concerned, the tyres were okay. Piquet had pitted several laps before and degradation wasn't an issue at that point. So no one was acting carelessly. It was just one of those things that can sometimes happen in motorsport. Tyre degradation is a combination of wear, load and heat cycle. As the tyre wears, it starts to allow more slip, which in turn loses traction and therefore temperatures increase due to friction; all the time the tyre is shedding more rubber, which is evident on TV as 'marbles', small chunks of rubber discarded at the side of the racing line. Sometimes, however, the degradation has far more catastrophic effects, such as my massive blow-out.

It was Goodyear and the team's call and I was comfortable with their decision. Besides, in those days, making a pit stop was very complicated and all sorts of things could go wrong – a nut could get cross-threaded, a wheel could fall off, it could be tricky – so in many ways I was relieved they didn't call me in. I was just thinking, *Stroke the car home, third is all you need, only 19 laps to go.* Because of the lap times we were doing, I hadn't lost much grip and wasn't putting huge amounts of stress on the rubber; it was just that none of us expected the tyre would delaminate and explode in the way it did.

Even within the confines of a blow-out, I was unlucky. A tyre exploding is in itself no big deal; you can often get back to the pits, change tyres and go back out. The problem was the force of the explosion was so violent that it broke the rear suspension and also tore the rear brakeline off. So the car was on three wheels with very little braking. At over 190mph, that was one hell of a moment, let me tell you.

The first I knew of the problem was when the car instantaneously tried to turn sideways into the wall. I had to opposite lock it, the physical movement of the car was so incredibly violent. Bear in mind the tyres were a lot bigger in those days. I remember pressing the overtake boost to get past the Ligier of Philippe Alliot so that I could follow Alain into the corner, and shortly after that the tyre just let fly. It felt like a bomb had gone off.

At that speed, I could've had a terrible accident and been seriously injured, which I instinctively knew, so I used every bone in my body to wrestle the car to safety. Self-preservation kicks in; you just know that if you crash the car at that speed, with a wall so close by, it is going to be a biggie. So I fought to control the car in any way I could. Sadly for me, I did manage to control it and I came to a halt in a safe run-off area. Why sadly? Because the reality was that, if I had crashed, they may well have put the red flag out, and, as the race was already over two-thirds completed, they would've taken the result from the positions the lap before and I would've been crowned world champion! That never crossed my mind. I was trying to avoid slamming into a wall at over 190mph, not mentally flicking through the pages of the rule book. To date, I'd driven the best part of 15,000 miles in F1 races and here I was, only 44 miles short of winning the world title. James Hunt, commentating on a pit-lane camera shot of me, said, 'Poor Mansell, that is terrible . . . at the last moment,' while Murray said, 'There's the unfortunate Nigel Mansell, bathed in sweat, his face a mask of tragedy.'

That incident was *very* hard to come to terms with. It felt so unfair. As I mentioned, Williams won the Constructors' Championship that year, which was an amazing achievement especially when you consider that Frank's terrible car crash could have derailed the team before the season had even begun. However, Williams was a special team and everyone, from Frank and Patrick Head down, did an incredible job for the entire season. Sadly, in my opinion, Alain didn't win the drivers' title, we lost it. Prost even graciously said himself that he felt sorry for me, having himself twice lost the title at the very last race of the season, so he understood how I would be feeling. 'Nigel was the one who deserved it the most,' he said. I'd lost the title by just two points.

I wasn't world champion. We had lost it. I use the royal 'we' deliberately because it was an accumulative combination of factors throughout the season, mixed in with some very bad luck. Looking back on it now, with much water having passed under the bridge, I actually feel sorry for Goodyear because it wasn't just that one race in Adelaide that cost us the title. They didn't deserve some of the negative publicity they received after that incident. There were probably up to 20 reasons throughout the whole year: mechanical failures that could not have been foreseen; strategy errors; driver errors on my part; and, of course, just sheer bad luck when that tyre exploded and caused the specific damage it did.

There is no question that what put us out of that particular race was the tyre exploding and, had it not exploded, then I would have been world champion. That is true – but there were other factors. The problem for Goodyear was that it was such a visual event, so dramatic and so high profile that naturally the focus was on them and their tyres. If we had got everything right – and I include myself in that – I believe we could've won that title. Losing the World Championship in 1986 still hurts to this day, I am not going to lie. Even now, nearly 30 years later.

CHAPTER 10

RED 5 PUSHES ON

After Adelaide, I did contemplate retiring, but I love winning and to call it a day with that graphic tyre blow-out as my last Formula 1 moment would not have sat well with me. On the day, Captain Mark Phillips was there in Adelaide and I'd like to personally thank him for consoling me in the way that he did. Once back home, I was further comforted to a degree by the fan letters and encouragement I received. Looking back a few years later, I felt that the outpouring of support after the tyre blow-out meant that it was the moment perhaps that I became the 'people's champion'. Although I didn't win the title in 1986, the majority of F1 fans said that morally I was the world champion. I definitely felt a shift in support for me after Adelaide.

There were some nice accolades too, such as the BBC Sports Personality of the Year (I later won that prestigious award a second time in my championship year, 1992). However, the loss in Australia bit deep. Back home, as I reflected on the year, the championship slipping out of my grasp, my dejection was compounded by the terrible loss of our lovely friend Elio just a few months earlier.

On a personal level, 1987 was a very testing year. Rosanne was pregnant with our third child, Greg, but the pregnancy didn't go well. She was hospitalised for over a week with a threatened miscarriage during the second half of the pregnancy. It was a really frightening time.

When I look back now, I am not quite sure how we got through that time because I was racing all around the world, and for the last number of months Rosanne was totally immobilised. However, we did get through it, by staying strong and soldiering on. In the day and age we were brought up in, you were expected to face whatever you were presented with; you 'got on with it'.

Back in the world of F1, in 1987 I was very competitive and won six races, with eight pole positions, 14 front rows and 61 points, but I still did not win the title. I suffered several mechanical failures, including a broken exhaust, a failed weld on the turbo, a wheel nut coming off and some engine problems. These issues cost me four wins, including what would have been my first ever triumph at Monaco. As an aside, that race was never particularly kind to me. In the early days, without any question, Monaco was the most physical circuit. Mainly because of the anxiety level – there were no run-offs, nothing, you either got round the corner or you had an accident! And if you wanted to be quick, then you'd have to really hang it all out there. It is true that sometimes we'd come into the pits and the logo on the tyre walls had been rubbed off because we were driving so tight to the barriers. Monaco was a great place to race, but very unkind to me. I should've won there at least three times. I came second but never won. I had several pole positions, too, but Lady Luck was elsewhere – but then I don't mind because I had Lady Luck on my side so many other times.

In 1987, I also had what you might want to term 'a heated exchange' with the late great Ayrton Senna, at Spa that year. It was one of those moments when, in my opinion, Ayrton didn't really have the respect that is necessary at that speed. I was racing hard and he blocked me when we went on the same corner at very high speed and we could easily have had a bad accident. That really concerned me. I was pretty furious.

After the race I went to the pits to have a 'polite' word with him, shall I say. For the first time in my career, I saw the red mist. I will never forget the late Sheridan Thynne – the commercial director of Williams, God rest his soul – he initially stood in my way to stop me going to Ayrton's garage, but he later told other people that as soon as he saw my eyes and the thunderous expression on my face, he jumped straight out of the way. (Sheridan was another truly fantastic, loyal supporter and great friend, a real gentleman.) He and a few others followed me to the Lotus garage.

Once I got there, I had what you could softly describe as 'an altercation' with Ayrton. With one arm, I had him pinned up against the wall by the neck, his feet off the ground. Then four people each grabbed an arm or leg and dragged me away. As they did, Ayrton had a couple of swings at me too. I watched him hit me but I didn't feel a thing at the time.

It was pretty heated and we exchanged a few words of mutual encouragement. However, I felt I got my point across. The fascinating thing was that although it was a massive dust-up, the FIA did not fine me for the fracas at all, despite the fact they were handing out lots of penalties at the time for various incidents.

After Spa, I have to say I noticed that Ayrton started to show me a really healthy respect, because he knew for certain that I didn't like to be messed with. In fact, from a racing point of view we became very close and both enjoyed being formidable competitors. All through this period, there were four main protagonists in my opinion: Senna, Prost, Piquet and me. A formidable foursome. It was a special time.

Fast-forward to three months later and I was 19 seconds in the lead in Hungary when all of a sudden a wheel nut unzipped itself and fell off. I lost the race. The words devastating, shock and disbelief spring to mind. I thought to myself, *What have I got to do to get to the finish line sometimes?* In any sport, if you are doing a sterling job and then it is just snatched away from you, it is hard. There is nothing you can do. What I will say is that the great thing about the Williams team was that, when something like that happened, nine times out of ten they were so disappointed for you and for themselves that no one had to say anything to anyone. It was a combined, collective disappointment. There was a real team spirit in that garage. By the way, after the wheel nut came off and I lost the race, I got back to the hotel and my beautiful daughter, Chloe, told me not to worry as she'd got me some dried flowers. That put a smile back on my face.

Although 1987 was littered with problems and frustrations, looking back now my memories of that season always centre on one of the proudest moments of my career – my famous win at Silverstone in mid-July. This victory came after being 29 seconds behind Piquet with 28 laps to go, and was topped off by the overtaking manoeuvre that most people still ask me about to this day, when I double-bluffed Nelson down Hangar Straight. Red 5 beat White 6.

Nelson had previously endured a poor week at Paul Ricard and was perhaps also keen to avenge my win at Brands Hatch the previous year. However, Frank sportingly stuck firmly to his no-team-orders rule and just asked that we didn't crash into each other in any on-track battle. Piquet narrowly took pole in front of a huge partisan British crowd, who I was determined to win the race for.

Nelson was leading and I was comfortable behind him when a wheel-balancing weight came off, creating chronic vibration in my car. Eventually, I had to pit on lap 36 and, when I re-emerged, I was nearly half a minute behind with 28 laps left. It was a mountain to climb but I set about my business.

I pretty much had to do one qualifying lap after another to catch him; it would have to be a record-breaking drive, hauling one second a lap off a world champion in a very similar car. I knew I had to maintain a record-setting pace and not make a single mistake. After just a few laps out of the pits, I started to plan my overtaking manoeuvre. Probably 20 laps out, I'd say, I was doing the maths, as early as that. The clawback was relentless, even with my fuel gauge and my pit-board team warning me about low fuel; every lap, bang, bang, bang, I was chipping away at him. I was actually hoping to get some bigger chunks off him earlier but I couldn't because – although he is a very indifferent person – he was doing such a great job of maintaining his own fast pace. His engineers were telling him that if he could maintain his pace then I would struggle to catch him. The problem for him was that I wasn't doing race laps, *I was doing qualifying laps*. In the next sequence of laps, I broke the lap record 11 times and I am very proud of that fact. Although it was an awesome deficit, once I settled into the groove and started to make inroads, I was on a mission. I could see that if I maintained the qualifying pace and drove flawlessly without any errors, then maybe within two laps before the end of the race I could be in snapping distance. I also knew I would only have one chance, because if you screwed it up that late in the race you wouldn't get another shot.

The power of the crowd at Silverstone is just incredible. I was *so* determined to win that race for them. As each lap clocked by, it was a case of executing finer and finer planning, little by little, just honing my idea and prepping the overtake. As I said, I knew I would have one chance and one chance only. It was so exciting. Rosanne was expecting Greg at the time and she later told me, 'I thought I was going to have the baby there and then.'

I knew on each lap where I was quicker; I knew I'd have to get past safely because I suspected that, if there was any opportunity for him to knock or force me off the circuit, he would. It is very difficult when you are trying to keep a rival behind you, because they are chasing your tail and hunting you down; they are always looking forward at the rear of your car and the track, yet you are constantly having to look in your mirrors, then back at the track, then the mirrors again. It was this unavoidable dilemma that I manipulated to overtake him.

I knew how he would be feeling inside his cockpit. I also used to like to go off in the lead if I could control the race, of course, but being first can be very draining. When you are leading a race you have moments of sheer, absolute panic and anxiety. I think you are at your most sensitive ever when you are the lead car. You are listening and feeling for everything that could possibly go wrong; you're micromanaging everything in that car, the tyres, the brakes, the suspension, the position on the circuit; you're playing the percentage game. You give more room here, you go in tighter there so you have more room coming out on the exit; you brake a little bit earlier, you give yourself more time, a greater degree of recoverability. What you don't want to do when you are in the lead is fly off the circuit and spin, or go in a trap and throw the race away. So the pressure of leading a race as opposed to chasing is completely different. I *loved* chasing people, hunting them down.

If you are chasing somebody, then you can use them as a brake, you can see in the distance where they are braking and you can use them as a guide – you don't have to keep looking at the side of the track to know where your brake points are. If they have a wobble in a corner, you are forewarned that maybe there is some oil or water there. So automatically your mind is being programmed by their car, just by watching them. And not only that, you can identify where their car is strong and where it is weak, so by the time you catch them, your mind is pre-programmed to know where your strengths and their weaknesses lie.

In many ways it is far better if you are in second or third place, provided you are not losing contact and you know your car is just as quick if not quicker. Then you can follow the leader at a distance, to conserve your tyres and fuel; you are in their slipstream a little bit, which is fantastic (as long as it doesn't hurt your car, because if you get too close it induces understeer, which means your tyre consumption on the front will increase). The whole thing is a balancing act. You have choices and, of course, those choices change from circuit to circuit. That's when you plan your game of chess. I found that whole element of strategising between race leader and chasing car fascinating: hunted and hunter.

You don't realise when you are in the thick of your career how much information your brain is able to store. In fact, it has only really been through the process of writing this book, sitting down here quietly in my study recounting these stories from all those racing circuits so many years ago, that I really began to understand the level of skill and programming power our brains were displaying in those cars. Wow – it's incredible what the human brain can do, when you think about it.

Anyway, flitting back from my desk in Florida in 2015 to

Silverstone in 1987, I was breathing down Nelson's neck with two laps to go. The crowd was phenomenal; the energy they gave me was immense. Naturally, the British fans didn't want him to win it. I am British; he is Brazilian. That's understandable. The Mexican wave undulating around the circuit, lap after lap, was going almost as quickly as I was!

As I approached, I knew he would try to block me and I didn't want to zigzag behind him down the Hangar Straight, so I'd decided that I had to sell him a dummy. With only a few feet between his rear and my nose, I moved slightly to the right and sure enough he moved to block. Then I disappeared from his mirrors towards his left side and, as I suspected, he moved to his left to block me. What he didn't realise was that I already had the closing speed and was in his slipstream, and so was primed ready to go back the other way. By the time he realised I wasn't where he was expecting me to be, I was parallel with him and it was a fait accompli – he could do nothing. It was mighty close going into Stowe at very high speed, but I had the advantage and took him for the win. I don't wish to sound cocky when I say this, but it was a brilliant execution of a dummy, and I think Piquet hates that fact to this day. The *Daily Mail* called it 'one of the most memorable races in F1 history'.

Of course, the context of the overtake made it all the more special. It was my home grand prix; the British crowd was always so fantastic to me, I just had to win. Then, on the slow-down lap, my car ran out of fuel. I'd had the turbo on full boost and, in fact, my fuel gauge was reading minus two litres, but there was no way I was going to stop! So when I did finally run out of fuel at Club Corner, I was swamped by hordes of fans – it was just the most amazing feeling, to be embraced by them. British fans are among the best anywhere in the world. As I mentioned earlier, some people called me the people's champion, one of the proudest things in my whole career. I have got to echo the words of Ayrton: there's nothing better than being cheered by your own fans and being applauded doing the best job you can for yourself and for them. That's what I felt my job was: racing wasn't just for myself; it was for them, too. That certainly applied on that special day at Silverstone in 1987.

Silverstone has a very special place in my heart. Obviously, it was my home grand prix and I have some fantastic memories there, not least my four wins. Silverstone was a fantastic circuit for me on a number of levels. Firstly, the track itself. I'm talking about the old Silverstone in particular, which was just the most awesome circuit in the world. Wow, that was just so fast! It had a sequence of corners second to none; very fast, very demanding corners. When you came out of Becketts, well, straight in front of you there were concrete sleepers. David Purley went in there head-on once and it was estimated he was pulling in the region of 180G, which I believe is the highest G accident ever survived (he decelerated from 108mph to zero in 26 inches). You had to go through there as quickly as you possibly could then down the end of Hangar Straight at full pelt. With the right tyres you'd turn into Stowe in qualifying flat out at 200mph. In those days, you had six-inch catch-fencing poles with strands of wire wrapped around them, and if you went off you'd go straight into that mesh. Potentially, you could be hit on the head with a pole or even decapitated, which sadly did happen at some other non-F1 motorsports around the world, which is why they were rightly banned. You'd go into Club flat out, through Abbey flat out, and so on – it was just the most exhilarating lap. The fastest sequence of corners anywhere in the world. If you were good, you could go round there in about 1 minute 13 seconds. It was so quick, so dangerous but, boy, so, so exciting. I absolutely *loved* that circuit. Now, of course, there are run-offs and some of the corners have been altered in line with new safety regulations, which has clearly slowed down the cars. We all used to love the sheer speed you could enjoy at Silverstone. As I mentioned earlier, Keke Rosberg did the then fastest ever average qualifying speed in Formula 1, with an average speed of 160mph. I saw that happen and it was incredible. What a lap, Keke!

Silverstone also has very fond memories for me and my family. There was an area renamed Mansell Village, which was designated for camping, but they used to rope off this little section for us and that's where we'd park our motorhome (not a very salubrious motorhome, I might add, especially the year it leaked and we were in a foot of water). Our friends used to bring their caravans and trailer tents and we would create a big circle, like a wagon train, with barbecues in the middle. The journalists used to come and join us, and we'd play football matches, too.

We always had loads of friends and family come to Silverstone. Some years, I would end up buying as many as 250 tickets just to make sure everyone got in. They all congregated on Copse Corner, on that little mound, so I have to admit I would be speeding around the track in the race and quite often looking out for my friends and family. You could pick people out, faces that you knew and wanted to see. Sometimes I would even wave at my children. Over the years, I made some pretty bad exits out of Copse because I was looking for my children, exiting at about 170mph and shouting under my helmet, 'Woo-hoo, Chloe! Leo! Greg! Helloooooooo!' Just delightful.

You'd think that with the sound of an old F1 engine you wouldn't hear much of the crowd. Absolutely not the case. At

Silverstone, sometimes the sound of the cheers was astonishing. If you needed a lift in the race, the crowd always seemed to know and they'd respond. I'm not sure if anyone has ever studied whether home support like that effectively cut a few tenths from your lap times, but I certainly felt like it did. Their support for me was christened 'Mansell mania' by some and, I have to say, I feel very blessed and privileged to have had such amazing fans championing me for so long.

The fans used to come around our motorhome and camp nearby. There wasn't the same level of security back then. The general public had incredible access; it was so much more relaxed. That actually applied to the pits as well, because for all the politics and rivalry, we would all just generally wander around. Sometimes drivers would pop into another driver's motorhome for a chat; it was very laid-back. There was so much less of the paranoia about taking photographs of cars. Don't get me wrong – there was plenty of looking at the back or front of the cars, getting a sneaky peek at designers' 'secrets' or a new piece of technology, but there wasn't the same level of security to prevent this. Of course, it's not just Formula 1 that has changed in this way in the last 25 years; the world has too. It is through no fault of anybody's; it is just the way of the modern world. You don't really see drivers leaning on a fence having a bit of banter together as much now, which is a shame. These days, they have their own little worlds, these absolutely incredible motorhomes that are like beautiful apartments. I think some of the drivers probably spend more on their motorhomes than F1 was spending in the early eighties!

In many ways, the Formula 1 fans were our security system; they were very protective of us. That seems quite strange to think of now, with the intense security around sports stars all over the world in the modern era. However, back then it wasn't like that, and I have to say we were privileged to have had that intimacy with the supporters, who were just the best fans in the world. They had total access but they were respectful, and when it was time to eat or go to bed everyone gave us our space.

I really related to the fans. They have paid money to come and see a show, to support their chosen driver or team, and what you need to do, regardless of how competitive you are, is the *best job you can*, not only for yourself but for them. Even if their team or driver is going through the doldrums and not winning, what they have to be able to take away is that their guy tried, he gave it his all; the car was crap but, boy, it was exciting!

Every year at Silverstone we made it one big British Grand Prix party from start to finish. We didn't even fly off or go home on the Sunday night after the race, partly because the traffic in the old Silverstone could leave you in a big, muddy jam for five hours, but also because we loved the experience so much. Win or lose, we would stay late. Silverstone was just the most wonderful circuit for me. Happy memories.

As a quick aside, away from the races I did earn a label for not being that exciting at times because I never partied. Until I won the world title, I hadn't achieved what I wanted to achieve, so for me there was always more work still to do. Now, when I look back at some of my race wins, I wish I'd hung around for a party after the race, like we used to at Silverstone. I did have a few great parties, though. Ferrari were always fabulous at celebrations and, of course, Colin too, but perhaps I should've gone to a few more. In 1994 I went to an incredible party that certain teams were at and I have to say it was probably one of the best parties I've ever been to in my life. I have never laughed so heartily from that day to this. It was just a crackerjack evening.

Getting back to Silverstone, the BRDC (British Racing Drivers' Club) are a great body of people and have made a fabulous modern circuit at Silverstone. Yes, I might say these corners are slower and so on, but that is a safety necessity and all part of the modern era. The actual facilities are now exceptionally good and they are constantly looking to improve, there is no resting on their laurels. In terms of what they have done with Silverstone, I take my hat off to them. What a fabulous achievement.

I loved racing at Brands Hatch too. It was a great driver's circuit but, from the point of view of the fans, it didn't come close to Silverstone. For me, that Northamptonshire circuit is the pick of the bunch, the home of grand prix racing.

As I write this, all these wonderful memories are flooding back of those great weekends at Silverstone. Happy times, lovely people, amazing races and very proud wins. It is actually quite astonishing sitting here reminiscing about it all; it feels like a lifetime away. I didn't realise that you live several lives in a lifetime and everyone has a number of chances. Silverstone in 1987 and, indeed, every time I raced at that fabulous circuit were certainly fantastic moments in time for me. Extraordinary, very dear memories.

I also hold incredibly fond memories of my wonderful friend, Murray Walker. It was in 1987 that he famously asked to see a bump on my head after the Austrian Grand Prix and then when I took off my cap he proceeded to accidentally poke the bump! It's a very funny and famous clip. For me, Murray Walker is everyone's dad, the father they never had. He is the most genuine, charismatic, beautiful male human being you could ever wish to meet. To this day, to my knowledge he has never properly fallen out with anyone or had a bad word to say about anybody. No doubt there are a few people he doesn't actually like too much, but he is such an incredible gentleman and a consummate professional that he can be charmingly polite even to someone he's had a run-in with, completely defusing any animosity. Even the strongest will can only bow to Murray. He has such a way about him – I put him in the class of Morecambe and Wise, I do honestly. I find Murray can be naturally very funny, just getting everything wrong, sincerely wrong, which is so appealing and endearing. Then you wait for him to gather his thoughts and correct himself and he does so with such style and grace. There is never any impatience or grumpiness. He is an absolute joy.

I will never ever forget the interview he did in 1993 when he came to our home in America after I'd won the world title over there. We had a massive BBC satellite wagon crammed full of all this technology set out down the road, and they took a long time perfecting everything to get ready for the interview. Then it was time for action, at which point Murray started with his opening line, 'So, Nigel Manson . . .'

I just looked at him and said, 'Did you just call me Nigel Manson? I'm not a mass murderer! It's Man-sell, Murray,' and he said, 'Did I just say Manson?!' We all broke into laughter. He is just a gem.

Murray and James Hunt made for the most fabulous commentating team. I was really quite a fan of James Hunt. He was very flamboyant; he did a lot of things I wouldn't do, granted, but his driving style really appealed to me and my sense of competitiveness. Of course, in yesteryear he was able to do many things that modern-day drivers would not, such as drinking, smoking and womanising. To paraphrase a famous motorsport quote, motor racing used to be dangerous and sex was safe, but now . . .

Anyway, James was very good to me in the 1980s, very supportive. I appreciated his support and respected him for his talent and his achievements. He was not just some handsome playboy racer; he was the real deal. He was very direct; if he thought someone was a berk on the track or in the pits, he would say so. He had his moments when he criticised me, which was, of course, his prerogative. Obviously, that outspokenness wound up some people, but I always thought at least he was being honest. You might not like his opinion sometimes but he was always being straight with you. There were no doubt many fisticuffs behind closed doors as a result, but you could never say he was two-faced. He told you how it was.

As for his driving style, I would say he was very cavalier. Was he as calculated as he might have been at times? Probably not, but that is what made him James Hunt and we should applaud him for that. The sport was hugely saddened when he died and he was a massive character to lose from the pit lane.

On a lighter note, I would like to say that I think James's relationship with Murray Walker in the BBC commentary box was just magical, arguably one of the best – if not the best – the sport has ever seen. They had many formidable years working together and it was a very sad day when that duo ended. Murray will say that James and he almost had physical punchups in the commentary box, fighting over the mike, because in the early days there was only one microphone. James would want to say something but Murray was already talking, and then other times Murray, in his unflappable way, would get a driver's name wrong and James would be eager to correct him. Eventually, they both got their own mikes so that problem was resolved, but the dynamic between them was fantastic. What an iconic commentating team. I should say as well that, although I suggested Murray might occasionally get facts wrong and make me smile unintentionally, I must make it clear that in my – and many other people's – opinion, he is the greatest motorsport commentator of all time.

There are so many funny stories to do with Murray, but perhaps the most memorable interview I ever did with him – and there were hundreds, if not thousands, as well as the TV commercials we made together – was in Rio in the 1990s. He was in sublime form. It was one of those interviews where he didn't put a foot wrong – every question was superb, he took the conversation off at fascinating tangents, the verbal sparring between us was so enjoyable and interesting, he was incredible. The ebb and flow of the interview was arguably the best TV piece I'd ever done, it was just fantastic. When we finished, Murray put the microphone down and said, 'Nigel, you already know this but that was fantastic. Thank you for that, it was a really splendid interview.' And off he walked.

Several hours later he came up to me in the pit lane, rather sheepishly, and said, 'Nigel, can I have a word, please?'

'Yes, of course, Murray. Always, for you.'

'You know that interview we did today?'

'You mean the one that you said was fantastic and was easily one of, if not the best we have ever done together?'

'That's the one, yes.'

'What about it, Murray?'

'The microphone wasn't switched on.'

Another one of Murray's moments.

In the second half of the 1987 season I was unhappy with my engines and called meetings with Frank and Honda to discuss why I often felt I was down on power. Despite my misgivings about the power issues, and me saying I would leave the team if it was felt to be in the best interests of all parties, Frank backed me by saying he wanted me to stay on for 1988, which was excellent, but I felt that Honda were not giving me their very best. It was a difficult time behind the scenes. A low point was probably in Mexico. I was coming round the last corner and across the start/finish line 2–3mph faster than Nelson, but then at the end of the straight I was something like 15mph slower, even though I was carrying less wing. So I should've been at least the same or faster.

I was terribly unhappy and down on overall lap time, so I kept telling the team, 'Look, we are both going for the World Championship – this needs to be resolved.' A chip was changed in my engine and magically I was 10mph faster. I know this sounds like stating the obvious, but it was so incredibly crucial to get the right engine. The engine is the donkey that pushes you along. Once you have got an engine that is working relatively well then you are also looking for that power unit to be consistent and reliable. You want as much punch out of the corners and as much power down the straights as you can get, and you want that performance *reliably*. It is no good flying around the first 30 laps, only to break down halfway round the race. The settings of your engine can make or break a race. In my era, drivers were closely involved with picking the engines. I would not want it any other way. The same went for gearboxes. If I found a gearbox that for whatever reason felt silky smooth, I'd earmark that one or even identify the man who built it, and I'd want that specific box as often as possible.

Unfortunately, despite having been in contention for the title again, my season ended early when I had a big smash in first qualifying at Suzuka, in Japan. That brilliant circuit has incredibly fast sweeping corners, but if you step one inch out of line on a corner and touch the curb when you are on full lean then the car will swap ends on you. Not just at Suzuka, at all circuits. Sometimes the margin for error is less than an inch.

At Suzuka that day I was pushing hard in qualifying and that's what happened, causing an accident on a corner where there was nowhere to go. I was thrown into the wall at 160mph, went airborne about 12 feet in the air, spun 360 degrees and landed badly. This is where you have 'lucky' accidents and 'unlucky' accidents: my car landed with its wheels either side of the kerb, so the seat area of the car landed directly on the kerb itself. Therefore, no wheels touched the circuit first to dissipate any energy, and the entire force went up through my seat and into my back. I was later told they calculated the impact force up my spine to be in the region of 75G. This crushed some of my vertebrae. The pain was horrible and I was having trouble breathing, which I later found out was due to fractured ribs.

They rushed me to hospital where I was kept for some time, and it was not a nice experience. The first couple of nights I was in intensive care, and I witnessed some horrific things, including two people dying close by my own bed.

I never really had the success I feel I should have had in Japan, because I love the circuit. I think Suzuka is a fantastic driver's track and the people were wonderful. However, it never really panned out for me there. I used to stop off in Hong Kong to dilute the time-zone issues, but I always struggled. In my heyday, the British Army gave me a Gurkha bodyguard, who used to follow me round Hong Kong and help me organise everything. I got very friendly with the Gurkhas and the military – what a great body of people and so much fun. I can't thank them enough for their friendship and time spent looking after me.

However, in 1987 I did not have such a good time. I was flown home, seriously injured and facing another spell of recuperation. As a result of this injury, and my previous back and neck injuries, I got even shorter, so I am now three-quarters of an inch shorter than I was aged 21.

Eventually, Piquet would win the 1987 title, and he then moved to Lotus. In 1986 I had won five races; in 1987 I'd enjoyed six wins. Yet my title hopes were over for a second year running. A week after I returned home from Japan, our third child, Greg – about whom we had worried so much – was born. After all the concerns, we were blessed with a healthy baby.

After the big smash in Japan saw me missing out on the world title for the second year in a row, a few people questioned whether I'd still have the hunger, but that was never going to be an issue. I trained hard in my recovery, even going to a clinic in Austria to attain peak fitness. I was ready for the new season. In 1988, however, I was not so competitive and, like the rest of the grid, was beaten comprehensively by the all-powerful McLaren-Honda of Senna and Alain Prost, which pulverised all opposition. Honda and Williams had parted company and the manufacturer had moved to McLaren, where that partnership would enjoy record-breaking success, winning 15 grands prix out of 16 races. Our normally aspirated Williams was no match for the turbo engines and it was an uphill battle all year. Patrick Head and his team had created a beautifully designed and incredibly complex FW12 car, but, until turbos were outlawed at the end of the season, we were always going to struggle. Reliability was an issue and ultimately we just didn't have the same grunt as the turbo cars.

Part of the FW12's potential was the active suspension. However, it was unpredictable at first and could be a real hand-ful. Active suspension was another technological development that, like ground effect, could be pretty frightening at first. To hugely simplify a very complex system, the active suspension constantly monitored load from one wheel to another, the idea being to keep the ride height as controlled and level as possible (initially it had been devised to help control the skirts used in ground-effect cars).

Early active suspension was very dangerous because when the computer and control system failed, it could throw you off the circuit or down the straight or round a corner at any time. Both my team-mate at Williams, Riccardo Patrese, and I had umpteen experiences of that, which doesn't exactly build confidence in a driver! The most famous example was when Riccardo and I got really cross with one particular engineer at the same time. He'd put the data on his computer and said, 'It looks all right to me,' but after the car had tried to kill us a couple of times that's not what we wanted to hear. So we voiced our opinion quite strongly!

The system was devastatingly scary at the beginning, but in the end we got everything working quite well. We still had some failures, but when they happened we managed to go into failure mode, as opposed to what I used to call killing mode. A failure mode wasn't very comfortable, it wasn't very pleasant, but at least you had a chance of stopping the car and not running into a wall or being smashed up.

That 1988 active suspension system was obviously very advanced for the time, but compared to the modern-day systems it was completely primitive. The suspensions they are using in F1 in the modern era are so sophisticated; they are astonishing pieces of engineering. Someone once said to me that there are the equivalent of about 15 laptops of processing power and computer tech on a modern F1 car. In the early 1980s, I don't think there were that many laptops in the entire pit lane . . .

The Williams team worked extremely hard that year. They even somehow managed to convert a car to passive, old-school suspension for me at Silverstone, after my active suspension had failed three times. They did an amazing job and I was able to bring the car home in a wet race in second place behind Senna. There was to be no repeat of my 1987 heroics, but it was a great result for the whole team, as we had all worked so hard against the odds. However, aside from a few highlights, 1988 was largely a season of disappointment, rendering me with just 12 points and no wins. There was disillusionment, I am not going to lie. Having come so close in 1986 and '87, to trail so far behind in 1988 was obviously frustrating.

Then, for 1989, I signed to race for arguably the most famous and historical Formula 1 marque of them all: Ferrari.

CHAPTER 11

AMAZING TIMES AT FERRARI

Driving for Ferrari is a very special experience. The cars and their track record speak for themselves, but it is not just that – the whole culture around the team is mesmerising. Just meeting Enzo himself was an absolute honour and I am extremely proud to be able to say I was the last driver that he personally picked before his sad passing in August 1988. I'd had conversations with Ferrari previously, in the mid-1980s, about joining the team, but here I was, finally driving for this famous F1 marque. Like Colin Chapman, Enzo Ferrari commanded the utmost respect and I feel privileged to have raced for them both. Enzo told me he thought I was one of the finest drivers he had ever signed. To know that I was following in the footsteps of other Englishmen who'd driven for Ferrari, such as Peter Collins, John Surtees and Mike Hawthorn, only added to the honour. I was so proud.

Previously I have spoken about an incident with Enzo at a restaurant, but the anecdote bears retelling because it really shows the charisma and power of the man. One night I was invited to a very lavish dinner with him and various members of the Ferrari team, and it was fascinating, the people-watching was brilliant. The Italians around the table were all talking at a thousand miles an hour; there was jovial, excited chatter going on all around. Then, suddenly, from where he was sitting at the head of the table, Enzo just lifted up his thumb and index finger and *in an instant* the entire table fell silent. The first time he did this I was stunned. He said something to the gathered guests, then the moment he finished the chatter started up again. Later on, though, he did it once more – fingers went up, again all the chat around the table stopped instantly, but this time he was just grabbing the salt. The power of the man and the respect he commanded were legendary – all I could think was, *Wow!*

Another time, I'd been testing the geometry for them on a new road car, the Testarossa. I did my work and commented what a beautiful machine it was; I really loved this Ferrari. A week later, a shiny new Testarossa turned up outside my home. The same happened with a beautiful red Ducati motorbike I'd mentioned I loved, which soon appeared outside my home. Then one time we were going down to Estoril for testing and I piloted Enzo in his magnificent Falcon 900 private jet. It really was the bee's knees – what a plane! I mentioned several times how I thought this was the best plane I had flown for a long time, what a marvellous piece of engineering it was. I really made it clear I loved it as much as I had the Testarossa and the Ducati.

I'm still waiting for the plane . . .

My two seasons at Ferrari saw mixed fortunes. I was honoured that they gave me the number 27, which Gilles had used when he drove for them previously. I was excited about the possibilities for the season ahead. With turbos banned, Ferrari had come up with a highly complex and ingenious new car for the 1989 season, so I was expecting a year of development, which was fine.

One notable element was the semi-automatic paddle-shift gearbox, which at the time was revolutionary, but for me it meant almost relearning how to drive in certain instances. I enjoyed finding out how to wring the best from this new system, though, and certainly the lack of physicality involved in changing gear was a huge bonus. The theory was wonderful – being able to keep your foot down on the throttle and change gear, even around corners. At that point, you still had to synchronise the shifts down and the wheel sensors weren't bulletproof. If you called for a gear at the wrong time, you could mechanically over-rev the engine. If you did that then the pistons would hit the valves, basically breaking the pistons, blowing the engine up a few laps later! So in those early cars you still had to be very mindful of your correct moment to change gear, even with the semi-automatic box.

However, it was the beginning of a revolution. It was wonderful, I have to say, to be able to keep your hands on the steering wheel all the time, because we were still without power steering, so that was a huge help. I was actually a big fan of the old-school manual gearbox. I enjoyed having to manage the engine so precisely; I enjoyed the physicality of changing gear and understanding when the revs were just right, that was a great skill. However, I totally loved the emergence of the semi-automatic box. Nowadays it is so sophisticated that in theory it is impossible to change down at the wrong time, to select the wrong gear. Maybe that's going too far, I don't know.

Anyway, back at Maranello in 1989, I was concerned in pre-season testing about a lack of power. The complex gearbox was always a worry and proved to be prolifically unreliable, but I remained optimistic. However, we got off to the most incredible start at the first race of the season in Rio.

That race was more than a fairy-tale script; it was a miracle. People use the word 'miracle' flippantly, but what is a miracle? For me, a miracle is something that is so out of the ordinary and against everything that you think could possibly happen, yet somehow it happens. In my life, I have been on the edge of several miracles unfolding before my eyes. One of these was winning my first ever race in a Ferrari in Rio in 1989.

People often ask me how I won that race. The honest answer: I haven't got a clue! We were testing all through the winter, but the Ferraris were so unreliable that my new team-mate, Gerhard Berger, and I couldn't complete more than five laps before the things broke down. Potentially, we knew the car was quite good, but the semi-automatic gearbox failed *all the time*.

At Rio, my Ferrari broke down in three out of four practice sessions. It got worse. We used to have warm-ups before each race to check the cars out, and therefore give you a chance to fix any problems. In Rio, for the season opener, I went out in the pit lane on my warm-up and I didn't even make half a lap. It broke down within a few corners. This was my first race for Ferrari and here I was, sitting on the corner of the track at Rio, with all the stands full of fans towering over me and they were cheering and throwing stuff at me. They were obviously supporting Nelson and Ayrton, I understood that, but that atmosphere was pretty intense! I was waving and smiling back, trying to keep calm, all the time thinking, *I hope they don't start throwing bricks.* Joking aside, I was disconsolate – really quite down but trying to put a brave face on it. I just felt I was doomed to failure before I started; I had no chance.

Well, we went into the race and I have to say that Rio that

year was, in terms of feelings, probably the most unique race I have ever had in my life. Despite my very low expectations, after a few laps I found myself going along okay. *It won't be long, the car will break down soon*, I said to myself.

I started overtaking a few cars and found myself in third place. However, I was actually really annoyed because I was thinking, *Don't you dare let me get up into third place and then blow up!* But the car kept going and going, and a few more laps went by and then I was up into second place. Now I was going to be *really* annoyed when it finally blew up. Every lap I was waiting for the car to break down, but then a few more laps went by and I overtook to get into first place. I was in the lead! You are supposed to be happy in the lead, but I wasn't, because I was so angry with the car, fearing it was going to blow up and I'd have to retire while leading. I tell you what, I have never driven a car so gently and so perfectly as that day in Rio.

I actually started talking to the car out loud. 'Come on, keep going, don't you give up on me now, keep going, pleeeease ...' Lap after lap, I urged this car not to fail. It was like some mantra of desperation: 'Please don't break down, please don't break down, please don't break down.'

Then on lap 40 my steering wheel came loose.

The steering-wheel bolts came loose and the thing almost came off in my hands (something that had happened to me once in a Formula 2 race). I couldn't believe it. All this time I'd been praying – literally – that the semi-automatic gearbox wouldn't give up on me and now the steering wheel had almost fallen off. So I shouted in the radio, 'The steering wheel's coming loose, the steering wheel's coming loose!' It was bordering on the comical. Again, I don't remember laughing at the time.

I slammed into the pits and they had a spare wheel ready. I threw the old one off, the mechanic pushed the new one into place then, with an urgency that would come to cause him considerable pain, he smacked the steering wheel into the column really powerfully ... promptly stabbing himself in the palm with the long, thin, sharp-edged team radio switch that I'd had fitted (because I had trouble holding a button down around corners).

I dashed out of the pits with a new set of boots and a new steering wheel and I was just thinking, *What is going to happen next?* Then I started panicking about the gearbox and the conversation started again: 'Oh no, please don't blow up' – back to my old routine, I was begging the car not to fail. Then I got back in the lead and ... oh, I don't know ... I haven't got a clue what happened that day ... but we won the race. It was probably the single most unlikely win of my entire career.

Everyone was over the moon. If you look at the stats, it took Gerhard and me a hatful of grands prix before we even managed to finish another race because the car was so unreliable. I'd even changed my flight home to an earlier one because I was so convinced that I'd be out of the race really early. As it was, I missed my flight but secured Ferrari one of their most improbable race wins for a very long time. That victory was actually the longest distance the car had ever covered.

At Imola, my Ferrari team-mate Gerhard Berger had a huge crash when he smashed into the same fateful corner that five years later would tragically take Ayrton Senna's life. The car actually exploded into flames and Gerhard was burnt in the ensuing fire. It was a very serious incident. They stopped the race and all the drivers were back in the pits waiting for updates about Gerhard and what would happen next. I went to see Gerhard because thankfully he was conscious and said he was okay. Remarkably, he even had a bit of a laugh with me. What a fantastic driver. I said that I needed to know what had happened, as there had been talk of the front wing failing.

To the layman with no knowledge of F1, a front wing breaking or snapping looks like a relatively minor fault in relation to the rest of the car's size. Far from it. When that happens, you lose all the front end of the car and almost invariably you end up having an accident where you are just a passenger, a missile going into the wall or the barriers. So after Gerhard's nasty crash there was conjecture that it was down to a front wing, but because the car was in a million burnt pieces, verifying that was impossible in the circumstances.

When I returned to the pits, everyone was very worried about Gerhard and emotions were running high. James Hunt came up to me looking quite intense and said, 'Nigel, unless you know exactly what has happened to Gerhard's car, you should not go back out if the race restarts. You would be taking your life into your own hands if you go back out there without knowing what has gone wrong.' He was really quite forceful.

He was adamant and we talked about it at some length. I am a big fan of James and was very flattered that he was worried in that way. I think his concern that day reflects a very admirable side of James; he was a passionate and caring individual. He was also a former world champion, so I took his opinion very seriously indeed. After he'd left, I went to the Ferrari team and explained his viewpoint. Ferrari were very sympathetic and said, 'Look, the call is yours, we will put the responsibility on you. If you are not comfortable and want to withdraw, we will withdraw the car and back your decision completely; if you want to race, we will race.'

In the pits we did everything we could to figure out the problem that had caused Gerhard's crash. We were jumping up and down on the front wings – we'd actually had a new front wing that weekend, so they had already been beefed up. It wasn't totally confirmed that it was the front wing that failed, not least because, as I said, there was nothing left of Gerhard's car to see. Without forensically examining the wreckage for metal fatigue and crack detection and all the clever ultraviolet testing they can do, it wasn't possible to be certain. Besides, even if it had been possible technically, there simply wasn't enough time, as they only stopped the race for a short while. Eventually, I decided to race. James respected that decision but he still held his own position and I admire him for that.

Just to finish off that story: when I say I raced at the restart, I did so with considerable trepidation – it wasn't any kind of caricature of 'Nigel Mansell the Aggressor' flying around the circuit, laughing in the face of death. Not at all. I was very wary indeed. My decision was made because of what I explained earlier about being a fatalist. When there is a massive accident like that and your team-mate has been burnt and seriously injured, lucky to walk away with his life, in fact, if you then decide to jump into an identical car and go racing again, then first you have some very serious questions to ask yourself. Common sense dictates that until the team knows what is wrong, you shouldn't drive the car. My view was, without being gung ho, that if it was going to happen it was going to happen. I got back in the car but after 23 laps a gearbox failure put me out of the race. As much as I love to compete and win, I can't say I wasn't relieved. It later transpired it had been the front wing and a similar failure happened to me in Monaco going into Casino Square.

The other highlight of the 1989 season for me was my second win for Ferrari, at the Hungaroring. After qualifying in 12th, I jumped four cars at the start and then gradually picked my way through the field towards the front, until I was behind only Senna with just over 20 laps left.

People often ask me what I consider my best overtaking manoeuvre to be. It's not a simple one-choice answer. I certainly feel that the most spontaneous overtake I have ever had the pleasure of doing was passing Senna that day at the Hungaroring in my Ferrari, a move that enabled me to win the race. I boxed him in with the backmarker Stefan Johansson as we came around a right-hander. It was a split-second move and James Hunt quite rightly commented at the time that I didn't have very long to make the call. I had to get round Senna as well as Johansson, but thankfully it all worked out well and I went on to win the grand prix. Actually, I have to be honest: although I say it was spontaneous, I had thought about the possibility of using backmarkers many laps before, when the race was panning out and it was clear that slower cars were possibly going to come into play. So I did think about the possibility of such a move, but not the exact location and moment, and when we came around that corner, I seized the opportunity and went for it.

Of course, that move would not happen in the modern day because backmarkers have to move out of the way. In that era, backmarkers would often get out of the way, of course, but they weren't bound to do so; they were allowed to race if they chose to. So it was a risk, because Stefan's car was a third element that might cause a problem. Thankfully, I was able to manipulate the move so that Stefan's car effectively boxed Ayrton in. Many people have cited that as one of my greatest ever wins, which is always nice to hear.

There is a great saying in motorsport that if you have to think about something on track then it is already too late, and if it's not too late you are too slow. Either way, you are no good. Overtaking manoeuvres like that one are totally instinctive. If you are a world-class driver operating at the very top of your game, you adapt instantly to whatever is thrown at you. It is true that you never know exactly what will happen until the precise sequence of events unfolds, and that is when your racing instinct comes into its own.

The 1989 season was somewhat littered with retirements, six through reliability, plus I was black-flagged twice and suspended for one race. If I look back at the races I did finish, we did well. Two wins, four more podiums and two fastest laps. Set against a backdrop of McLaren-Honda dominance, it was a strong season for the team if you take the new car and severe competition into account. It felt a little more modest for me, finishing fourth on 38 points, but even though I hadn't won the title, driving for the Tifosi was always going to be special, even so.

To be nicknamed '*Il Leone*' – the Lion – by the fans in a country where Formula 1 and motor racing means so much was incredibly special. It's a bit like receiving accolades from the Queen or your government – a 'money can't buy' achievement. The Italian racing fans even made me a one-off bronze statue of a lion and later awarded me the Golden Helmet, a very prestigious accolade voted for by the public. At times they made me feel like they were my home fans. At the end of 1990, they even sent me a trophy inscribed with the words, 'Our World Champion in 1990'. Wonderful.

To drive for Ferrari means you are godlike in Italy. In that country, if you are four or 104, you know who drives for Ferrari. I had heard about this special treatment before, of course, but experiencing it first-hand is really fun. It's like a passport to everything for free and the most amazing times. They literally won't let you pay for anything. From that point of view, Ferrari was, for me, without any question the best team to drive for in Formula 1. They took care of everything – your own doctors at the circuit, your own masseuse, your own chef, anything and everything was done for you. Nothing was too much trouble. They were among the most wonderful years of my life and I would have loved to have been at that team a lot longer. Even today, in my sixties and long-since retired, I travel the world and Ferrari fans come up to chat to me. They still call me *Il Leone* and treat me with the greatest respect.

I have for many years been a special constable in the UK, and also worked with the Australian and American police forces. I will come to this in more detail later, but with regard to Ferrari there was one incident I absolutely loved that really shows you how Ferrari F1 drivers are seen as demigods. I had been testing at Maranello and working at the factory, and was on a quick lunch break. I needed to pop to the shops to get a teddy bear for my boy Leo, who was only a toddler. I didn't have much time, so I left my racing overalls on and jumped in my Ferrari Testarossa, then zoomed off towards the shops.

There was a lot of traffic, so I was blasting around the outside, overtaking everyone, 'utilising my professional skills as a racing driver', shall we say. As I hammered down this one particular straight, I got to the end and was pulling back in when I suddenly saw some police cars. For some reason two soldiers were also standing by these vehicles, complete with sub-machine guns and pistols, looking extremely unhappy with me as I screeched to a halt.

I was pulled over by the three policemen and I have to say I was pretty nervous. They were so armed up, I thought I might be looking at a long time in a very harsh Italian jail. That wouldn't do much for my F1 career at Ferrari.

They came marching over, looking really stern, machine guns at the ready. *Crikey!* I thought to myself as they approached my car, *I'm in trouble here!* As they got to within about six feet of the Testarossa, I wound down the window and that's when they saw my face, my moustache and my bright-red Ferrari racing overalls.

They stopped instantly in their tracks, absolutely dead on the spot. Two of the police immediately walked out into the road and stopped all the traffic, while the remaining officer and the two soldiers waved me back and onwards along the now empty road ahead. As I drove past, bemused, smiling, relieved and stunned, they all stood to attention and crisply saluted me.

By the way, Leo loved the teddy bear and it now sits in his daughter's nursery.

CHAPTER 12

THE 1990 SEASON: A 'RETIREMENT' YEAR

In my era of Formula 1 you had to – quite literally – look at yourself in the mirror each morning and ask yourself if you had what it took to hang it all out there on track. Could you go into a corner that had previously taken someone's life? Could you push that new part of the car to the limit even if failure could throw you off the circuit and into a wall? Could you fly down a straight with concrete barriers either side? You had to answer these questions all the time, in testing, qualifying, racing. One way I did this, and all other drivers will have their own version of this ritual too, was by having a very strict race-weekend routine.

Every top driver will have a regime and a safety net of certain people around them who know how things need to work on race day. My routine would depend on the race we were going to: is it a European or transatlantic journey? How long is the flight? What is the time zone you are in? For example, if it was in Australia I would need a minimum of three days before driving to acclimatise. Japan was another tricky one. For Europe, you might have your own plane but you'd still go there a minimum of the day before.

When I got to the track, I'd go through all the engineering reports and check my car. I had my own personal checklist to make sure the engineer and the mechanics had done any tasks that had been carried over on a work list from the previous test or race. We would have a briefing about what the weekend was potentially going to be like, discuss the car's settings – we didn't have the data-logging technology, of course, so we did everything ourselves with engineers and the team.

Depending on the circuit, specifically whether I knew it well or not, I would walk it, run it or ride it, maybe even drive it if I could get hold of a car. I actually preferred to walk the circuit because you would see more, and it was also a bit of exercise. I always tried to make sure that I was mentally comfortable and happy, and if there was something bothering me, I would discharge that frustration or concern to my engineer or to a team member who could make a difference. I would always try to do that the day before the race, because then you offload your anxiety rather than take it to bed with you, which might affect your psyche and your disposition on the grid. Most importantly, if the worry was something I could not affect myself, then I would hand over to the right people to make sure the issue was dealt with properly. Then, the next day, I would make sure that the task had been carried out.

The night before a race I would always go out clubbing, usually drink a minimum of ten pints of high-strength beer and a few tequila slammers, and then, on the way back to the hotel in the early hours of the morning, maybe get a burger and fries, or sometimes a kebab. Well, actually, that's not strictly true. On a few occasions I had half a pint, but normally I'd be teetotal, maybe have a relaxing meal with friends or family, then get an early night, around 9pm, sometimes earlier. I just felt it was more restful in a quiet hotel than if I was out in the open where people might want to chat or take photographs. Sometimes well-meaning people might say something that unsettled or annoyed me, so it was just easier to be in the hotel. I might sit in bed making some notes, ruminating over a few ideas, then lights out, ready for the next day.

On race morning I would normally get up quite early to beat all the traffic into the circuit, as early as 5am or more often 6am. You see, Colin, fudge factor. I had a code with Rosanne when I was racing: depending on how I got up in the morning, I would be able to tell her that 'today was not a good day'. So if there was anything she wanted to have a go at me about – kids, dogs, damp coming in through the roof, maybe our family car tyres needed changing – unless it was an emergency, she knew to leave me alone. *I love you but it's not a good day today. I will be hot to trot tomorrow*. If you are not careful, your nearest and dearest can get the brunt of your edginess.

I had such a great relationship with my engineers – David Brown at Williams and Maurizio Nardon at Ferrari – that I would trust them totally with my life. If they said to me that everything was okay and they had something covered, then I was relaxed. If an issue wasn't resolved, they would work very hard with me to get the best result that they possibly could.

I would have some breakfast then we would have a warm-up. I would then eat specific foods before the race that I knew were good for me. After that, I would make out that I needed to go for a little nap, but this was really just so that I wouldn't be bothered. I would sit in the motorhome trying to keep my energy to myself so that I could concentrate on doing the job. Then they'd call me for the race.

This was how I personally prepared for a race, but each

driver will have their own very strict approach and discipline, a set routine, and nobody must disrupt that unless it is for a very important reason, a genuine emergency. All their energy needs to be focused on the race and nothing else; no nervous energy needs to be lost by having anxiety or distraction. That is why I used to say to Rosanne all the time I was racing that unless there was something really serious going on with the family back home, any news could wait until I'd finished the race. That sounds harsh, but it is a necessity of driving at world level. If something very sad has happened, then the people around the driver have to make a judgement call. Will telling them before a race make any difference? It will certainly affect their race. It might even put them at risk if that driver is not able to deal with the bad news and they have an accident, because they weren't focused enough in a potentially dangerous environment.

I can remember one specific example of this with my own family. I always phoned Rosanne before a race. Just before I got into my race overalls and headed for the grid I would phone her; that was a part of my routine. This was in the days before mobile phones, but I would always find a way to get through to her. On this particular race day, just before I called, unbeknown to me, Chloe – who was about five at the time – had run into the bathroom at home, tripped on a rug and smashed her head on a marble top. She'd opened up a big gash in her forehead and was obviously really shaken up and upset. Chloe was sent off to the hospital and some close friends (who are sadly no longer with us) helped out Rosanne. Some weeks later, Sid Watkins took the stitches out for Chloe at Silverstone!

Anyway, back on that race day, I phoned Rosanne as usual and, although she said everything was absolutely great – 'The kids are fine', all that – I could just tell in her voice she was hiding something; my instinct told me that something was wrong. She insisted but her tone of voice told me different. Sixth sense, intuition, call it what you will. I really pushed her, asking, 'Something is wrong, isn't it?' but she wouldn't have it; she stood her ground, there was nothing for me to worry about. She knew that telling me would not change anything. I couldn't help Chloe; I was thousands of miles away. All she would do by telling me would be to distract me, which in a 1980s F1 car at 200mph could be a very dangerous thing to do. Rosanne knew the score.

I do think motorsport is different from most sports in this sense. If a golfer is distracted by some family news from home before he tees off, then the worst that can happen is he will have a really bad round. He might not make the cut. If that distraction happens to a racing driver or Superbike racer, he could get killed. To extend this further, I think it means that racing drivers are able to hone and narrow their focus so intensely compared to almost any other sportspeople (with a few obvious exceptions in dangerous sports, such as boxers and Superbike racers). In the majority of sports, you don't go to work and consider you may get seriously hurt in a way that will change your life, or that you could possibly be killed. With motorsport there is always that chance, even with all the safety standards that are now in place.

I would go as far as to say that it brings an almost unfair advantage, because if a racing driver doesn't concentrate or pay attention going round a racetrack then he will get bitten on the ass real quick and will get hurt. So a driver's motivation to concentrate is immense. Drivers are, if you like, self-policed, because they have to do the job properly otherwise they will be too slow and perhaps not be employed, yes, but more importantly they could get hurt. No one really wants to get hurt so there is a lot of self-policing and self-belief in motorsport.

In most other sports, you can have an off day and you won't get hurt. In fact, in many other sports you can simply pull out. Take golf again: if you have had some bad news or feel unwell, then pull out, miss that tournament, get well and go again at the next competition. In F1, you can't do that because if you miss a race you lose points, you fall behind. If you have some difficult family news, or get the flu at the wrong time, or you eat something bad, you have to carry that through the weekend and still perform.

The worst race I went into health-wise was in Hungary. I had a temperature of 105 because I'd caught chickenpox. I still put the car on the front row. That race was awful, though. I had to pull out halfway through and I was hospitalised with a blood disorder. Turned out I'd effectively boiled my own blood. That day in Mexico when I'd had Montezuma's revenge after Murray Walker's party was another time I could *really* have done with a day off . . .

Anyway, being serious again, this is why people in motorsport need a different mind-set, because the level of risk sharpens their focus. In my opinion, other sportspeople suffer because they find it harder to sharpen their awareness for key events, where they don't hone their levels of performance to the highest point. In motorsport you simply can't afford to screw up big time because it might kill you. Self-preservation is an incredible motivator.

In September, Alain Prost announced that he would be joining me at Ferrari after a very acrimonious spell at McLaren-Honda with Ayrton Senna. That move, as I later found out, would lead to my position in the team shifting dramatically. Of course, I had heard the rumours about Prost, which had surfaced earlier in the season, but I was confident in my ability and felt that, in a straight, fair fight, I could beat him. In the past, he had been fair with me and spoken with respect away from the track too.

However, events did not unfold like that. I had number one driver status but that altered when they brought Alain into the team. I have to say, Ferrari were very honourable and beautiful people. They told me that the goalposts had moved. Unfortunately, over the course of the 1990 season, Alain worked very hard at motivating the team to support him. He was always a very political driver, and I quickly felt the emphasis shift away from me. Naturally, this was demoralising and disappointing.

It was a season with little joy on the track. I had just one win, in Estoril, Portugal (which put me level with Sir Stirling Moss on 16 grand prix wins), and four podiums, and came only fifth in the title race behind Senna, who was now a double world champion.

As a quick aside, Stirling remains hugely charismatic to this day; an amazing character, who can make you laugh so easily, too. Four times the World Championship runner-up and often the underdog; he should have won it but unfortunately he didn't, and yet he is still so bouyant. Having been a bridesmaid three times myself, I know how much it hurts, and the way he carries himself is just incredible. He is also a mine of information and the thing I love about Stirling is that, no matter what subject he is talking about, he states it as it is; he doesn't pull any punches, but he does so with grace and style. Eloquent and funny, entertaining and informative, I have got a special place in my heart for Stirling. I don't think he is political in any way; he is a genuine sportsman, a true racing hero. So to be level with him on wins with that Ferrari victory in Estoril was a real joy.

When I surpassed his total, he came up to me shortly after and said, 'Thank you very much, Nigel, thank you kindly.'

'Why, what have I done?'

'Well, now you have bagged more race wins than any other driver who hasn't won the title in the history of Formula 1! At last, you have taken it away from me. That is one record I don't mind losing. Thank you.'

We really laughed, it was so funny.

Getting back to that season, it's interesting that, with the passage of time, if people ask me about the 1990 season they don't want to know about all the politics with Prost, the manoeuvring behind the scenes, the intrigue – they want to know about me overtaking Gerhard Berger on the Peraltada Corner in Mexico.

With three laps to go, Gerhard had come down the inside of me on the main straight with all four wheels locked up. I looked in my mirror and felt that if I turned into the corner he could have T-boned into me and I would have been out. In my opinion, he'd abruptly pushed his way past me in the most forceful manner. I wasn't happy with this move, not happy at all, and so from that moment I was determined that I had to regain the position. I thought to myself, *There is no way I am going to give second place to someone driving like that.*

We proceeded to fight tooth and nail until on the last lap I was dummying one way and the other. I have to admit there was a little bit of red mist involved in what I did next. I thought, *Screw you, I am not backing off*, so I drove flat out at 180mph around the outside of Berger on the Peraltada Corner and screamed into second place. It was a very danger-ous manoeuvre. Going round the outside of anyone at that speed is friggin' dangerous. They only have to move a bit and touch you and you are gone. I wasn't thinking that, though. I was just determined to pass him and get into second and, besides, the adrenaline and the exhilaration of that move was so exciting.

I finished second behind Prost, but as far as my overtaking move was concerned, I didn't think anything more of it. Anyway, on the slow-down lap, the fans were all going berserk around the circuit. On the actual Peraltada Corner they were standing up and clapping. I was a little perplexed, to be honest. I thought I'd come second but maybe Prost had retired on the last lap and I'd won?

That feeling gathered momentum when I got into the pits. Prost must have broken down ... As I entered the pits almost everyone – drivers, team managers, mechanics – were clapping me in. I thought, *I must've won, right?* I got out of the car and all these people were congratulating me. One of my mechanics said to me, 'Nigel, I cannot believe what you have done!'

'Er, what have I done?'

'Peraltada ...'

That's when I realised that I hadn't won; they were just so stunned by the overtake.

'Oh *that*! Yes, that was pretty hairy!'

Those moments are pretty magical. When your peers, these world-class talents, engineering experts and Formula 1 legends are clapping a move you have made – even if they don't like you perhaps – then it is a lovely feeling. These were people who had seen everything, done everything, yet here they were applauding me for this manouevre. Wonderful.

Mexico was the highlight of the year for me, but with all the behind-the-scenes political upheaval surrounding Prost and Ferrari, I did not believe that I had the opportunity to compete on a level playing field anymore. At the British Grand Prix that year, I found out that Prost had liked the look of my car more than his so they were switched, which really disheartened me further (although I was re-energised to beat him and put his car on pole). However, during a bitterly disappointing race, a gearbox failure halted me, so shortly after the grand prix I announced my retirement from Formula 1.

I had been number two to Keke Rosberg, then to Piquet and now it seemed to Prost. Remember after Elio died and I had resolved only to continue in Formula 1 if I had a genuine opportunity to compete? This feeling was now more relevant than ever. I was risking my life and felt I deserved the opportunity to go for the world title, but that seemingly wasn't going to happen. I didn't want to make up the numbers. I was tired of all the politics. I had been so close to the World Championship and had it snatched away on more than one occasion, so when Ferrari swapped cars at Silverstone, the gas went out of me and my motivation dissipated. It was exacerbated by the fact that the history and heritage I had with the British fans was something very precious and pure to me. We weren't hard up financially; I had fulfilled so many of my ambitions and I was happy to retire, even though I'd not won the title. So I made my announcement and retired from Formula 1.

However, there was, of course, another twist in the tale for me. Frank Williams started enquiring if I would drive for his team in 1991. There had been much intrigue about where Senna was going to drive in 1991, but eventually he signed for McLaren. Given the great times I'd previously had with Frank and his team, there was certainly a synergy in us working together again. I was obviously pleased that someone like Sir Frank was interested, but in my mind – and I can't stress this enough – I was genuinely retired.

Eventually, after Frank enquired some more, I began to contemplate the idea of a swift return. I spoke to Rosanne and eventually we decided to talk to Frank about the circumstances of any drive. I said I would come back for him but only on very specific conditions: with number one status; certain guarantees in the paddock and in testing; wages and other terms were discussed too. I really wanted to make sure that if I was to return to F1 then it was to be with a genuine shot at the title. Sir Frank said at the time that what I was asking was 'impossible', and I was okay with that. I respected his right to do what he felt was best for his team, just as I had my right to look after my career and family.

Then, three weeks later, I found out that the impossible could happen after all and the Williams team agreed. This was potentially brilliant news. I personally felt that the combination of being the number one driver with the very best of the best presented to me, along with Frank, Patrick Head and the team behind me, and with the car I had heard about being developed, meant that finally, after all these years, my moment might be approaching.

CHAPTER 13

THE MOST SUCCESSFUL RETIRED F1 DRIVER

I really had trouble in the winter time before rejoining Williams for 1991 because of the emotions I'd gone through when I retired. I'd made a public announcement and in my head I was an ex-racing driver. I felt I had retired for all the right reasons and genuinely felt at ease with my decision. Then, suddenly, I not only had a drive but I had a proposal that potentially could take me to a world title. Yet in the past I had been on the receiving end of situations where I felt events did not pan out as expected, so I was also wary of getting too excited.

I was criticised at the time for coming out of retirement, but I was used to barbed comments from some quarters of the specialist press. The funny thing is, in some ways I stayed retired in my mind, so as far as I'm concerned I am the most successful retired driver in the history of the sport, because while I was retired I came back to F1 for two years, and I went on to two motorsport world titles back-to-back. I was a happy boy!

In that winter, I was determined that if I was going to come back I'd be fitter, stronger, leaner and more focused than ever before. We were living in America, so the countless transatlantic flights were tiring but there was a feeling that the team could make a big impact in 1991. Living in Florida meant the conditions for getting fit were excellent; I could almost train 24/7. I worked so hard; the lightbulb went on in my head to make this opportunity count.

I was also aware of my age – I was approaching 38. The clock was ticking; I realised that I had only a finite amount of time left and that was a precious commodity. I knew that I wasn't going to get this time back again, and so I grasped it and I worked my little ass off.

Pretty soon after I first sat in the 1991 Williams, the excitement levels started to rise. They were working with Renault and Elf, and the brilliant designer Adrian Newey was also on board. Couple that with Frank and Patrick's expertise and vast experience and it felt like a very strong team indeed, certainly one capable of winning the world title. My already high spirits were lifted still further when I was awarded the OBE by the Queen, which is something I am exceedingly proud of.

In pre-season testing I challenged the team and also Elf to push the boundaries and strive harder and harder. There were new fuels from the likes of Agip, which were seemingly providing considerable power advantages, and we could not afford to miss out on this development. So I really pushed Elf hard.

Speaking of pushing fuel suppliers to raise their game in pre-season, I won't say which team but another well-known F1 outfit once put some of the very special racing fuel in a small rental car they had, for fun. The little car ran really well for about five minutes, but then the whole engine collapsed and the car imploded because the fuel had effectively melted every seal and gasket!

*

Although the start of the 1991 season was plagued by gearbox problems as the team worked on the exciting new semi-automatic box, we all felt the FW14 had the makings of a championship car, not least because of the highly impressive aerodynamics. The team were working relentlessly to resolve any issues and the atmosphere in the garage was brilliant. A few people, including my race engineer David Brown, had commented that I was a quicker and more accomplished driver post-Ferrari, and I would have to agree with that, which was very reassuring. After retiring in the first two races and crashing out of the third, I got my first result with a second place in Monaco. By then I felt the car was wonderful and really believed I had a chance to push for the title.

One common ailment that can really impact on your race is hay fever. Sometimes, my hay fever was so bad that my eyes were watering inside my helmet and I'd be sneezing as I cornered at 160mph, it was really difficult. When you can't breathe very well it affects your performance.

In order to try to resolve this I went to Harley Street and found out it wasn't just pollen. I am allergic to apples and oranges as well, for example, among other things, so I have to be very careful. Cooked apples are fine but raw can send me into an anaphylactic shock. When I was racing I even underwent a two-year programme of injections to try to alleviate the hay-fever symptoms, but it didn't really work, even though I had to have the injections every two weeks under very specific conditions. At the start of the two years they told me it had a 90 per cent success rate. Well, I'd like to say it is still very sniffly over here in the other 10 per cent!

Years later, after I had finished racing, I went to a doctor who was supposed to be the latest bee's knees in the field, and he said he could cure people with allergies. He took a load of bloods and tested me, then called me up and said, 'It is all in your mind.' I disagreed but he said he was convinced, and to prove his point he wanted to run some controlled tests. 'When was the last time you had a Granny Smith apple?' he said.

I reluctantly agreed and so Rosanne went off and bought a Granny Smith. They made some small prick marks in my skin and ran three tests with water, raw apple and antihistamine. Within 20 seconds my lips were numb, in 30 seconds my throat was inflamed and I was having trouble breathing. Obviously they had the correct antidotes on hand, but I was not impressed! Later, the doctor actually apologised to me and said he'd failed to do the one thing that they were always taught – to listen to the patient.

A few other drivers had similar problems with hay fever, not just me. I think it doesn't help that all racing drivers were exposed to some pretty serious fumes during their careers. It wasn't just my nostrils that were sore sometimes. I'd noticed that my moustache seemed to be catching some of the pollen because at times it was very sore to touch and was covering a raw rash. So in 1991 I shaved off my moustache. When people asked why I had done that I told them it was for aerodynamic reasons.

1991 was a great season. Riccardo Patrese was my team-mate that year and at first he was out-qualifying me, so I really had to be on top of my game. A second place in Monaco – my highest finish at that fabulous track which has traditionally not been so kind to me – was a big boost in May and after that my season went very well. I really enjoyed driving the car and we picked up some great results. Despite the early reliability problems I would go on to win five races and earn four podiums. The Canadian Grand Prix brought me some vitriol from certain critics, who accused me of switching off my engine when in the lead. Actually what happened was the gearbox just went into neutral and I couldn't get in gear. Eventually, although I was revving the engine, trying to keep it going, it stalled. It was probably one of the hardest races to lose because we had such a fantastic lead at the time.

Nonetheless, we played catch-up with Ayrton for the rest of the season and pushed him hard, winning three races in a row in July. This included my third British Grand Prix win, which I earned despite wheel balance and gearbox problems – by this stage of my career it would take a gargantuan effort by another driver to stop me winning at Silverstone; I *adored* racing there, even after it had been redesigned. Mansell mania, as they called it, was in full swing! This famous win even earned me a congratulatory fax from the prime minister, John Major.

On its last lap, Senna's car ran out of petrol and he was left stranded at the side of the track, in front of all the British fans. There had been talk of 'bad blood' between us, which was nonsense. Yes, we were rivals, of course, but there was no personal animosity. Now he was stranded trackside after one of his rivals had swept to victory.

So I stopped my car and gave him a lift back to the pits.

It was just one of those spontaneous things: I came up to the corner and saw him out of the car, standing on the track. I just felt he was having such a hard time, and I could transpose myself straight away and imagine Ayrton thinking, *My rival's just won, I'm at his home grand prix with 100,000 of his fans, my car's run out of petrol and I am stranded – this is not good!*

When the tables were turned and I was racing in Brazil, it wasn't always easy. Remember when I had been racing at Ferrari and there were even bottles thrown at me on the grid when I broke down in Rio? It wasn't pleasant. That reaction in Rio wasn't entirely a surprise, because the two main people I was fighting all the time – Nelson Piquet and Ayrton – were Brazilian, but it was still very uncomfortable. Obviously, throwing stuff isn't acceptable but, to be fair, all great fans of any nationality will be rooting for their home boys. The proper fan will appreciate good sportsmanship; if their home driver's rival comes through and wins in the right way, they will applaud it. At Silverstone that day, no one was throwing things at Ayrton, but I really did feel for him.

So I picked him up. It was just a simple gesture of empathy. He walked over to the car, climbed half-aboard and patted me on the head by way of thanks. An official tried to pull him off, but Senna waved him away and off we went. The crowd was spilling on to the track and it was just a great moment. I was criticised afterwards by some of the media for allowing him the chance to look into my cockpit and potentially see if my Williams car had any secrets he could utilise, which was, of course, complete nonsense. When we reached the pits he just got off, patted my head again and gave me a thumbs-up. It was a nice moment and the images are regarded by many as among the most iconic in Formula 1 history, which is also very pleasing.

After Silverstone, we kept pressing even though Ayrton's lead meant there was very little room for error. The Williams team was just wonderful – so focused, so determined; we were a mighty force to be reckoned with. There was quite a degree of racing tension between myself and Ayrton at times, and let's just say the drivers' briefings before races occasionally got quite heated . . .

Then, despite all the team's efforts, in Portugal I suffered one of the most unfortunate retirements of my entire career (only two years after a pit stop problem and missing my box in the same grand prix for Ferrari). Coming in for a pit stop, the right rear wheel did not get fixed on the car properly and within yards of leaving my box it span off, leaving me stranded on three wheels in the pit lane. The team ran over, lifted my car up physically and put a wheel on, but that was against regulations and inevitably I was later black-flagged. This was a very serious blow to my title hopes.

My intense rivalry with Ayrton continued in Barcelona. Our famous wheel-to-wheel battle in the Spanish Grand Prix, where our two cars were centimetres away from each other at speeds approaching 200mph, perhaps sums up more than any other moment the intense rivalry between myself and Ayrton. That level of competition and sheer will to win is what grand prix racing is all about, surely? On this occasion, the victory was mine. In Suzuka, at the next race, I was hunting Ayrton down but a spin into a sand trap meant that Senna was the champion. Ultimately, Ayrton's early-season points advantage was too great to overhaul, and he took the title by 24 points, with me coming in as bridesmaid for the third time with 72.

Despite being disappointed to lose again, I congratulated Ayrton on his title win. I just thought it was the right thing to do. At the end of the day, I am a thoroughbred sportsman and, win or lose, I will congratulate those who have done a better job and have won the day. You should always be what I call a courageous loser, never a bad loser. Congratulate your adversary, learn your lessons and make sure you do the best job you can next time to beat them. I think Ayrton really appreciated that gesture. When you are fighting tooth and nail for a championship, you are very focused on one another but I had to hand it to him. Fair play.

At the end of 1991 we raced in Adelaide in a monsoon. I am not exaggerating; this wasn't a 'bit of rain', this was a monsoon. The weather leading up to the race had been lovely and sunny, but that all changed for race day itself (two years previously Adelaide had also seen a very wet race). The deluge was so severe that they stopped us after just 16 of the scheduled 81 laps, and with the result being declared from lap 14, this still stands as the shortest grand prix race ever. For me personally, it was a rather painful one.

The track was carnage; cars were sliding all over the place. It was raining heavily at the start but we all got away reasonably well. I started on the second row and before long there were cars smashed into walls all round the circuit. I made ground up to second but both Ayrton and myself had to take evasive action with cars littering the track in several places (back then, they didn't always take the debris away). There were no safety cars either and the potential for aquaplaning was horrendous.

At one point the visibility was so bad that I asked my engineer if he could see from the TV pictures whether the track was safe to overtake on at a certain point. On lap 16 I was coming down the straight, pulling out to overtake Ayrton in his slipstream. Perhaps, in retrospect, we were racing too hard, but I obviously wanted to beat him and Ayrton was always super-competitive – we were racing like crazy! Anyway, I pulled out just at the wrong time and aquaplaned straight into the friggin' wall, totally out of control, and hit it really hard. I knew I'd broken my left foot; the wall crushed the cockpit, which smashed the end two toes and splintered the bones in my foot. Oh my word, it hurt!

The car came to a rest and I just sat there waiting. I was in agony and I was going, 'Crap! Crap!' I was really upset. *I've broken my foot, I'm upset. I am out of the race, crap!* I must've been dazed. I wouldn't say I was concussed but I was dazed with the pain. It was excruciating. When pain is that severe it can cause you to pass out. I was trying to come to my senses, opening my eyes, and I saw the red flags and then the doctor's car pulling up to where I was. The next thing I knew the brilliant F1 doctor, Sid Watkins – known as Professor Sid or sometimes just Prof – rushed up to the car and said, 'Nigel, are you okay?'

'Yeah, I'm fine.'

Now, Sid was a brilliant man, a lovely guy and a legend in our sport. He'd previously given me a hard time when I had wanted to race with injuries that he felt were not safe to get in a car with. He always looked out for the drivers' welfare and we all respected him enormously. In Adelaide, the rain was still teeming down on us both and Sid was obviously concerned.

'Nigel, are you sure you're okay?'

'Sid, I'm fine, honest.'

'Well, why haven't you got out of the car, you've been sat there for a few minutes?'

I looked up at him and it was pouring down; the rain was sliding off his face and I was drenched. I said, 'I've been racing and I'm tired, Sid. It's raining hard out there and it's much nicer in here!'

Luckily for me, there was some confusion about the race finish so, as I said, they backtracked to lap 14 and took the results from there, which meant even though I'd spun off I still finished second. Result! We only got half points due to the shortness of the race, but I was more than happy with that. There was talk of restarting the race, but this caused great consternation among the drivers, and to be fair the conditions really were atrocious. As it was, Ayrton's race win and Gerhard's third place gave McLaren the constructors' title that year. Ayrton was pretty vocal about the difficulty of the wet weather. He said that, in future, he would not start a race in those conditions again, although he also said he understood the pressure the officials were under to start the race and made the point that the drivers chose to get in their cars of their own free will. He had a point. I just remarked on the amount of debris on the track and that I felt the race should have been stopped earlier.

After the race, I headed back to our new home in Clearwater, Florida, and my foot was really quite swollen during and after the flight. I went straight to the hospital where the doctor said, 'The foot is broken and needs operating on straight away.'

Mindful of the need for winter training to get me ready for a season where I knew I had a crack at the world title, I said, 'Woah! Hang on – what is the recovery time for that?'

'Well, there is residual damage from a historic break, so it's not straightforward. You will be on crutches for three months.'

'Three months? You gotta be kidding me!'

'I am not kidding you, Mr Mansell. Three months.'

'In that case, my foot is fine.'

He looked at me and said, 'Mr Mansell, your foot is not fine, it is broken!'

I was three months away from a crack at the Formula 1 world title so I said, 'I am sure I can work with it,' shook his hand and hobbled out of the room.

It wasn't quite as simple as that. Initially, they wouldn't let me out of the hospital so I had to wait for my good friend, Dr George Morris, to turn up and when he did I said, 'George, I can't be out for three months. Is there any way we can shorten the rehab time down?'

George said, 'No, it's three months, Nigel. Period.'

'George, I appreciate your expertise but I am not prepared to do that.'

'Look, okay, I understand your position,' he said. 'We have to advise you to have the operation immediately. The bones are splintered. It is going to be incredibly painful if we do not operate, but there is no threat to life. I am warning you, though, you won't be able to walk on that side at all.' Reluctantly, George watched as I checked myself out without any surgery.

Basically, through the winter of 1991 and into 1992, I had only one pair of boots I could wear because of the injury. What we did was make some bespoke carbon-fibre inserts to protect the damaged part of my foot. I walked funnily but those inserts kept the pressure off the broken bones. I also had implants made for my racing boots, whereby I could put pressure on the foot in the cockpit without it absolutely killing me. During 1992 I discovered that over the course of each race the foot would gradually become increasingly painful, because the fractured bones were chafing internally.

Despite the broken foot, during that winter I trained *really* hard. In fact, I would say harder than I had ever done before. I lost a good deal of weight, so that at my pre-season weigh-in I was the lightest I had ever been in Formula 1.

When the races started in 1992, I was immediately devastatingly quick; I was focused like there was no tomorrow. I won the first five races. I knew I was in with my best shot ever of winning the title, the one thing I had dreamed about all my life.

CHAPTER 14

1992 – THE CHAMPIONSHIP YEAR

Most people get opportunities in life. Sadly, some people are guilty of not seizing those moments. Life is about grasping the opportunities that come your way, taking that chance and running with it. Some people think they will have more opportunities further down the line, so this one particular moment is not that important but, of course, they are often wrong. You have to embrace it *now*. When you get a moment – like the one I felt I had in 1992 – it is gold dust.

Going into 1992 I was my lightest, fittest, most focused – I was ready to embrace the opportunity. I felt I had paid my dues, with all those years in inferior cars or as a number two driver. I'd surpassed the great Sir Stirling Moss for grand prix wins; I was closing in on Jim Clark and Jackie Stewart's tallies; but above all I wanted the world title. Senna and McLaren were likely favourites, Ferrari were always hovering around, and Benetton-Ford were also a force to be reckoned with.

The FW14B was a brilliant car, refined in the wind tunnel, and an improvement even on the brilliant car of 1991. It also had a more reliable active suspension system, which underwent over 7000 hours of testing. The electronics guy at Williams even called his experience of one particularly gruelling test at Estoril as 'The Eight Days War', because it was so intense and focused. The resulting car was over two seconds faster than the preceding passive car. It was also proving to be reliable. Now I was *really* excited.

I dominated the first race at Kyalami, winning by 24 seconds from Patrese, and nearly 35 seconds ahead of Ayrton. As I've said, I won the first five grands prix in a row, also scooping pole at the first six races. A loose wheel nut scuppered me in Monaco (destiny again!), but generally I was feeling fantastic. I sensed that I was almost unstoppable.

The fourth grand prix of the year was in Catalunya in Spain and it was very challenging. One aspect that yesteryear and modern drivers share is terrible visibility when it rains. I remember some dreadful conditions for a few stand-out races in my career, weather that really tests your skills and nerve. The tropical storm we raced in at Adelaide in '91 was shocking. I think Monaco, when I crashed out in the lead, was shocking too – and very disappointing because I was leading on Casino Square. The monsoon race in 1994 in Japan was another incredible one – boy, that was unbelievable. Those are the three races that I can distinctly remember being severely challenging because of the weather.

It is no exaggeration – if it rains when you are driving a Formula 1 car, you really can't see much at all; it is very dangerous. The biggest problem when you have a really heavy downpour is not so much the rain; it is when you aquaplane. Wet-weather tyres work very well, so normally you do retain grip. However, if you then aquaplane your car goes from having some sort of grip and control to zero grip and zero control – you are a complete passenger. Aquaplaning is like being on ice.

You just slide straight away and once it starts, until the car gets some grip again or adhesion to the circuit, you just speed up all the time, so it actually magnifies; it gets worse before it gets better. I can't say hand on heart that you enjoy those races; you *survive* those races.

I won quite a few races in the wet. I think the outstanding race I had in the rain was when Michael Schumacher was in his Benetton-Ford catching me a few seconds a lap at Barcelona in 1992. I couldn't figure out why he was catching me so quickly. I managed to catch a glimpse of him in my mirrors and I realised that he was taking totally different lines, in the process almost losing control of his car on the outside of the circuit at times, searching out these different lines. I thought, *Well, I had 15 seconds on him, now it's down to five. I've gotta push now, but surely he can't sustain this?* However, he did. So I started to push. I almost lost the car on a couple of corners – it slid out to the edge of the circuit and I thought I was going off, and then all of a sudden there was so much more grip out there! From having a few whoopsies, I then changed my line quite significantly and went two to three seconds a lap quicker myself. Then I even started to pull away from Michael. I didn't get any credit for it; the press said I was playing with him. What a load of nonsense – he was driving fantastically. I had to relearn real quick where he had the advantage. Fortunately, I was able then to find the time and to go on to win the race. That was one of the best wins I had that season, because I felt extreme pressure from this young guy coming from nowhere and catching me quite quickly, and I was thinking, *I am going pretty flat out here – what am I doing wrong?* He'd found better grip in the corners and until I worked that out he was catching me. That shows you what a brilliant, intuitive racer Michael was and for those reasons I am very proud of that victory.

I'd heard from Frank as early as Mexico back in March that Alain Prost might be a new team-mate for the next season. With my experiences of Prost at Ferrari this was not a prospect I was particularly enamoured with. I told Frank my opinion in no uncertain terms, making it clear that I was not happy about this possibility. Not happy at all.

At the time, I didn't allow these conversations about Prost to distract me from my mission. In Spain, I won my 25th grand prix, equalling Jim Clark's record, a very proud moment indeed. By winning the next race in Imola, I became the first driver ever to win the first five races of a season, another record. I would win nine times that season, securing 14 pole positions out of 16 races in the process. Quite quickly, Senna was trailing me heavily in the points and he was pushing hard, not least during a very controversial incident when, in my opinion, he took me out of the race in Canada as I tried to pass him. He didn't agree with my view, of course, but I was not a happy chap about that one!

At the end of every single race in 1992, I basically went into a dark room and virtually cried because of the pain I was in from my broken foot. I did get hammered by certain elements of the press, who said I was overdramatising, which was ludicrous. I was driving with a broken foot! It was annoying at the time, of course, but looking back now I would only say that they had no idea of the physical demands of driving a car all year with an injury like that. I raced the entire year with that broken foot, and had no surgery until after the season had ended. I put that down to a dogged determination because I knew I was about to have the opportunity to win at the highest possible level and get to the top step of the World Championship. Like I said, those opportunities don't come along that often – embrace them. Remember, I had already

191

been the bridesmaid three times before and I had been number two driver for three world champions – Piquet, Rosberg and Prost. I had smelt it and almost tasted it for so many years but never got there. However, in 1992 I really felt like this was my time. My window of opportunity was there and I was not going to let anything get in the way, not even broken bones.

I won another British Grand Prix that year and with the growing sense that I could be on my way to the title, it was a special weekend. I was extremely focused, very quick all weekend, and scooped pole position, fastest lap (in fact, 11 fastest laps) and another Silverstone win. And, yes, it is true that Ayrton Senna was stopped by police for speeding in his Porsche on the M25 and they asked him, 'Who do you think you are? Nigel Mansell?'

After my Silverstone win, fans poured on to the track and it was just the most euphoric moment. It also meant that I had secured my 28th grand prix win, which was the most for any British driver in F1 history, finally surpassing Sir Jackie Stewart. I was just so proud. The crowd reaction was spontaneous; it was really wonderful, a fantastic day. Apart from running over a couple of people's toes . . .

By the time I reached Hungary, there were several permutations that would mean I'd lift the world title, but there was really only one that mattered: I was one win away from the title that I had craved for so many years (in fact, second place would do). It was not a circuit famous for overtaking opportunities, so it was by no means a simple task. Nonetheless, I was just 77 laps from being world Formula 1 champion.

You should have guessed by now that lifting the title in Hungary was never going to be straightforward! The circuit was ridiculously dusty and on the Friday I had a fire in the engine bay. I also got caught up in someone else's accident but eventually landed safely on the grid in second, behind Patrese. I slipped from second to fourth at the start, with Patrese, Senna and Berger ahead of me. After passing Gerhard and Riccardo, who slipped down to seventh after a mistake, I was in the second place I needed for the title. That's when I got a slow puncture ... *Blimey, what do I have to do to win this title?*

The pit stop was executed brilliantly by the team – the whole Williams team had been tremendous all year – but it still dropped me down to sixth with 16 laps to go. Then Schumacher retired in fifth with wing damage, and I got past Häkkinen then Brundle, and after talking to Patrick on the radio to confirm the position I needed – still second – I took Berger and settled into the slot that would give me the world title with 13 laps left.

This time there were no crashes, no tyre blow-outs, and I made it to the finish line in second, behind Ayrton, to take the title. Crossing the line as Formula 1 world champion was just the most incredible feeling. I had done it! Finally, after all the years, the battles, the sacrifices, everything that Rosanne and I had gone through, I was the world champion. I just felt total disbelief. I had done it.

I was world champion with five races of the season still remaining – Britain's first F1 champion for 16 years. I'd totalled 108 points, 52 ahead of my second-placed team-mate Riccardo Patrese. I'd recorded an unprecedented five opening wins, the most pole positions in one season with 14, the most fastest laps, the most points, the most wins with nine and a new British record total of 30 grand prix wins at that point. It was total domination, to be fair. I had finally done it.

On the podium, Ayrton was very nice to me and at one point he leaned over to me and whispered into my ear: 'Well done, Nigel. It's such a good feeling, isn't it? Now you know why I'm so difficult sometimes. I don't ever want to lose the feeling or share it with anybody else.'

I've mentioned already how I am a huge fan of Sir Stirling Moss. He's a lovely man and Susie, his wife, is wonderful too. After my World Championship win, I bumped into him and he was so generous and funny. Remember, this living legend is a man who was bridesmaid four times and, if you recall, back in Estoril he'd thanked me for surpassing his number of grand prix wins without being world champion.

When I saw him that day after winning the title, I playfully said, 'Stirling,' – he was not yet 'Sir' – 'I believe I previously took your record for winning the most races without being crowned champion. Well, it gives me great pleasure to now hand that accolade back to you.'

He leaned towards me with a delightful smile on his lips and said, 'You bastard.'

Winning the F1 World Championship was wonderful, it really was. The Williams team did a magnificent job that season with a fabulous car – my favourite, you might not be surprised to hear! – and I was totally dominant all year, so I am very proud of my achievement. It was the completion of one part of my life and dreams, and it felt especially good because I had been so close on all those previous occasions. Numbness, happiness, elation, so many emotions. I wish my mom and dad had been there to see me step up on that podium as world champion, I really do.

The days immediately after winning the world title were incredible, fabulous, a joy. I had finally done what I set out to achieve all those years ago. I was the champion. It felt so good! We had a belated birthday party for Chloe, and Murray Walker came over to the Isle of Man to do a BBC special about my championship season.

However, at the same time, my drive for 1993 with Williams

The closest finish ever recorded in Formula 1. After a huge battle with Ayrton Senna, he just pips me to the chequered flag in the 1986 Spanish Grand Prix.

With my Williams team-mate Nelson Piquet. Our working relationship was difficult at times.

Piquet is behind me as I close in on victory in the 1986 British Grand Prix, my fourth win in five races.

The devastation is clear on my face after an exploding tyre forced me out of the grand prix in Adelaide at the end of that season, costing me the world title.

Making a point to Murray Walker. In many people's minds, the two of us formed a Formula 1 double act.

One of my favourite victories: the 1987 British Grand Prix. I'd just gone ahead of Piquet after pulling off a special manoeuvre on Nelson.

In agony after taking 75G through my spine following a crash in qualifying on the Suzuka circuit in 1987 – it brought a premature end to my season, as I finished runner-up once more.

My time with Ferrari couldn't have got off to a better start, as I win my first race – at Rio in 1989.

After this spectacular crash in the French Grand Prix, I still managed to finish second, but overall I completed just six races in that season.

Sharing a light-hearted moment with Alain Prost during the 1990 season, but his arrival meant the Ferrari team became more focused on him.

A great shot of a great car at the British Grand Prix, after which I announced my retirement.

John Townsend

Working with the Williams team once again in 1991. With my engineer David Brown, Adrian Newey and Sir Frank Williams.

John Townsend

Clean shaven after I became concerned that my moustache was making me more susceptible to hay fever. Sir Dave Brailsford isn't the only one to look at 'marginal gains' to improve performance.

John Townsend

Giving Senna a lift after his car had run out of fuel at the end of the 1991 British Grand Prix. A spontaneous gesture of goodwill.

Nigel Mansell

Celebrating my win at the 1992 Spanish Grand Prix with runner-up Michael Schumacher, where he showed what a brilliant driver he was.

John Townsend

The crowd poured onto the Silverstone track after I'd won my 28th grand prix, taking me past Sir Jackie Stewart's British record. The fans were, as usual, awesome.

With five races still to go, my second place at the Hungarian Grand Prix means that I am finally world champion. Standing to attention to listen to the National Anthem was a moment I will keep with me for the rest of my life.

was still not secure. The mid-season talk about Prost had not been welcome. The negotiation challenges I faced after I won the World Championship have been well documented, not least in previous books. To summarise what happened: I believed I had agreed a provisional deal to drive for Williams in 1993 but, as the season ran on, a formal agreement was seemingly delayed. Then it became apparent that Ayrton Senna was possibly in the mix for a drive, which really unsettled me. There was even talk of him offering to drive for free, while my critics were very negative about the money being speculated upon in my deal.

Even though Prost would be the other Williams driver, I was excited about the possibility and the privilege of being able to defend my world title and of building on the enormous success we had all enjoyed at Williams in 1991 and 1992. However, we couldn't seem to find a way to reach an agreement. Obviously, I had my view and Williams had theirs. Unbeknown to me, the relationship with the French sponsors was quite significant to Williams' future.

Bernie Ecclestone was fantastic as usual and tried to do all he could to help resolve the issues. He was always a great supporter of mine and wanted me to stay in F1, but even when I ultimately chose to race in the USA he told me that, if that was my decision, then I should at least go out there and win. Sadly, the situation with Williams could not be resolved and so destiny decreed that I would not be racing for Frank's team and defending my world title in 1993.

At Monza, I called a press conference where I announced my retirement, even though a Williams representative made last-minute attempts to dissuade me. My lengthy statement attempted to explain why I was retiring from the sport of which I was world champion. 'Due to circumstances beyond my control ... I have made this decision with some regret, but not without a great deal of thought.' I explained my position and that since the saga started 'relations with the team have not been good'. I acknowledged it was Frank's prerogative to choose his drivers for his team but stated that I still felt very disappointed. I finished by thanking Williams and Renault for their support to date and wished them well for 1993. I also suggested I may look to America for my next racing challenge.

I'm not going to repeat myself here but suffice to say I felt incredibly deflated, dejected and very disappointed that I wouldn't be defending the title I was so incredibly proud of. I was criticised by some for leaving F1, while Williams were also criticised by certain parts of the media and public alike, with some even demonstrating outside the factory, but in a statement they said they felt 'deep regret' that I had chosen to retire and I had a 'special place' in their team's history. They also said I 'richly deserved' the title but pointed out, as was their prerogative, that they felt they had to preserve the wellbeing of the team. So, as I've said, destiny decided that I wouldn't be blessed with the opportunity to defend my F1 World Championship.

I have a very healthy respect for Sir Frank and certainly what he has achieved in Formula 1 is absolutely remarkable. Obviously, as with many relationships, we had some disagreements in our time working together, which I have touched on here. Clearly, when I thought his decisions were not in my best interests, then we had strong differences of opinion. Conversely, Sir Frank always said he had to put the interests of his team first. The Williams team is one of the finest in Formula 1 and I am extremely proud to have been a part of that history. I think, after his accident, to go and win the constructors' title in the same season typifies the bulldog spirit and culture of excellence that Sir Frank creates in his team.

There were still races left in the 1992 season. After

announcing my retirement, hydraulic failure curtailed my race at Monza, albeit only after setting the fastest lap. I won the next race in Estoril, a record ninth win that was overshadowed by my team-mate Riccardo Patrese's awful accident when his car went airborne, which thankfully he emerged from unscathed. Riccardo finished second in the championship and Williams won the constructors' title. It was a hugely dominant performance from the whole team all year. Unfortunately, after Estoril I had two retirements for my last brace of races for Williams, in Suzuka and Adelaide. The first was an engine fault, the second was an accident, when Ayrton's car hit me from behind and took us both off.

So, despite being the reigning F1 world champion, I retired from Formula 1. The day after my title season ended, I came back home and was admitted to hospital for the operation on my long-suffering foot. I was on crutches for three months and recuperated in time for the new motorsport season, which, as destiny had decreed, would not be in Formula 1. As you know me by now, you perhaps won't be surprised to learn that, for all the considerable disappointment of not defending my F1 world title, I would immediately bounce back, across the Atlantic, in what some people considered was the fastest and at times the most dangerous motorsport of all: IndyCar. Exciting times ahead!

CHAPTER 15

COME TO THE WILD WEST

In sharp contrast to the disappointment of not being able to defend my F1 title, I was very excited about the prospects for a new career racing in the USA. I had previously been made offers to race over there, but at the time I was still intent on becoming the Formula 1 world champion. First of all, I have to say we would never have come to America without the support of Paul Newman. My new team boss, Carl Haas, was doing all the negotiations, which were fairly protracted as these things tend to be, but we got there in the end, and I signed for the revered Newman/Haas IndyCar team. Once or twice, when there was a bit of a stall in the process, Paul Newman phoned me and we had some really nice chats. He said to me, 'Nigel, you will love it out here – it's like the Wild West! It's so exciting to race and your family will love it too; they will all be included. I will give you my personal word that I will support you and do whatever is necessary to try to win the championship. Come and have some fun with us – come and have an adventure!' How can you say no when Paul Newman phones you and says that?!

Very soon after we arrived in the States to race, I realised that being Formula 1 world champion counted for very little over there. People in the American racing world knew about F1 and, of course, respected my achievement, but among the wider American public that wasn't really the case. I think it's fair to say that, back in the UK, I was one of the most well-known sporting faces of that period along with the likes of Frank Bruno, Nick Faldo and so on. One time, Frank and I were the only sportsmen invited to a dinner at Number 10 Downing Street to meet Bill and Hillary Clinton. That gives you an idea of the profile I enjoyed in the UK.

In America, however, it was nothing like that. When I went over there, I was insignificant. In the UK, we have a population of about 65 million; in the States, it's over 300 million. The country is so vast and there are so many high-profile sports. We came from being a big fish in a small pond to being just a tiddler in a massive ocean of sportspeople. There are literally tens of thousands of sporting heroes in America – golfers are ten-a-penny, baseball players, NFL players, basketball stars, thousands of professionals, proper sports megastars who are paid fortunes.

Yet my relative anonymity was a pleasure because I could take my children out for a pizza or go to the cinema or play with them at the park, whatever, without being recognised or asked for photographs or whatnot. I was allowed a completely normal family life and that was really lovely.

I was very excited about my first season in IndyCar. Several drivers got in touch to wish me well and welcome me to IndyCar, even though I would be racing against them, which I thought was wonderful. I had been told by several veterans of the series that it would take two to three years to get the hang of IndyCar, the oval racing in particular. This

US motorsport that was so different in many ways to Formula 1.

Well, I won the IndyCar title in my first year.

IndyCar was amazing – it demanded incredible race craft and I just embraced the whole spectacle. At the time, it was the biggest auto racing in America and possibly challenged F1 in certain races, it was so popular. On a practical driving level, the cars were different to F1 cars, even though they might look similar. They were heavier, less nimble, possessed higher top speeds but less downforce, less G-force and were generally less high-tech, with manual gear changes, inferior brakes and passive suspension.

My first season in IndyCar was such an eye-opener and I had a fantastic time. After a very busy off-season, when I'd had the foot operated on and also fulfilled the hundreds of obligations that a Formula 1 world champion enjoys, I was fit and ready to start my racing life in the USA. As I mentioned earlier, I'd been told it took drivers several seasons to get used to oval racing – by contrast, I had decided I wanted to win the title in my first year. That way I felt I was 'defending' my world title.

In pre-season testing we were very fast. That first test in Phoenix was a bit of a culture shock, very different to the Formula 1 races I was used to. The skill levels of the pit crew were as good; I clearly had an exceptionally talented and well-drilled team. The car felt good, well balanced – which in the ovals is paramount – and I really felt like we had a great chance of making an impact. By the time we flew to Australia for the season opener, I was extremely excited.

At that first race, I put the car on pole position and, despite a stop-go penalty for running under yellow flags, pitting for a suspected puncture as well as running on fumes for the last few laps, I won my first ever race in IndyCar. The car ran out of fuel within 100 yards of passing the finishing line – talk about fine margins! I was the first rookie to win an IndyCar race from pole and the first driver to win on his debut since the amazing Graham Hill in 1966. I know it was a long way off, but I really felt like I could go and win the title. You would be forgiven for thinking that this whole IndyCar lark was easy ... Well, after what happened at the very next race, a gaping hole in my back that has since made medical history will tell you different.

To get off to a flyer in Australia was amazing and I returned to America for the next race at Phoenix full of optimism. However, in Saturday practice I suffered my biggest ever accident – a smash that could so easily have proved fatal.

I honestly don't remember a lot about the worst accident of my career. In Saturday's practice session I was flying along, setting fastest times and really belting out there. Then I flew into turn one at 187mph, probably marginally quicker than I had gone before, and the car just instantly swapped ends on me, which is the single most dangerous thing that can happen on a high-speed oval. There had been some aerodynamic changes to the car and there was heat build-up in the tyres too. Also, I did go very slightly higher than on previous laps, so it was a combination of factors perhaps that caused the crash. What I do know is that I paid the highest price possible when the car backed into a concrete wall at that massive speed. There was no chance of trying to catch it – I was gone, just a passenger. The impact was catastrophic and knocked me out immediately. When I hit the wall, my speed was so great that it smashed the gearbox into the back of the car and my spine was next in line for the shock wave.

I blacked out and the rescue teams rushed over. It was a colossal accident. Where the car had hit the wall there was a three-foot hole punctured through the concrete, the first time in IndyCar history that this had happened. I was rushed to the medical centre and the experts started surveying the damage to my body. The monumental force of the impact had opened up a cavity in my back. The doctors were very concerned and I certainly knew I had caused a lot of damage when they explained to me that they'd never seen this type of injury on a patient that was still alive. Apparently pathologists had only seen this on corpses from plane crashes. The shearing force of the impact had been so great that it had replicated a degree of damage that only occurs at several hundred miles an hour. Massive and constant fluid build-up was a major problem, which meant I had to be repeatedly spiked with tubes and pipes to have my back drained.

There was only one thing to do: bounce back! Would you be surprised if I told you that, less than two weeks after the accident, I was qualifying and pulling 5G at Long Beach? People told me there was no way I could race that day – instead, with the help of a lot of ice packs, medical care and commitment, I put the car on pole and eventually came third. To be fair, the doubters were almost right; there's no way I should've carried on racing in 1993, let alone achieve what I was about to do, but I did. That was through total determination to win on my part, but also through having great experts around me.

The doctors in America were fantastic and there are four I want to mention in this book: Dr Terry Trammell and Dr Steve Olvey (the IndyCar medical officers), Dr George Morris and Dr Mike Piazza, who all put me back together – each one of them had a hand either at the racetracks or in surgery. In America they got you back out on the track pretty quick! I owe a debt of gratitude and a huge thank you to those people and everyone else who cared for me. Without their expertise I wouldn't have been racing at all and I certainly wouldn't have won the championship, so I can't thank them enough for their friendship and professionalism.

After the big smash, that next race in Long Beach was the funniest and hardest race I contested on the way to winning the championship. Why? Because they had to draw blood off my back so that I could even get in the car. This had been happening frequently at the local hospital during my recovery, but the fluids were still building up on the race weekend. My good friend, the golfer Greg Norman, was there and saw it. They drew all this fluid out of me and then they pumped me through with neat anaesthetic, after which I drove half of the race not feeling my feet because they were numb. Trying to drive a race car at 200mph on a notoriously bumpy circuit while not feeling your legs and feet is not something I would recommend!

I was off the pace a little bit at first, but after about an hour the feeling in my lower legs started to come back. I had a bit of a scrape with Al Unser Jr, which put him out of the race, and also lost second gear. However, I was gradually getting quicker and quicker, so that by the end of the race I came third and got on the podium . . . and those points got me across the finish line at the end of the year. That's commitment.

After Long Beach, they operated on me and had to put 148 stitches in and around the gaping cavity to try to pull my back into place. There was a lot of internal cutting needed and all sorts, it was a real mess. I had a 12-inch section taken away from my back because all the flesh was rotten and manky; it all had to be cut out so they patchwork-quilted me back into shape.

Looking back at my treatment, I was effectively a total guinea pig. In fact, Dr Terry Trammell wrote about my injury as a clinical test case, because it was rare, possibly unique, that anyone had survived such a tear and cavity of that size in their back. Best of all, the injury was so unusual that it has since been named in medical journals as the 'Mansell Lesion'. Pretty cool, eh?!

Ten days after my operation I was racing at well over 200mph again, this time at Indianapolis, my first oval race. My back was killing me; the stitches, fluids and soreness were unbearable at times, but I had no choice. I felt I had a chance to win the title and lying on a bed at home recovering was not going to get me the points I needed.

Following the smash at Phoenix, I was more acutely aware than ever of the dangers of oval racing. People think that because you are an elite racing driver, you don't get nervous or frightened. Not so. In terms of my career, the races that made me most nervous were mostly the ones in America, on the ovals. Don't get me wrong – there were, of course, plenty of times in F1 when I felt vulnerable and nervous. However, oval racing was a whole new level of jeopardy that took some getting used to.

When I went to race in the USA I was taken out of my comfort zone. The racetracks were all new to me, the faces were as well, but I was reasonably comfortable with that change. You can switch teams quite regularly in motorsport so everything can alter overnight, and I had done that several times before. What was a particularly new challenge for me was the *ferocious speed* of these IndyCar races.

During my whole F1 career, there was never a time when I felt a massive jump in terms of performance from one season to the next. The turbos were fantastic, of course, and I've also talked about the brutality of ground-effect cars. However, I did feel a substantial leap in terms of speed was when I went to IndyCar, on the superspeedways.

While I was racing IndyCar, my fastest average lap was 233.75mph – that's *an average*! That is close to 100mph faster than the average of an F1 car. This included two entire laps with my foot flat to the floor. That is insane. At one oval race, the slowest I came down to was 229mph! And yes, before you ask, that is scary. The top speeds of those cars were just ridiculous. The acceleration of IndyCars is slower than F1 and their ability to corner at high speed is not comparable, but in terms of sheer top speed, they are like missiles. That is why, if anyone touches another car on an oval or if there is any kind of mechanical failure, you have a massive accident. That's before you take into account that there is a concrete wall 25 yards away from you at all times. With so much dense traffic, it is also easy to lose downforce if you get too close to the car in front, and then you are also going to meet the wall at a very high speed, sometimes peaking at 250mph. For these reasons, it is the most dangerous racing in the world, bar none.

That made me nervous. I am not going to sit here and pretend it didn't. I was confident of my skills, of course. If you are not confident at that level then you are a liability to yourself. However, I was very nervous of something going wrong on the car. If you are averaging speeds in excess of 230mph, and if something goes wrong – a wheel comes loose, the suspension breaks, or even just an aerodynamic piece of the car falls off – you are in big trouble. There are also other cars around you that might accidentally nudge you, or maybe experience a failure and be thrown into your path. If one or more of the above happens, then you are going to have a massive accident.

The speedways were, for me anyway, more frightening than Formula 1. F1 was still mighty dangerous in my era, but that risk is not necessarily in your face all the time, lap after lap, corner after corner. You will go around an F1 track and there'll be slow corners or a chicane, so you go down to 60mph and accelerate out; and, although that is exciting and challenging, it is not fast, you are not going to hurt yourself even if you make a big mistake on those slower parts of a track. With the super-speedways and oval racing, you are nearly always averaging over 200mph, so you are covering the length of a football pitch every second, for as much as 500 miles. At that velocity, things can go very, *very* badly wrong. There is no reprieve.

Of course, you can't think about that all the time otherwise you would be mentally crippled with fear. You put the fear to the back of your mind, but the knowledge of just how danger-ous it is stays with you in the form of an underlying nervous anxiety. It was always there. I didn't have that in Formula 1; I didn't feel the same corrosive sense of anxiety that I experienced on the speedways. There is very rarely a small accident on a speedway. Fact. There is no fudge factor. You either do it right or you do it slowly. The alternative is a massive accident, as I found out to my cost in Phoenix in April 1993.

At my first Indy 500 I managed third after a few driver errors, including a poor restart after a green flag. I was still proud of third, though, especially given the state of my back. I even kissed a wall at 220mph but thankfully got away with that, although it was pretty scary for a few seconds! However, I was back to win-ning ways in Milwaukee, my first oval win (the first Brit to do so since 1966, when Graham Hill won at Indy). There then followed a run of form that brought me three more oval wins (Michigan, New Hampshire and Nazareth) as well as several podiums. A mid-season push by our biggest rivals, Penske, saw them gain ground, but those oval wins and the podiums re-energised my title push. I am told that my win from pole in New Hampshire – on my 40th birthday – is regarded by many as one of the greatest IndyCar races of all time.

By the time I arrived in Mid-Ohio I was on the cusp of scooping the title, but suspension damage after I was hit by another car dropped me to a 12th-place finish and put paid to that. IndyCar then rolled into Nazareth for the penultimate race of the season, and this is where I finally clinched the title.

Of course, like the time in Hungary the year before, my title-winning weekend was far from normal. We turned up to qualify and it was pouring with torrential rain, which even turned to snow and sleet. Oh my word! I thought, *What is going on?* Due to the inclement weather, we weren't able to do qualifying, so the grid was lined up in championship order. I remember the race was a freaking nightmare. Nazareth was probably my least favourite of all the ovals, because you were literally inches away from hitting a wall almost all the time. Holy crap!

The high-speed traffic was so jammed all the time, the risks so high, it was horrendous. The race was fierce and included the fastest one-mile battle in IndyCar history. Fortunately, I was able to take command and the win. Only Scott Goodyear finished on the same lap as me. On the team radio after I'd crossed the finish line, I wasn't sure if I had won because the fight for the title had been so close, but the team made it crystal clear: 'Nigel, you are the champ!' I was a rookie and I had won the 1993 IndyCar title.

So, it didn't take me three years to learn the ovals in America – I won four oval races in the first year on my way to winning the title. No one could get their head round that. I'd never been on an oval track in my life. At the first time of asking I had won one of the most challenging and dangerous motorsport crowns. This triumph made it back-to-back F1 and IndyCar world titles, and for one glorious week in September 1993, before the new F1 champion was crowned, I was both

Formula 1 and IndyCar champion simultaneously – a unique achievement that hadn't been done before and certainly not since. The revered Jim McGee was my team manager and he said that it was 'a feat that may never be repeated'. Being awarded the Driver of the Year, as voted for by the American public, topped off an incredible year. Crucially, I also felt as though I had defended my Formula 1 title, too. That debut IndyCar championship is something I am incredibly proud of: 1993 – what a year!

CHAPTER 16

FUN TIMES IN INDYCAR

When I was racing IndyCar, I was fortunate to get to know the great Paul Newman very well. We became good friends not simply because he was part of my team's management, but also because of various charity projects. During our time living in America, we have been heavily involved in fundraising for all manner of good causes. One particular ongoing campaign was started to help less fortunate children enrol at the excellent St Paul's School near our home in Florida. This was not an inexpensive school, so we raised money that was put into scholarships for students from poorer backgrounds to get the best education. One lovely idea was the so-called Tree of Life, which had bronze, silver and gold leaves that you could buy, each one costing progressively more money. This concept seemed to strike a chord and it raised several million dollars over the years – money that went into supporting the education of children who might not otherwise have had the opportunity to go to such a fabulous school. So it was a wonderful campaign to be involved in.

Each year, Paul Newman would come to our house in Florida

to help out when we held charity evenings. As part of the fund-raising push for the school in Florida, we also developed a golf tournament and were very thankful that KMart and Dirt Devil, plus loads of associated sponsors of the team, donated product. We were completely blessed and surprised that Paul Newman, wonderful man that he was, managed to give up his time for several days every year and come and stay in our home with us. Back then, we raised several six figures every year and had a great time; we opened up our home to hold the charity event, as well as using my beautiful local golf club at Belleair. It became a huge success and that charity tournament still goes on to this day, 25 years later. Due to Paul's unstinting support of our school fundraising push, I now support the Hole in the Wall Gang charity run by his daughter; it was Paul's charity and very dear to his heart.

However, I tell you now, pretty much all of the women in our social circle were completely useless for anything on the weekends when Paul Newman was visiting. One time, our housekeeper answered the phone and it was Paul – I think she had to have a sit-down after! We couldn't do anything with her for the rest of the day. He was a gorgeous man, a megastar and a legend in his lifetime, and a dear friend. And his eyes were a very deep blue, I can confirm that!

We still have a beautiful home in Florida to this day. We have got an outside grillroom where you can cook up some food, sit and sip a glass of something nice. Well, to our alarm, one day I was grilling some big steaks and having a lovely time when a rat ran across my feet. We are lucky to live by the water and we'd heard you can occasionally get rats coming up off the shore after fruit trees and food. It wasn't uncommon but we hadn't seen it before, so it was an unpleasant shock. Rosanne mentioned it to a friend and pointed out that, because we had children and pets, we didn't want to put down any poison. So the friend told us we should get some mothballs, which can apparently deter rats.

So Rosanne headed off to the big hypermarket in town. It was a massive local supermarket but was a little down-at-heel, probably due a refurb. She went and found a trolley, picked up a few bottles of wine while she was going round, some bits and pieces, and then got the mothballs as well. She went to the till and the checkout lady was chatting away as she rang the stuff through. Rosanne observed she had very carefully manicured nails – not something I would have particularly noticed! – and she was chatting away, telling Rosanne about her hot flushes. It all sounded quite comical and fun. Apparently, she even made a wisecrack, asking if Rosanne was old enough to buy the wine.

Now, by her own admission, Rosanne had not got dressed up to go shopping. She had a very hectic day, with a million and one things to do, so she'd just thrown on some casual clothes because she didn't have time to mess about. As the checkout lady came to the mothballs, she looked particularly intrigued.

'Do you mind me asking what you are going to do with the mothballs?'

'No,' answered Rosanne, 'a friend of ours says they are good for deterring rats.'

'Oh, I see, yes, I have heard that – and snakes, apparently,' said this lady, rather quietly. 'Are you by the water?'

'Yes, we are as it happens . . .'

Then, with a sympathetic half-smile, she said to Rosanne, 'Do you live in a trailer?'

Racing in America was a lot of fun and I was treated extremely well over there. When I won the back-to-back championships, in 1992 and 1993, the Ford Motor Company were delighted with the Indy triumph and so they kindly presented me with a very limited edition 7-litre Mustang as a gift for winning. This car was just fantastic, bright red, soft top – wow, it was a beauty! They were incredibly sought-after and very rare vehicles.

At the time we had a lovely man called Donald working for us who'd been helping out for many years and was a really great guy. He helped me win the championships in many ways, because he took care of so much stuff that might otherwise have distracted me. He was an ex-military man and very on the ball, really helpful to have around.

Anyway, that Christmas his car had broken down, so he was stranded and unable to get to the shops to buy all his presents. He very politely asked me if he could borrow one of my cars. I think we had three or four at the time, so it was no bother to me, I was glad to help out. I was thinking about which one was best to give him for the day and then I thought, *Why don't I treat him and let him take the Mustang?* He'd previously said the Mustang was his dream car, so I did exactly that.

As you can imagine, Donald was delighted. He couldn't believe his luck and so I was really chuffed too – it was a lovely reaction to get. Anyway, off he went with his wife to one of those gigantic shopping malls. American malls are so big it's about a two-mile walk from your car to the shops! He was gone some time and after about four hours I started to wonder where he was.

Then the phone rang. It was Donald and he was out of breath.

'I'm so sorry, Nigel, I'm so sorry!'

'What's the matter Donald – are you okay?'

'I'm so sorry . . .' He was really in a panic about something.

'Are you all right, have you been ill or something?'

'No, Nigel, it's not me. It's the Mustang.'

'Oh, okay, what about the Mustang?'

'It's been nicked!'

It turned out the car had been stolen. It was such a sought-after vehicle that someone must have seen it and waited till Donald was in the mall and then stolen it. We never saw the car again. So the moral of the story is: if you own a limited-edition, 7-litre, bright-red, soft-top Mustang, don't let your mate take it Christmas shopping.

While racing IndyCar in Australia, there was a local Ford dealership run by a very nice chap who used to loan us courtesy cars quite often and generally looked after us. Over time we got friendly with him and his girlfriend and had a couple of meals together. Then he invited us to go horse riding one day. Rosanne loves riding and I am okay with it, so we said yes.

It was only a couple of days before the next practice session for a forthcoming race, so I thought it would be a lovely way to relax before the madness of the race weekend. He was a lovely guy and along the way we started swapping stories. He told me that he had previously been a semi-pro golfer and had been thinking of turning full-time. He was practising like crazy and really feeling that his game was in great shape.

Anyway, one day at the driving range he noticed this big lad, no more than 16, with a shock of white-blond hair, hitting the ball ferociously. He was dropping his shots inch-perfect by the pins and smashing the balls miles up the fairway in the most remarkable way. My pal from Ford told me he watched this and just thought to himself, *Boy, if that's how some amateur kid can play these days, there'll be loads out there like him. I've got no chance, I'd better change my career plans!* So he decided not to turn full-time pro and instead followed a different career path altogether. It was only a few years later that he found out that the blond 'amateur kid' was actually Greg Norman, one of the greatest golfers ever to walk the planet!

I had a fantastic afternoon, except Rosanne was on a horse called Bourbon and, let me tell you this, don't follow Bourbon up a hill. He farts like there's no tomorrow! We got the giggles and were like, 'Holy crap, how does anything fart that much?' Worse still, I found out to my peril that if you got too close you could get a few of Bourbon's spin-offs too. I was used to 'dirty air' from my racing career but nothing like this. It was dreadful but so funny! We were trotting and walking, not galloping, through brush, and even stopped off by a stream for some food. The whole trek was probably about three hours each way and we had a great time.

The next day, I got my stuff together for the race weekend and I noticed I felt a little bit stiff, but not too bad. Well, long story short, come the actual morning of the first practice session, I couldn't even lift my leg over to get in the race car. I couldn't move it! The mechanics were looking at me hobbling over then trying and failing to even lift my leg up to get into the cockpit of this state-of-the-art ballistic missile I was supposed to be racing. They even tried physio on me in the pit lane, but it was no good. My very experienced team manager, Jim McGee – who'd been in IndyCar since the 1960s – came up to me and, because he knew me by reputation, said, 'Nigel, what on earth have you done now?' When I told him I'd been horse riding he just rolled his eyes and laughed. And how did this ultimately get sorted so that I could race? Well, they had to *lift* me into the cockpit.

This wasn't the only time I arrived at an IndyCar race with . . . how can I put it, 'non-racing injuries'. The other time I turned up really sore was for testing one week. I was groaning and in pain, but I didn't want to say anything to the team about why this was. What I didn't realise was that Jim was in earshot of my yelps, so he came over and, once again, said, 'Nigel, what on earth have you done now?'

'Ah, well, I touched the wall in Phoenix in testing, Jim. It wasn't a big crash, just a nudge, but I have pulled a muscle near my ribs.'

He narrowed his eyes and looked at me suspiciously.

'Testing? In Phoenix, eh? *Really*?'

Later on, I was getting really hot and sweaty and I needed to take off some layers. As I pulled my top layer up over my head, Jim came over again.

'Nigel, let me see your side, just to check it out.'

'No, it's okay, Jim. I'm fine . . .'

'Nigel, let me see your side.'

I lifted up my shirt and he looked at my bruised ribs, which had been the source of all this pain and grumbling.

'Nigel, I am not an idiot. If you did that when you had that shunt on track in Phoenix, how come the bruises are shaped like someone's knuckles and a handprint?'

I had to own up – I'd done my brown belt karate grading the week before, which was a full-contact session and the sensei had lathered into my ribs. I later found out that I'd actually cracked two of them.

Jim just shook his head, said, 'You have got to be kidding me,' then tried to hide a smile and walked off, still shaking his head. As he walked away, I half-heartedly shouted after him, 'Hey, Jim, I got my brown belt, though . . .'

He didn't seem too impressed.

Did I tell you about the time my wife caught me kissing a supermodel? Oh crikey. When we were in Australia in 1992 with F1, I was in the garage and, as usual, there were a lot of people milling around. One of these was an invited guest, the supermodel Elle Macpherson. We were introduced and she was a lovely lady with very long legs, I have to say. Rosanne wasn't there at the time. Elle chatted with me for just a few moments really and then, out of courtesy, she planted a kiss on my lips, just a little peck. Just at that exact moment Rosanne walked into the garage. You can imagine, can't you . . . this went down like a lead balloon.

Now, my Rosanne is the most wonderful, warm, beautiful human being I have ever met, but boy, let me tell you, she knows how to exact revenge! She was in no rush either, as I will explain. A full year later (yes, a year), we were back in Australia again, this time with IndyCar, at Surfers Paradise where they had a resort called Sea World. This one particular trip we were invited to do a photo call. By coincidence, who else was there for the photoshoot that day? Elle Macpherson.

I had started the day doing all these tricks with dolphins, riding on them and being photographed by the media – it was great fun. Then they said to me, 'Nigel, shortly Elle is going to be doing a photoshoot with some other models in swimsuits. She has requested, would you mind going on stage and being involved in some way, please?' Rosanne was in earshot at this point and I was thinking, *Oh crap!* However, I do remember Rosanne agreed it was a good idea and, in fact, looked pretty relaxed about it for some reason, which I thought was weird.

Anyway we got over there and they said, 'Look, we want to do a little bit of a fun sketch, so the plan is to take you on stage blindfolded – we don't want you getting too excited with all the women in bikinis and all that.' So I got up on the stage, in front of loads of people; they introduced me to this big crowd and everything was sounding great. Then they said, 'Nigel, Elle would really like to give you a kiss,' and I was like, *Oh, my word, not again!*

Next thing I know, I am being given the biggest, sloppiest, most disgusting kiss ever! The breath stank, it was rancid. The slobber was all over my face – it was the most horrendous kiss ever.

That's when they took off the blindfold and said, 'Nigel, please meet Elle Macpher-Seal!' It was a two-tonne elephant seal.

Rosanne had exacted her revenge.

What could I do except laugh? Brilliant fun.

CHAPTER 17

BOUNCING BACK AND MOVING ON

The 1994 season in IndyCar proved to be much less of a fairy tale, as our cars were well down on performance compared to the might of the Penskes. Early testing suggested our car was even faster than the '93 Newman/Haas that had won the title. Driving with a number 1 decal on your car's nose was special, something I had always dreamed about but which had eluded me to date, because it meant you were a defending champion.

However, as the season unfolded it became apparent that a defence of my title was unlikely. Although I snatched two pole positions, I was unable to win a single race, with a combination of reliability issues and bad luck gradually eroding our chances of defending the title. Worst of all was a horrific accident at Indy in late May. Dennis Vitolo did not slow down enough under a yellow flag and smashed into a line of cars going into the pits. I was at the front but his car went airborne and ended up on my roll bar. I was lucky not to have been killed. Eventually, I would finish eighth in the title race, which was won by Al Unser Jr in his Penske.

However, any disappointment I felt over my 1994 season was overshadowed by the awful deaths of the great Ayrton Senna and Roland Ratzenberger at Imola, on that fateful weekend in 1994. Ayrton's death sent shock waves around the world of motorsport as well as the world in general. The terrible double tragedy also started a safety revolution in the sport I love, which I will come to later. At the time, the deaths had a massive impact on the world of Formula 1 and, although I was racing in America at the time, there were massive repercussions for my family too.

Ayrton was blessed to be, if you like, what I call in the elite category, so whatever was the best car, the best engine, he could get it. Racers like that have the ability to be in the right place at the right time and are able to utilise that for even more wins. Add that to his fantastic talent and you have a very powerful combination.

Obviously, Ayrton and I tangled on the track a few times and, on occasion, off it, too! I didn't agree with some of the things he did on track against me at times, a few of which I have already spoken about. However, over time we came to respect one another and there was a dignified, healthy acknowledgement of each other's skills and passion to win. Part of that was because we both tried to intimidate one another more than once, but it just didn't work.

When we were hammering down the main straight at the Spanish Grand Prix just a few centimetres from each other at approaching 200mph, that mutual respect was evident. Ayrton and I had many vivid moments on the track, and there were times when we disagreed very strongly about what had happened. In that instance in Spain, we both knew exactly what we were doing: he was trying to intimidate me and I was trying to intimidate him. It was brinkmanship of the highest quality and intensity.

And there was the race I lost in Monaco in 1992, when Senna was chopping and changing in front of me all the time. With the present-day regulations he would've maybe had half a dozen stop-go penalties for blocking, but the point is I could've quite easily run into the back of him and punctured his tyres or broken his rear suspension. Maybe I'd have broken my front wing but I could've perhaps had that changed and still won the race. However, sportsmen don't do that. To drive at Monaco like we did and not touch one another was pretty impressive on both our parts, although, in hindsight, perhaps I should've just tapped him! Seriously, though, it was another example of the respect drivers had – even the most intense rivals.

We earned that respect for one another because invariably we were having accidents together and winning races from one another; and – this works both ways – when you realise that the intimidation factor doesn't work on a driver, you gain a healthier respect for them. I always had a respect for him but initially that wasn't reciprocated. On a few occasions, he thought it was his right to push through but he started to realise he couldn't do that.

Racing against Ayrton was never dull and I am proud that I was able to beat him on numerous occasions. As I mentioned earlier, I still rate my overtaking manoeuvre in my Ferrari, when I boxed him in behind Stefan Johansson, as one of my best ever, and part of that pride is that it was executed against one of the sport's all-time greats. Ayrton was not an easy man to overtake! Once I got to know him, he said a few things to me that were really telling about his total passion to win and his fascinating personality.

When Ayrton died in 1994, it was a huge shock. Someone I cared about and looked up to as one of the best drivers ever had just been killed. The shock was compounded by Roland dying too, and then a few weeks later Vitolo's car smashing on to mine in America. It all felt so incredibly dangerous.

I've got to align myself with the rest of the world here – I was one of the many people, racers, fans, the general public, who thought Ayrton was bulletproof. I honestly believed he was untouchable and indestructible. When you have got the immense natural ability that Ayrton possessed, it is possible to feel that way; he had the talent to back it up. The problem is that if Lady Luck is not on your side and destiny takes over, you can get hurt. What happened to Ayrton was a completely freak accident, a one-in-many-millions chance. The possibility of that terrible accident being repeated is so minuscule that it can't even be calculated. Lady Luck, destiny, call it what you will, was tragically not with him that day and that was just terrible. When his fatality happened, it rocked all the drivers in totality. More than that, Ayrton was a global figure in sport, so his death was felt way beyond the confines of the paddock. Ayrton was a complete driver, a racer, a thinker, a politician, an incredibly talented man who would leave no stone unturned to find a way to win. His death was one of the single most monumental events in modern racing, a terrible tragedy and a massive loss to the sport and the world.

On a personal level, Ayrton's tragic death would come to alter the course of my career and my family's near future. The events of 1994 have been widely chronicled, but for the purposes of retelling the tale, Senna's death led to a dramatic shift in my future plans. We were comfortable as a family in the USA; my children were enjoying school and it was a lovely life. My brand was strong and, although the 1994 season had not been as good as 1993, there were exciting times ahead. I felt like we had our future mapped out. There had even been talk of my own IndyCar team.

However, destiny decreed that the route we thought we were taking as a family and in my career was not the one we were now going to follow. As I have said before, I thought I would be racing in the USA for some time, but circumstances changed and I was therefore available to race in Formula 1 once more. It was obviously very flattering that the pinnacle of motorsport, F1, wanted to see me racing again. It was not what we had expected but I was excited to see how the cars had changed in the two years I'd been away.

Behind the scenes, I have to emphasise it was a massive effort for my family to relocate back to the UK – new schools, new friends, new home. Our children were still young so it was a really big deal. Of course, the ultimate perspective on this is that it could have been me sitting in that car that smashed into the wall in Imola. Fate decided that it was Ayrton. Mine and my family's life was turned upside down in the aftermath of that awful weekend in San Marino. I'm not going to pretend it wasn't a major upheaval in our life, because it certainly was. Ayrton, though, was terribly, dreadfully unlucky.

Unavoidably, we were now faced with moving our entire family back to the UK but, as with all the other challenges Rosanne and I have faced, we grabbed it with both hands and went for it. You move on, you have to. As I keep saying, it is all about the bounce-back. You have to move on and work out how to extract the most positive outcome from your new set of circumstances, however unexpected they may be.

In terms of my racing career, that meant being back in the seat of a Williams Formula 1 car. With the frightening experience of the Vitolo car almost landing on my head in Indy coming only a few weeks after Ayrton and Roland had been killed, I don't mind admitting that I did wonder if I was tempting fate myself. I am sure in the aftermath of Imola most, if not all, the drivers in the Formula 1 paddock thought the same.

However, as I have mentioned, I am a firm believer in fate and, to add to that, I still loved winning. I was, as you now know, bitterly disappointed at not being able to defend my 1992 World Championship title, so there was the feeling that here was a great opportunity to race again at the very top level. In a statement to the press, I said, 'Formula 1 has gone through tragic times in recent weeks. Against that background and bearing in mind our successes in the past, it was perhaps inevitable that speculation would take place about the possibility of people trying to persuade me to return to F1 – despite all the problems that would cause. After all, I have often said that, in motor racing, anything can happen!'

So it was that in the middle of the 1994 IndyCar season, I made a guest appearance for Williams-Renault at the French Grand Prix at Magny-Cours. My plan was then to race the final three grands prix of the season and hopefully continue in 1995. I was overwhelmed by the size of the crowd that turned out to testing just before the French Grand Prix in July – more than 15,000!

Getting back into a Formula 1 car was a bit of a shock, but I quickly familiarised myself with the Williams-Renault. Most notably the active suspension that I had worked with in '92 was banned, as was traction control. During qualifying, Damon Hill drove brilliantly and nicked pole off me by less than a tenth of a second (0.077 seconds to be precise). When he came back into the pits, he said to the team, 'I had to absolutely drive my balls off to do that!' My engineer David Brown just laughed and said, 'That's what Nigel does all the time!'

In the race itself I retired through a gearbox failure. However, in my mind I knew I was fast and was therefore excited about the three races coming up later in the year, after the IndyCar season had finished. I was tired flying back and forth and those races were very challenging, but I really enjoyed myself. I was competitive, even though I was bumped by Rubens Barrichello in the European Grand Prix and later span out; this was followed by a very strong fourth in Japan. At this race, my main rival on track that day, Jean Alesi, affectionately told me I was 'very quick for an old man'. Haha!

The final race of 1994 was in Australia. I put the car on pole but all eyes were on the fantastic battle between my Williams team-mate, Damon Hill, and Michael Schumacher for the world title. Damon is a really nice person and I was thrilled to be able to support him to try to go for the championship in late 1994. He is a gentleman and was never afraid to say if another rival was pushing him about. Damon was a great driver. I wouldn't describe him as a racer; there are very few people I would class as thoroughbred racers, but he was an absolutely excellent driver.

I like Damon immensely. I think he has a cool head and he can sometimes be misunderstood, which is unfair. I love Damon and his family, and I think to have achieved what he has done in the shadow of his father, the great Graham Hill, is truly outstanding. The challenges I am sure Damon has had through his life and career, along with his mother and wife . . . they are a wonderful family and just outstanding examples of how to behave.

In Australia that day, I was following Michael and Damon as they went into the fateful corner and I could sense Damon was aching to get past. I must have been in the best seat in the house! I was urging him not to get tangled up with Michael. When those two came together and Damon's race and title hopes were ended, I was able to push through and go on to win the race. But, as pleasing as that was for me, I was devastated for Damon. Of course, there was much controversy in the aftermath about Michael's intentions when his car hit Damon's and took him out of the race. Two years later, Damon thoroughly deserved to win the title in 1996 and I was thrilled for him when he did. I really enjoyed those races, and Frank later said I was a lot of fun to deal with in Japan and Australia. This was to be my 31st and last grand prix win, a British record that would stand until Lewis Hamilton took it from me in 2014.

I felt my performances in late 1994 had proven I was still at the top of my game, was still quick and still very hungry. Ultimately, however, Williams opted for David Coulthard, who had previously been a test driver for the team. I was obviously very disappointed. Adrian Newey was later quoted in the book *Williams*, by Maurice Hamilton, as saying that, 'If Nigel had been in the [FW17] for the whole of 1995, I believe he would have won the championship.' That's obviously wonderful to hear, but at the time I was bitterly disappointed not to be in a car that I knew was super-quick and capable of vying for the title. However, that wasn't to be our destiny.

Fortunately, I was able to bounce back straight away because there were a number of openings in Formula 1 available to me elsewhere. In the recent past, Ron Dennis of McLaren had expressed an interest in working with me and, when it became apparent I would not be driving for Williams, that interest was reignited. Previously we had been quite intense rivals, but once we met in person – as with other people I've told you about – we got on well and a deal was done for 1995. McLaren had had a poor 1994 but I was very excited to be driving for such a famous team, and Ron had been exemplary in all our negotiations and early work together.

It has been well documented that the McLaren car that season was terribly uncompetitive. The car had inconsistent handling problems, and in testing I immediately found it very disappointing to drive. Worse still, the cockpit was tiny and it was difficult for me being bashed and crushed as I was driving. My detractors found much merriment in this fact. I had signed for McLaren very late, which didn't help, but my team-mate at McLaren, Mika Häkkinen, also really struggled with the claustrophobic cockpit. In fact, he likened the car to running the London Marathon in a pair of shoes that were too small. Eventually, McLaren decided to redesign the seat and cockpit, which meant I had to sit out the first two races, with Mark Blundell being brought in to cover for me.

At San Marino, I made my return to the track and the race was modestly successful. I finished tenth but I was two laps down on the winner, Damon Hill, and my concerns about the car continued. Two weeks later in Spain this was compounded when I retired on lap 18, as I felt the car was not driveable. That trust that I spoke about, the confidence you need in a car, was just not there. Watching Damon and David Coulthard driving the Williams in 1995 was hard, because my car didn't even fit me. It was incredibly uncomfortable, very uncompetitive.

So I made the decision to stand down from McLaren and I departed from F1. I walked away and by that point, I have to be really honest with you here, disillusionment had totally set in. I felt like I had been pushed pillar to post on more than one occasion in my career, and been given possible opportunities to win World Championships only for them to evaporate.

By 1995, I felt, rightly or wrongly, that the whole world was on my shoulders. I felt that some people were taking from me and not giving any support, but I didn't show anything of what I was feeling. I guess I reacted just as I did when I lost my mother. I was very private with my feelings. Again, I didn't want any emotion to be perceived as a weakness. Looking back, I really needed some understanding, some support and some encouragement; it would've helped enormously. However, I didn't open up to people, so how could they know I needed their help and support? Not opening up to Ron about my feelings is something I regret. I should've maybe said to him, 'Look, I am going through this challenge at the moment and I would welcome your support.' However, I didn't, so Ron never knew how I was feeling. In the press release at the time, he respectfully said I had been 'entirely straightforward and totally professional' in my business conduct.

I have been very frank with you in this book and I have to tell you about something that I never realised until recently. I can see now that my whole life I have suffered anxiety attacks. No one knew, I hid it all, during my Formula 1 career and also since. I have learned to spot the onset of an attack and have become pretty good at thinking my way through each episode. When the anxiety levels are about to hit me hard, my heart starts pounding, the adrenaline floods into my body and makes everything even worse – it's like someone jumping out of the dark and scaring you suddenly. A chronic anxiety attack can last for quite some time. It is really pretty unpleasant.

I have learned that a lot of life's anxieties can be avoided by better planning and preparation. Remember that morning I was late for a meeting with Colin Chapman? I had thought a four-hour fudge factor was enough but clearly it wasn't. If you are going for a meeting, allow enough time. If you need to prepare notes, don't do them the night before. Put the meeting in context: how important is it? Should you be this anxious? Try to control the anxiety by not sabotaging yourself.

I think the vast majority of people feel this way at times,

anxious, uncertain, worried, even frightened. Maybe to different degrees, but they all do. I know some very successful and accomplished people who suffer terrible anxiety. We are all guilty of it – you put yourself under the cosh when you don't have to. In moderation and when it is justified, it can be a good thing, because that's how we motivate ourselves. But when it is not justified and you don't need to do it, it can be very damaging. The biggest single person who gets in your way is often yourself; so if you are reading this and relating to any small part of what I have said, then just get out of your own way. Then you start to *breathe* a bit more.

Looking back, in 1995 I regret not going to good people, such as Ron, and explaining myself. I'd had to move my family back from America, find a place in new schools for the children, settle into a UK life all over again; then I didn't get my Williams drive, followed by the McLaren problems – it was all so much to process and deal with.

Being older and wiser, I think talking to a few close people would have been a good course of action. They may well not have seen it as a weakness, but possibly seen it even as a strength and a mark of honesty. Who knows, my career may have come to a close in a different manner. Anyway, destiny took me on a different path once more. Besides, with a whole new life in front of me outside of Formula 1, I would soon bounce back.

After I retired from Formula 1, my life would have, at times, even more drama, happiness, some sadness, and certainly challenges that were more demanding than anything I had ever faced on track. In many ways, my story was only just beginning.

PART II:

FORMULA 1 –
THEN AND NOW

CHAPTER 18

PAST AND PRESENT

In terms of motorsport, Formula 1 will always be my first and greatest love. As a fan, I watch the races and love to see the evolution of the cars, the drivers' battles, the stories, the whole drama; it's so enthralling. Specifically, though, I am very proud and enthused to be an FIA steward, a job I love and take very seriously (I also sit on the drivers' commission). My role as a steward has an added benefit: it gives me the very privileged position of being able to compare and contrast the era that I raced in with the modern sport of Formula 1 in the 21st century. It is always a fascinating and stimulating discussion.

I am delighted to say that in the modern era, the stewards in F1 do an absolutely exceptional job. This is one area of the modern F1's development that I don't think is always given enough credit. It was a brilliant idea to put ex-drivers on the stewards' panel. I believe that the current drivers find this immensely reassuring, because unless you have sat in that cockpit and felt the emotional white heat and sheer intensity of a battle on track, unless you have had to make those split-second decisions and been through the same high-speed dilemmas, it's not possible to *fully* empathise with the drivers' view.

I have seen a few instances where at first glance an incident seems very clear cut but actually, as a driver, you know there were complex and extenuating circumstances. I think the current crop of drivers like having ex-racers around, for that reason. The non-racing stewards on the panel are amazing too; they have such a level of experience and objectivity that they add an immense amount to the decision-making process. In my opinion, that blend is an excellent balance.

What is absolutely fantastic is the assistance the FIA give the stewards in being able to make the right decision. The FIA governing body and the policing of the sport is done in such a way now that there is no place to hide. They are incredibly fair and very good people; there is meticulous discipline but also great camaraderie. In many ways, it is also a thankless task, but the FIA provide the stewards with so much amazing footage that we are able to see exactly what happened. The digital information available is just sensational, too. The stewards are allowed to call on footage from on-board cameras, from other cars, front, back, it's absolutely brilliant. Sometimes you see an incident on TV as a viewer and you think it is pretty clear cut, but the stewards may get to see alternative angles and read digital feedback which reveals that, in fact, the initial opinion was totally wrong. The FIA family are second to none; it is a very well-oiled machine.

I enjoy my work as a steward very much, just as I do being a special constable (which I will come to later in this book). You are there as part of a governing body and what you have to do at all times is be very fair and even. When I am a steward, it doesn't matter who the driver in front of me is, what team they work for; I judge the situation on its own terms. It has to be like that, a level playing field. You can't penalise one team or driver but not another. No matter what sport you are talking about, you have to interpret the rules for the incident that has just happened, regardless of the personalities or context of the championship and so on. So I pride myself on objectivity and take the job very seriously.

Of course, as a steward you can't win! It is an impossible task. Someone will always be upset with the panel. Drivers sometimes become very agitated if they don't get the outcome that they want. I understand that; I have been there and, like I did, they all want to win. I have also seen times when teams and drivers know they have done something wrong but still push for a favourable decision. In those cases, you have to be very firm and say, 'It is not our mistake, it is yours – you are in the wrong.' Rules are there for everyone to abide by. The current crop of stewards do a brilliant job of making sure that happens, to the great benefit and credit of the sport.

So, getting back to the comparisons between my era and the modern generation of Formula 1: let's start with the cars. I've already touched on the physicality of the cars from earlier in my career compared to the modern generation of F1 machines. Driving a Formula 1 car has been made exponentially less physical, in my opinion. That is not to denigrate the modern era of drivers at all; it is just my observation about how it has changed since I started driving.

The brute forces and physical demands that yesteryear drivers had to withstand were more rigorous than those the present-day drivers have to contend with. The most obvious difference physically between the two eras is the introduction of power steering. In the past, when there was no power steering on the cars, it was the man and the beast; the race car could bite you on the ass at any time. When you were in a corner pulling upwards of 5G and the car twitched on you, it was your physical strength hanging on to that steering wheel that kept the car from spinning. It's hard to put in words just how very violent it felt on the steering wheel; it was a brutal moment, something you might experience many times a race, all the time knowing that if you went off at extremely high speed then there was a strong possibility of a massive accident that could be potentially very serious or even fatal.

When power steering came into F1 it really was a revolution. The arrival and then rapid evolution of power steering has allowed a lot of younger drivers to come through into F1, young men who do not necessarily have incredible upper-body strength yet. So the demographics of the drivers' physiques have changed now: smaller is better aerodynamically, better from a weight limit point of view, better from a cockpit point of view, just better all round. This is partially why drivers as young as Max Verstappen are able to enter the grid aged just 17. In yesteryear, that would have been impossible; a driver of that age – when not yet fully physically developed – could never have controlled the cars from a physical point of view. (I will come back to the age of modern F1 drivers later.)

Cornering at speed was one challenge, but in fact just to drive the cars competitively at all was a physical challenge. Your upper-body strength and leg power had to be immense to sustain competitiveness. For example, to depress the heavy clutch thousands and thousands of times a race (4000 times in Monaco, for example), change the manual gearbox, hang on to that violent steering wheel, deal with the G load. It was so demanding on the racer's body and fitness that we had to monitor when to go flat out and when not to, because we couldn't physically sustain the former all the time. You had to pick your moments; that was all part of the strategy and race craft.

In a modern-era Formula 1 car, the drivers are exceptionally fit, absolutely. However, the physical demands placed on them are very different. For example, apart from power steering, you have elements such as the semi-automatic clutch (which I was fortunate enough to enjoy also). Their seats are individually formed around their unique shape using digital scanning and bespoke moulds in order to be ergonomically perfect. Well, in the earlier years of my career, we didn't even have seats! As I mentioned, in earlier cars we sat on the sheet-metal floor. You'd sit on the flat floor with just a two-piece foam set-up, which would be expanded around certain contours of your backside. But you always had to sit on the floor to get low enough to conform to the height regulation once in the car, so you pretty much had nothing under your backside. That was fine; it wasn't exactly a comfortable ride but you got used to it. However, as I found out to my cost, if you went airborne and had a shock wave for some reason – typically if you hit a kerb – that force shot straight up your spine.

Modern-day cockpits are still very tight, of course, but compared to the piece of foam under my butt back in the day, they are relatively luxurious. In many ways, the cars are actually built and designed around the driver, with their size and shape in mind. That is logical; if you make the cockpit an uncomfortable and difficult place to work, how can you expect the driver to get the best out of the car?

Necessarily, because in my opinion drivers had to be stronger back then, some of us were quite a bit bigger than the modern drivers. Fortunately, at the time when I came into F1, I had an advantage over a lot of drivers because I was really quite powerful in terms of my upper-body strength, and I could do things with a car that physically smaller, less powerful drivers couldn't. That was very important, because we didn't have a combined weight limit back in the 1980s when drivers and car were weighed together.

Of course, being broader and physically bigger came at a price. All motor racing, not just Formula 1, is essentially about power-to-weight ratio. If you were a heavy driver then competing against the lighter guys could be difficult, because on some circuits when they went out of the pit lane they were already effectively half a second quicker. They used to say that ten pounds in weight was worth a tenth of a second a lap. Over the course of a 70-lap race, that's a deficit of seven seconds. However, I was 40 to 50 pounds heavier than some drivers, which over the course of a race could equate to as much as 35 seconds. So that body weight was a plus in terms of strength and being able to manhandle the car, but it came at a cost.

In the paddock now you do see some very small drivers. Back in my day, myself and Derek Warwick were probably the biggest drivers. We are relatively tall, too, being around six foot. Many modern-day drivers are much more compact, shall we say, and they can be like that because of the incredible evolution in the driveability of the cars.

One really exciting aspect of this modern generation of F1 cars being physically lighter to drive is that, I hope, eventually female drivers will be on the grid. This is no slight on the women of the world, but back in the 1980s it was just too physically demanding for the vast majority of women to drive our cars. Now, however, I see no reason why that can't change. I have known some fantastic female drivers in the past, women with incredible driving talent who would certainly have made it given the right opportunity in F1. There is now more of a chance than ever before of a woman lining up on an F1 grid and I would absolutely welcome that development when it comes.

All these observations about how much less physical it is for a modern-era F1 driver are only the result of spectacular progress, let me be clear on this. It is the result of hundreds of absolutely brilliant engineers, designers, very clever minds evolving and perfecting intricate parts of the cars year after year. There has been an incredible change. While saying that drivers in my era were more physical, I think there has been a marvellous breakthrough in technology, making it physically easier for the drivers to do their job, so how can that be a bad thing? You cannot determine when you are born and I think it is great for them that the progress has been made in this way.

I have to defend the drivers here. Over recent years, I have seen some drivers who have had quiet races get out of a car looking as though they've just come out of a hair salon, no trace of sweat. Yet in my era we were all dying when we got out of the cars. However, that's not the fault of the modern-day driver. I would say to them: lap it up! Just think of me in my steel cockpit, with my arse aching from sitting on a slim piece of foam and being thrown around inside a hot, cramped metal box for two hours.

What about the actual car itself? I have spoken about the 1350bhp beasts and turbo missiles we used to drive compared to the engines of the current generation. Regardless of the power you have, though, getting that force down on to the track is the key, so an absolutely massive part of any car's success and performance is the tyres. The wrong tyres, or ones that have degraded, can ruin your day, potentially even put you in a very serious accident. Remember my first day testing for Lotus when I was five or six seconds off the pace? Much of that was down to tyres. What you want is a set of tyres that will stay with you and keep the balance of the car consistent for a good period of time.

In yesteryear, we used to get through tens of sets of tyres in testing and practice, to get three or four sets for the race, because we would want to identify the best sets. Top drivers can sense the tiniest of vibrations when they are hammering down a straight at 200mph and will be able to pull into the pits and say, 'The front right is no good.' Even the most minuscule vibration can be picked up by a quality driver. Back in those days it was still quite a challenge to balance the tyres correctly. Wheel weights could be crucial to your chances of winning or performing well; they were so crucial. Back then, it was very hard to balance the tyres and wheels to the proficiency that was required to have a really smooth car. Vibration is the enemy of a Formula 1 car and race driver because any kind of vibration is basically taking away grip, especially in the corners. The car is literally lifting off the track in minute amounts, but when you are running at that level of performance it can create very bad results.

If you want to get really detailed about this, it's a fact that under braking the tyre can actually twist on the rim. If, for example, they haven't fully wiped the soap suds clean off the wheels after they fitted them, there might be too much lubrication on the edge of the tyre. Then when you brake under intense load, the wheel rim stops in line with the brakes, but the tyre itself keeps turning. Then all of a sudden your car is totally out of balance. You haven't actually lost any weights; it is just that the tyre has moved maybe two or three inches on the rim. On more than one occasion, I had tyres move halfway round the rim, especially on the back. For me, utopia was finding a wheel and tyre mounted where you had *no* weights on it at all – that was perfect. Technically, the wheel could slip a little bit and you'd still be in balance. So the fewer balance weights you had to have on the wheel the better. Going into a corner at 180mph braking under about 5G and knowing, or feeling, that your tyre is still rotating halfway around the rim is not the most reassuring feeling for a driver!

The problem with vibration still exists today. When you hear a modern driver shout on his team radio, 'I can't drive the car!', it is often due to vibrations. It might be a flat spot on one of the tyres from locking up the brakes, or it might be another fault or failure. Sometimes in a car like that it feels like you are bouncing all over the place.

If you recall Silverstone in 1987, my wheel weights had come off and for the first number of laps I could barely drive the car. Then I made a pit stop and caught Piquet with only a few laps to go, moving at over a second a lap quicker than him. That was a particularly extreme example, but it wasn't unusual for wheel weights to detrimentally affect your performance quite substantially. Sometimes they weren't fitted properly; sometimes it was just bad luck. I have got to be fair to the tyre fitters now, they do a fantastic job. The recent changes concerning tyre degradation have generated much debate, with some critics suggesting drivers have to preserve their tyres more than they race their rivals, so it will be really interesting to see what happens with this in the future.

Another area that has seen monumental change is testing. I've mentioned before that in the early days at Lotus, if a designer had an idea, they'd draw it on an old-school draughtsman's board; then those drawings would be used to fabricate the one-off part, they'd stick that new part on the car and we'd go out and thunder round at 200mph. If the stopwatch said we were faster, then great; but if not, that new part would be binned.

Certainly in the earlier part of my career, we were always out on track trying out ideas. We weren't limited as far as the number of tyres, gearboxes or engines we could use in a season was concerned, which was a plus compared to nowadays. In the earlier years, we didn't have any of the computer processing power, so no simulators, no computer testing, no wind tunnels, shaker rigs – it was all done first-hand in the real world, on track. The lap time told us everything.

I loved testing. Yes, it was tiring, but it was exciting to be at the forefront of new technology in such a dramatic way. At times, in fact most of the time, there was an element of 'finger in the air' in terms of our tests, especially with brand-new technology. However, that was exciting. I've mentioned it could sometimes be scary too, like when Colin wanted us to try that bendable steering column, but mostly it was fantastic. If someone had an idea about some new aero, they'd build a one-off, or maybe one for each car, strap it on and we'd go out flying round the track. Like I said, lap times were everything.

What I enjoyed so much about testing in the old-school era was that you were essentially a test pilot. You were more than just a grand prix driver. You were working hand in hand with the engineers and it was always a small team (now a top driver will have a whole team of engineers, each with very specific responsibilities). In my early years, the engineer team was very small, two or three at the most. I spent many years working with the lovely, very smart David Brown as my engineer; he is a wonderful gentleman and I have a real soft spot for him (as I do for Maurizio Nardon, my Ferrari engineer. I liked working with both these men immensely).

I really enjoyed working with my engineers. Yes, I would be demanding of them at times, but that's because I wanted the very best car and they knew that. They were very clever individuals, amazingly adept at providing you with what you wanted. You'd work with the engineer, all the time; he'd throw ideas at you, you'd throw ideas at him, then you'd come to an agreement about what to try, have an order of things to try to make it better. It often went further than that. If there was an issue with the springs, the driver would come back in, tell his engineer and then the engineer might change the springs himself, there and then. If the job was difficult and there were not enough resources, then often the driver would help change the springs too. You can't get much more direct input than that!

Testing in my era seems prehistoric compared to testing nowadays. Testing started to change dramatically during my career but, in the modern generation, the testing and simulation technology have reached astounding levels. Technology such as computational fluid dynamics can tell teams how a part will perform before it is even bolted on to a car.

Wind tunnels did start to come in during my career (in the late 1970s), but they were very early incarnations of the technology and, like all innovative ideas, there were flaws. Back then, the racetrack was categorically more important than the wind tunnel. The wind tunnel might tell you that a specific part worked, but out on track you might get an altogether different reaction because the correlation between hypothetical and actual wasn't yet refined enough to be reliably accurate.

Initially, they didn't even have rolling roads so their accuracy could be quite limited. This is one area where Adrian Newey was an incredible perfectionist. His approach to wind-tunnel work was so particular, so meticulous. Other teams would be dealing with a calculation that was accurate to hundreds of pounds of downforce, but Adrian wouldn't be happy if the calibration wasn't accurate to within a few pounds, maybe 20 or so at the most. Back then, that was a big ask, but he knew that without accuracy the wind tunnels were effectively rendered only partially helpful, and potentially misleading. Some teams made big mistakes by not being as particular as Adrian with their calibration. This technology has improved immeasurably in recent years and now the wind tunnels are spectacular pieces of kit; their accuracy is astonishing and this is why teams use them so much. Some teams have two or three wind tunnels operating in different countries.

The testing technology doesn't stop once you take the part out of the computer world and bolt it on to a car. Whereas in my early career it was all analysed trackside in the garage, now the teams have telemetry that tells them every aspect of a new part's performance. They have engineers who aren't even in the same country as that new part! When we came in from a test lap, the engineer would be in the pit lane with his oily fingernails, pulling and prodding the part, looking at the lap times. Now, they can be thousands of miles away, reading telemetry off a computer screen and feeding that information back to the team at the circuit on a different continent. They can do a lap, get the feedback regarding, say, loads, temperatures and forces; then there will be interface between the remote factory team and the actual engineers at the circuit, after which the necessary alterations can be made on site. It's just remarkable.

This is all astounding, fabulous technology. My only concern with this rapid evolution is that it shouldn't be allowed to dilute the importance of the driver. Previously, the driver's input after a test lap was everything; they were the human feedback, flesh and blood telemetry, if you like. The engineers would listen to that opinion being voiced and act on the information. If a driver was poor at picking up faults or potential issues, then that team's performance would suffer as a result.

Now, there are many instances in which the engineers will tell the drivers what is going on – and sometimes that dilutes the impact of the driver's expertise. There are control systems that know that a certain part is going to fail long before the driver does. That's why the cars have so many adjustments on the steering wheel. Of course, technology is something of a genie's bottle; once you open up an idea, you can't put the lid back on. However, I do feel that the sport would benefit by focusing on the driver's skills and making sure it is the racers who are doing the racing.

The FIA are constantly trying to boost the spectacle and there has been criticism over the years about tracks with little over-taking potential. With this in mind, I think the introduction of KERS (kinetic energy recovery system) was a fabulous idea. KERS is a great piece of technology and I enjoy watching the clever racers utilise it. If the car in front has used his KERS and you haven't, then you come on to the straight and blast straight past, that benefit is due to your clever management of the car and the race.

I am less of a fan of DRS, if I am being honest. This drag reduction system is purely an overtaking aid, but it is some-thing that, once enabled, you can use every lap in the specified zone on the track. The issue I have with it is there is not enough driver skill involved. If you have fought your way to the front, or at least ahead of your rival, but then he is allowed to do 20kmh faster down the straight, every lap, where is the skill in that? Is that really a fair way to win a race?

When I was racing we had a so-called 'overtake boost' button, which you had to manage in a similar way – different technology but similar management. We had a button that you could press on the steering wheel which for three seconds gave you an extra 150bhp or 100bhp. Everyone had it. At that par-ticular moment the system would allow the boost to jump up another couple of bars of pressure, so that when you put your foot down it fed in a lot more fuel and BANG!

The caveat was that you could only use it maybe five times

through the race (not nearly every lap like DRS), because after that it was probably borderline whether mechanically you might damage the engine, or possibly even blow it up altogether. So you would use it wastefully at your peril. Used within the parameters and sensibly, it was a wonderful tool. The overtake boost was definitely an aid, but it was like brinkmanship. If you were racing hard with someone on the last lap, you wouldn't know if they had any boost left, so it was really exciting. If you'd already used your button, then you'd be history!

The start grid is another area where the driver's input should not be diluted. In the modern era, provided the driver has followed the instructions from his engineer on the lap to the grid and effectively prepared the car for launch, there's little chance of stalling the car. You release the clutch levers on the steering wheel, the bite point of the clutch is controlled by computer and the difference between a good start and a bad start is 0.2 of a second. In my opinion, that is too sterile. In my day, if you didn't get it quite right at the green light, the difference between a good start and a bad start was a full second or more. Get a really bad start and you could completely mess up your whole race. If you stalled on the grid, it was your error (unless the electronics had failed) and everybody knew. That's no longer necessarily the case, so in a number of ways I think we need to be careful that technology doesn't diminish the driver's importance.

The FIA are aware of this dilemma, of course, and the desire to keep the racers at the forefront of the performance was reflected in 2014 by a new regulation that forbids two-way communication that is perceived to offer performance information – for example, the lap times of competitors or remarks about other teams' strategy. That was a great idea. In my era we managed the car; we did not have the pit watching out for problems in advance to such an extreme degree, tipping us off so we could twiddle a dial on the steering wheel for an ailment that we might not even have noticed ourselves.

For me, there should be a complete embargo on two-way radio during a race unless it is a matter of driver safety. For example, if there is a fault developing with the brakes or tyres that could endanger the driver, then in that instance, absolutely, of course, allow two-way radio to alert them to the danger (in our day we had no such luxury); but otherwise, in my opinion, it should be left to the driver to race alone. I'm not sure how easy it would be to take away something from the drivers that they are used to, but it is a dynamic that I think would benefit the sport if we could just ensure there isn't too much help. The technology is incredible but we just need to ensure that the drivers are still the most important element of the story.

Arguably the biggest – and many would suggest single most important – change in Formula 1 since I was racing is the safety element. The evolution and development of safety standards in Formula 1 in the modern era is absolutely astounding. Frankly, I run out of superlatives when I am talking about safety in the modern era. The FIA have done the most remarkable job in making what could potentially be a hugely risky sport relatively safe. You only have to look at the massively lower number of injuries and fatalities since that terrible weekend at Imola in 1994. There was a 20-year gap before so many things conspired to cause the tragedy of Jules Bianchi's accident in Japan in 2014. Back in 1994, those accidents sent shock waves through the sport in so many ways, and I would suggest that those dreadful deaths ushered in the modern era of Formula 1 safety. Many lives have most likely been saved as a result. Easy to say and that's absolutely no solace for the families of those two fabulous drivers, of course, but since that dark weekend, the sport has changed immeasurably in terms of safety.

There are a number of ways in which F1 has massively increased the safety of the sport. Let's start with the circuits. In my very early racing days, if you came off a corner at high speed, there might be a metal mesh catch fence supported by wooden poles only a few yards from the track. There were sometimes trees nearby. The barriers were often just lumps of concrete. If you hit a concrete barrier or catch fence at high speed, you were in big trouble. This is what killed or maimed many drivers during my era.

Naturally, the solution was to remove the dangerous barriers and safety fencing. Install large run-off areas so that if a car loses control, there is a big area where the energy can dissipate and the car can come to a gradual stop. Hats off to the present-day circuits; by and large, if someone loses it on an incredibly fast corner, there is usually a really healthy degree of run-off before they hit something. If they do hit a barrier, these have been improved immeasurably over the years; now there are sophisticated tyre walls and cushions and so on.

The kerbs of yesteryear were much higher. When I was racing, some kerbs at certain tracks were massive. If you went over them at speed there was a very good chance you would break your suspension (and sometimes your back!). Some kerbs would even possibly write off monocoques, which could be very expensive. The kerbs were just like a cheese shredder under the car, ripping the guts out of the machine in a split second.

Fortunately, in the modern era the kerbs have been lowered, although this wasn't just motivated by reducing the cost of repairing damaged cars. At times drivers were hitting kerbs at high speed (often through no fault of their own) and their cars were being launched into the air, which resulted in some fairly horrific airborne accidents. Admirably, the governing bodies then moved to reduce kerb heights. Today, kerbs have been shaved down massively. They still batter a car and certainly shake the driver, of course, but they are thankfully so much more benign.

The FIA's relentless quest for increased safety has also seen all manner of less obvious safety measures introduced. Non-slip paint on the kerb, the HANS device to protect against neck injury, wheel tethers, larger mirrors, detachable steering wheels, raised front wings and plates, fire extinguisher improvements, higher cockpit sides, more sophisticated racing suits and protection clothing, helmet technology, massively evolved tyre wall specification . . . the list is long and ingenious. Another big part of the improved safety of Formula 1 cars is the materials and crash structures used. Take, for example, when Kimi Raikkonen hit Felipe Massa sideways-on at the British Grand Prix in 2014. Kimi crashed off down the Club Straight and it was very lucky there weren't more serious repercussions. Felipe's reaction time was a massive part of that incident not being far more serious; he must be given huge credit for putting the car into a spin to avoid a colossal impact. In addition, the incredible strength of the Ferrari meant that Kimi was relatively protected from the massive impact when he hit the barriers. I couldn't believe he walked away from that; in years gone by, his legs would've been smashed and his career would've possibly been over. It was just amazing that the Ferrari was able to withstand that impact so, again, full marks.

The medical expertise on hand is another area where safety has improved hugely. The faster the experts can get to a driver at an incident, the better his chances of recovery. The regulations now state that for a race to commence, the helicopter ambulance has to be able to fly above the circuit. Further, there are extensive emergency vehicles on site and more highly qualified medics for helping with driver extraction from the car in the event of an accident, including very particular rules about how the injured driver must be removed from his vehicle.

The racer in me sometimes wonders how much this necessary drive for safety has diluted some parts of the F1 spectacle. Don't get me wrong and I want to be *very* clear on this, *at no point should drivers' safety be compromised in order to increase the racing spectacle.* However, there are certain elements where I think the safety could be maintained – as it should – but the drivers challenged more. Specifically, as we have discussed, if you lose control of a modern F1 car on a fast corner, most likely there will be a large run-off area and you will be able to slow down, regain control then rejoin the circuit, often without penalty in terms of lost time. As a racer, I don't think that is entirely right. With the caveat that safety comes first, if a driver runs off through error, there should be some element of time penalty; he should know that if he makes more errors than his rivals, he will not win the race. In days gone by, on many corners, if you went off that was your race over. Certainly, you'd suffer a substantial time loss, at best.

Gravel traps were one idea aimed at slowing cars down if they slid off a track. There were specific reasons why gravel traps were discontinued, though: they can exhibit a number of disadvantages, such as pitching the car into a roll if it enters at a particular angle and speed; paradoxically, if a car entered at a very shallow angle at high speed, it sometimes skimmed over the surface, losing little speed and leaving the driver exposed to the risk of hitting a barrier at high speed. The large tarmac run-off areas in use in the modern era combat this by 'scrubbing off' speed more effectively and predictably.

It would be great to see some element come into play that meant a driver making mistakes and going off the circuit was negative in terms of his race position (*not*, I repeat, in terms of his safety, though). To be fair, the stewards are increasingly penalising drivers when they feel an advantage has been gained by running off the circuit, so it is clear they are aware of the need for vigilance.

The circuits have changed beyond belief. I have to say some for the better, some for the worse, in my opinion. Improved from the point of view of safety, yes – undeniable and to be applauded. In terms of spectacular corners and needing a presence of mind to hang on to the car in those corners, less so sometimes. Some of the tracks don't have any corners that can end your race anymore. In my opinion, those tracks have become too sterile. Some of the modern drivers who don't realise how lucky they are even have the audacity to say there's not much grip on the Astroturf when they slide off. Well, don't go on it then!

The pit lane is so much safer now, too. It seems hard to believe but in my era, on certain circuits, people in the team and the pits could be in as much danger as the drivers themselves. Back then, there was no speed limit in the pits, so we used to fly in at crazy speeds. I think the fastest recorded exit of a pit was over 180mph. There were no restrictions at all; we used to come blasting into the pits with our tyres blazing, then fire back out at mad speeds. It was a hell of a skill not to actually hit anybody, to come in and hit your marks then get out as quickly as you possibly could. It was scary stuff. Terrifying for the drivers and the mechanics alike, but yet again, through safety standards that have been introduced, the welfare of the pit crew is extensively protected.

We didn't have the technology at that time to limit engines in a very controlled way, but after a number of serious injuries in the pit lane, thankfully new regulations were brought in. Having 60–80kmh pit lane speeds is relatively sterile by comparison, sure, but from a safety point of view you cannot knock it. Pit lane minimum widths and the ban on refuelling have added to the safety improvement, of course.

In my day, we used to have an old saying: 'How do you know a really good driver? By how he comes back from a biggie.' The old school used to view it that, when a driver has had a massive accident, it was how he returned from it that was the mark of the man. How he nursed himself through the physical injuries, the broken legs, broken feet, broken arms, broken back; how he dealt with the psychological challenges, the impact on his confidence, and yet still be able to go back and do the job. How he recovered in terms of determination, how he trained to get back in the car and then how he mentally handled putting his neck on the line again having had such a big shunt. There are many examples of drivers who had horrific accidents in days gone by and then came back amazingly well. Just look at how Niki Lauda returned after the appalling injuries and burns he suffered in a crash in 1976.

With the monsters we drove in yesteryear, the cars weren't always safe, weren't comfortable, the tracks were highly charged and dangerous; you had to be more cavalier, you certainly had to be more calculating, and you had to be a lot more aware of the dangers going into notorious corners on certain circuits.

In the modern era there are many, many drivers who will go through their entire career without having a big shunt and, even if they do crash, they will barely be hurt. Consequently, today's drivers have less cause for fear in their cars, largely because the circuits have been made so safe. I have never had that luxury, so I acknowledge I can't personally state whether a modern-day driver battles with fear or not, but I do know that the physical risk my generation of drivers endured was at times cripplingly real and frightening.

I think this is tied in with another element of modern F1 that in my opinion feels very different from my era. I don't believe I am being over-sentimental here, but in my day there was an etiquette, an unspoken respect among drivers, that I am not sure exists in the same way anymore. In yesteryear, if you pushed someone off the track or had an avoidable racing incident, you could kill somebody. So there was (usually!) a real understanding and an appreciation that these cars were not Dodgems – they could literally take someone's life or maim them and finish a career. We knew we had to respect the risk that we were all collectively taking. Of course, some drivers occasionally got into trouble when they overstepped the mark, but there was an overarching mutual respect because of the risks we were all taking.

In the modern era, some of the drivers – not all of them, I must state – seem to think they are driving Dodgem cars and that occasionally bumping into somebody is fun. It isn't fun; it's dangerous, and totally disrespectful to themselves and to the other drivers. When you are supposed to be the best drivers in the world, you don't need to do that. You can drive hard and fast and show some great driving manoeuvres without contact; it can still be incredibly exciting without being dangerous or disrespectful. The new safety standards are absolutely fantastic, but one result is that some of the less sporting drivers now do not observe this etiquette; they are not as respectful to their fellow racers. That is a shame.

I digress. Getting back to the exemplary safety standards in modern F1, in this day and age, you have almost bulletproof cars – the safety on the cars is second to none, the technology on the cars is second to none, the safety standards on the circuits are second to none. Of course, this all costs a massive amount of money. The FIA have poured millions and millions of pounds into improving safety in Formula 1 and for that they must be commended. Hats off to the FIA, Jean Todt, Bernie Ecclestone, Charlie Whiting, the whole organisation, they are on it *all the time* – perfecting the safety year on year in tiny detail, learning year on year, never sitting on their laurels, always improving. They even resurface some of the circuits. Think of the cost of all this! The attention to detail for driver and circuit safety goes hand in hand, and the modern racer is very blessed with the team of people at the FIA who take the safety of those drivers very seriously indeed.

The most impressive element of these safety improvements is that the FIA are faced with a constantly moving target. One new regulation or track evolution is introduced but then, in the never-ending search for faster lap times and better performance, almost immediately the clever team engineers and designers create some new technology and there are suddenly safety issues that maybe didn't even exist before. The amount of money that has been spent on safety is enormous and I must congratulate the FIA on their dogged determination to make Formula 1 a sport where the risks are diminished and contained.

Of course, if you are travelling in a car at speeds of up to and over 200mph, you can never fully eliminate risk. In Japan in 2014, we saw the most awful accident in which Jules Bianchi was so badly injured. I was there that day and I can say it was a complete freak accident. I don't apportion blame anywhere because everyone was doing the most fantastic job. There was a freakish set of circumstances that all aligned randomly and caused that dreadful accident. Losing control of the car at the specific point that was probably the most dangerous place on the circuit under yellow flags, in the heavy rain, at a certain precise moment, meant that he came off in the exact place to collide with that recovery vehicle. You are talking about having the most ghastly luck; it leaves me speechless and my heart goes out to his family for what has happened. As this book went to press, we received the very sad news that Jules had lost his fight and succumbed to his injuries. I was proud and privileged to have met and spoken to him the day before his accident. What a sad loss of a very skilful and wonderful young man.

Thankfully, an incident like that is very much the rare exception. I often see crashes in the modern era where I think, *If that had been in the 1980s, he would never get out of that alive.* Even more so, I see big accidents where you watch the incident unfold with growing trepidation and yet the driver just gets out of the car, waves to the crowd and walks back to the pit. They walk away and everybody says, 'My goodness me, amazing.'

I have to qualify this and commend the FIA even more: F1 is probably the safest motorsport in the world, because of the strict safety guidelines, because of the controls and safety standards of the FIA and the tracks and the way Bernie runs the whole organisation – it is absolutely fantastic. The FIA have done a great job and that needs to be stated.

In the 1950s and 1960s, Formula 1 witnessed horrific carnage. In the 1970s there were multiple fatalities; in my era, through the 1980s and first half of the 1990s, things had improved but there were still many tragedies. The new era of safety was ushered in following that terrible weekend when Ayrton Senna and Roland Ratzenberger were both killed. If you look at the advances since then, Formula 1 is almost unrecognisable as a sport. Yes, some of the changes along the way have unintentionally reduced the racing spectacle. However, regardless of those arguments, F1 can now hold its head up high and rightly say it is the safest motorsport in the world.

Someone asked me recently how I thought my 1992 World Championship-winning car would stand up if it was to race on the current F1 grid. Obviously, it's a purely hypothetical question, but it is an interesting thought. All things being equal, with the drivers being of identical talent, I actually think in some ways the car would do quite well ... on certain circuits.

If we raced the old cars versus the new cars, on different circuits you'd have different scenarios. For example, modern F1 cars can corner incredibly well. Back in my era, we had those cars with 1350bhp, so in terms of sheer power, they were a mighty creation. Perhaps if we drove around the old Silverstone, with those very fast corners that we went round flat out, I'd be very surprised if we didn't kick the ass of a number of the present-day cars. Only because of the horsepower advantage, though. However, if you go to a medium/slow circuit, there's no question whatsoever that today's cars would kick the old cars into a cocked hat, because of the technology, the aero, the electronic assistance. There's such a better balance to the cars now.

If I was asked how I would improve Formula 1, I would definitely have a number of firm ideas. I acknowledge that power steering is an incredible aid and I don't think you can take that away now, but I would remove a number of the other aids. I would make sure that wheelspin came back into Formula 1. I would give the cars 30 per cent more horsepower.

I would make the tyres bigger and wider so that the cars have more mechanical grip. Yes, they'd be slower down the straights but you can compensate for that to some degree by having more horsepower. I think we need to make it more interesting under braking and through the corners, I want to see the drivers having to muscle cars around the circuit.

I would definitely attract more teams on to the grid – that's not necessarily as simplistic as saying there should be a spending cap. It is about making sure new teams have the ability to design and produce a car that is competitive. Formula 1 needs to be more of a level playing field. We have to make sure the sport remains exciting and attracts new fans, as well as keeping the existing supporters.

Another fabulous privilege of being a steward and being around the paddock is that I have met and got to know many of the current crop of F1 drivers. I've spoken earlier about some of my childhood heroes and also about my contemporaries in my own career, but now I'd like to chat to you about the modern generation. In my opinion, the modern F1 grid is excellent; all the drivers bring a variety of skills and styles to the table. Maybe I am biased, but I think a few of them would have struggled to compete with the great world champions of the past.

What do world champions have that separate them from other racers? An incredible determination, a dogged single-mindedness, they are so incredibly focused on winning. However, to be a champion it is not enough to just win. First of all you have to concentrate on being successful, then you have to be focused on winning consistently, but then you have to have the incredible ability to maintain this package for an entire year. People can do well and maybe win at one race weekend, but to put all the ingredients together that you need to be a champion, over the course of a whole year, is a very different challenge. World champions have the ability to see the bigger picture, and know what is needed to motivate everyone for a whole season, to keep up the winning ways and make sure they don't miss their opportunity.

Let's start with the most successful driver of the modern era, Michael Schumacher. Michael was a very cool cookie from day one. Some people hit the right team at the right time, and the Benetton was certainly a great car. Even so, Michael did an extraordinary job from very early on in his career. It was clear straight away that he was an athlete, a great driver, and a driver with a light touch. That combination was fantastic.

He was also blessed with a fantastic management team led by Willi Weber, who was able to get him the support he needed at the right time. When he arrived at Ferrari, there was a perfect storm of fabulous engineering, brilliant management, an amazing team principal and senior management at the manufacturer, plus this incredible young driver. When you win so prolifically, to then keep all that support and the team together, that is a talent in itself. Some people get the backing of manufacturers and the team for years; some enjoy it only fleetingly or for a season or two, and then the moment is gone. I would say I fit into the latter category.

Another point to make is that the unprecedented degree of reliability that Ferrari demonstrated to the world – not just to different manufacturers, but to the wider world – with years of no DNFs, was just mind-blowing. Ferrari has got to take great credit for that and Jean Todt has got to take great credit too, along with Ross Brawn and the rest of the team. For many years they were totally unbeatable. However, Michael still had to race each and every car, and he did that sublimely.

I believe Michael Schumacher moved the goalposts in Formula 1. He raised the bar with his fitness levels, his approach, and the reliability he was able to utilise. I would say he was a racer more than a driver. Of course, Michael had his moments where he did things on the track, in qualifying and the races, that some people felt were not appropriate. At those times, he was doing what he thought was required to win, but he attracted a lot of criticism for that. However, you should never let that take away from his wonderful achievements. I don't think that anyone will come close to seven World Championships for many years to come.

I always found Michael to be a very nice young man. Obviously he had his critics due to his approach to certain situations on the track. A Formula 1 paddock is a very highly charged place, full of drivers who are intensely competitive individuals, who want to be the best in the world, so sometimes tempers flare and people disagree. I certainly experienced that a few times, let's be honest!

With Michael, it was clear to all of us that this young driver was a potential threat to Ayrton's crown, so that ramped up the tension between the two of them. Michael stood his ground and said, 'Just because I am the new kid on the block and you are a champion, I am not going to be pushed about.' You have to admire him for that. He wasn't intimidated or apprehensive; he wanted to win, he wanted to be world champion, simple as that. If someone was a legend and the top of the tree, then Michael was even more motivated to overhaul them. Like I said, he was a true racer.

I was horrified when I heard about his skiing accident and the injuries he has suffered. Michael is in our minds all the time. I have admired Michael and known him as a friend and as a driver in a lot of ways for many years, and I admire his fight now. I know that all of Formula 1 and its fans are praying for him and hoping for some sort of recovery. What must never be forgotten is that what Michael achieved in his career was magical.

Jenson Button is a really super guy, extremely professional, very likable and a gentleman around the paddock. In my opinion he is underrated; I think he deserves more kudos than he gets sometimes. He is a world champion, don't forget. I think, on the one hand, Jenson is not an out-and-out racer, because he needs a car to offer something special for him in particular. But, when he gets that, he is absolutely one of the best out-and-out racers there is. That's not a contradiction in terms. Some people are out-and-out racers regardless of what car they are in. I put Jenson into the category of a driver who, when he's got everything perfect, is sheer brilliance. Better still, and perhaps more impressively, when he hasn't got everything perfect, I would put him into the category of being smart – he is *very* clever.

He won't push a car that he knows isn't up to the job. He should never be underestimated, certainly not by his rivals on track. I was delighted for him when McLaren renewed his contract going into the 2015 season, because now he can flourish. He can do a fantastic job; he has done so in the past and he will do so again. I have absolutely no doubt that, given the right car, Jenson could be world champion again. No doubt at all. I was 40 when I won my title, so he has time on his hands!

I am a big fan of Fernando Alonso, a big fan. For me, at the time of writing, Alonso is the sleeping giant of Formula 1. He did such a fantastic job for Ferrari. I know there were difficulties there at times, but I personally think he did an incredible job at Maranello. Now he is with Jenson at McLaren, where he too will flourish if he's given the opportunity. Both Alonso and Jenson will need to be patient because the new engine partnership with Honda will take time to bed in and get right, for sure. However, Alonso is from a breed of true racers, it is in his blood, and in my opinion he has the talent and experience to go on to win a whole number of World Championships. He is both more calculating and also more daring than most drivers on the grid, so I just hope he gets the opportunity to show exactly how good he is with McLaren. He has done brilliantly. I am a big admirer of him.

Sebastian Vettel is a great driver. At times there was an underlying feeling held by some of his critics that he won four titles because he was number one driver in a car that was massively superior to its rivals. The season at Red Bull in 2014, when Vettel struggled, notably against his new team-mate Daniel Ricciardo, was held up as further proof of this theory.

However, I disagree. I think Sebastian is a hugely talented driver. Yes, he has been fortunate with the support he's had all the way through his career. However, he is a protégé who has backed up his early promise and I think it is all too easy to denigrate his achievements. When he eclipsed my record of the greatest number of laps led in a season (mine stood at 692, Seb managed 711, albeit with more races), I sent him a note congratulating him and he accepted that very graciously and said some lovely things about me. In fact, he actually said that my note meant more to him than the actual record! There were various other records of mine that he took from me, but let's not talk about that!

At Ferrari, he will find a new lease of life. As I was writing the first edition of this book, he won the second race of the 2015 season, totally against the odds and faced with the utter domination of the Mercedes team. After the race he was tearful; it meant that much to him to be back on the top of the podium. Sebastian is an outstanding driver with such a lot to offer. When you have won four titles on the bounce then things don't go your way, you have to draw breath. I think Sebastian has done that and he has now got a fresh challenge which I think will go very well for him. Some of you may know that he does a very interesting impression of me, which really makes me chuckle, as indeed does his version of Kimi Raikkonen and a few other well-known faces around the paddock. If he wants to have a bit of fun, then I don't have a problem with that at all; it will probably be in very good taste because he's a nice guy. He is fresh, he is honest and he will be champion again, for sure.

Talking of Kimi, he has been around a long time now and is still a great talent. I think he can be incredibly outstanding at times and yet, by contrast, can go cold at other times. So for me he falls into the category of being a bit of a hot/cold driver. I am not sure what button has to get pressed to really set his race on fire, but boy, when he is on it he can be an astonishing driver. If he could be like that more often then what a force he would be.

For his first year, Daniel Ricciardo was absolutely superb; I am thrilled and amazed he has done as well as he has and he deserves wholeheartedly the opportunity to lead the Red Bull team. Daniel is a future world champion in my opinion, again given the right opportunity.

This brings me to my favourite driver of the current crop: Lewis Hamilton. Maybe that's because his racing style reminds me a little bit of myself – haha! Seriously, though, what I like about Lewis is that he is an out-and-out racer. I love that Lewis wears his heart on his sleeve, albeit a little bit too much sometimes. He is a courageous, extremely talented driver who gets the job done spectacularly well.

Lewis is a *huge* talent. Huge! He is already a double world champion and I don't actually believe we have yet tapped into his full potential. I believe he will go from strength to strength; there is so much more to come. I know, for instance, that I never tapped into all my talent because I didn't always have the elements around to help me achieve that. Lewis has an amazing team around him and an incredible car. From a driver's point of view, that environment is fantastic, it is utopia. It gives you a wonderful feeling knowing you are with the best manufacturer, the best car, with a team who are working brilliantly – you are on top of your game.

They have just defended both titles successfully, they are on the crest of a wave; they have the expertise of people like Paddy Lowe and Niki Lauda and the might of Mercedes. I was and still am a big fan of Niki Lauda. During his career and since, he has been a tremendous ambassador for the sport. What that man has endured, what he came back from to win again, it's just incredible. He is now, of course, a very successful business-man, truly fantastic. As a driver, he was a great thinker and planner; he could put it out there if he needed to, but he didn't unless he had to, so he very cleverly played the percentages. Therefore, it is absolutely no surprise to me now that he is involved in the running of such a fantastically well-oiled machine as Mercedes.

I would imagine that the team have been given the directive by the Mercedes board to be pathfinders and the leaders in F1 for years to come, so their drivers don't have to worry about a lack of investment. Are they going to leave any stone unturned? No. Is the reliability going to be there? Yes. Who is your team-mate? Nico Rosberg. He is a really nice guy; he is quick, he will fight hard but fair, he will keep you honest. I believe one day, if Nico stays the course and doesn't have any lapses, he could turn into a great world champion like his father, Keke.

Much was made of the long-standing friendship between Nico and Lewis and then how this was affected when they had their disagreements in 2014 and 2015. It's an interesting dynamic. Putting all the competitive rivalry aside for a moment, I had some great times with many drivers throughout my career. Elio and I had a good rapport, as I did with Keke. I had great times with Riccardo Patrese, too. However, here is the kicker to that fun part: race-car drivers are, first and foremost, rivals. Gilles told me this: 'Try not to get too close to somebody for two reasons: one, you have to beat him on the track, and two, self-preservation will have to kick in when they get hurt.'

So, you form relationships with other drivers but there is always an element of feeling you need to hold back slightly.

I think the person I got closest to, who I got to know and really admire as a human being, was Riccardo Patrese. What a lovely, lovely man, a very experienced grand prix driver, incredibly talented, very emotional in a positive way about his racing – enthusiastic, as he called it. We had some fun times together and I really enjoyed my time with him.

When you are in the paddock, immersed in that cauldron of rivalry and intensity, although you don't always realise at the time, it's so easy in hindsight to see how things can go wrong, how small incidents or arguments can blow up into big confrontations. I think it's also fair to say that over the years some teams have sometimes been guilty of actually promoting that kind of activity, because they think hostility and outright competitiveness is healthy for the team, because it pushes the car, the team and the individual and at the end of the day that is what you are paid for. Teams are not there to fuel lovely, warm friendships; they are there to win. That is fine as long as it doesn't get out of hand. In 2014, just as I started writing the first edition of this book, much was made of the rivalry between Nico Rosberg and Lewis Hamilton, and it almost did get out of hand. But I have to say, hats off to Mercedes, they just kept a lid on it, for the most part, not in totality, but they did a fantastic job.

You have a relationship with your team-mate, but at the end of the day you are still competing against each other like crazy. Many of my team-mates were world champions. As humans and competitors that champion breed has a different mind-set altogether. They are the best of the best and if you challenge them in any way, on or off the track, forget being a friend, you are the enemy. They are just outright competitors, winners, and if you go anywhere near being as competitive as they are, you instantly become a threat; you undermine their authority and that will be smacked down. So no Christmas cards from those drivers.

The dynamics of being a Number 1 or Number 2 driver is a fascinating element of F1. In the case of Mercedes, they appear to have a policy of allowing their drivers to race, so in that instance the Number 2 is potentially able to beat the Number 1. That was something which I actually enjoyed doing throughout my whole career when I was a Number 2. Obviously, when it comes down to the wire, the team may well favour the Number 1 driver, but as a Number 2 you have to make sure you do a better job every race and maybe get an improved contract the following season.

I'm not going to pretend it's preferable to be Number 2 – being Number 2 in anything sucks! – however, there are certain caveats that make that position enjoyable. You are grateful to be with a strong team, you know that if the Number 1 driver doesn't win and you put in a good race, then that may upset him but you have increased your status within the team. As a Number 2, everything you do is measured by your team-mate, but I always saw that as an opportunity to push him, I didn't feel the pressure he was under.

Of course, on the days when you beat the Number 1 it was fantastic. So being Number 2 is not necessarily as undesirable as you might think. I have to be honest, when I was Number 1 driver, I didn't really feel the pressure from the Number 2. I was very confident of my ability and I didn't really have any problems with my co-drivers. And when I was a Number 2, I was given the equipment to try to beat them. It is certainly a fascinating part of Formula 1.

I am pleased to say that it seems Nico and Lewis have managed to remain friends, which is great. Lewis and Mercedes are going to be the ones to beat for many years to come. Add in Lewis's enormous talent and you have got a spectacular opportunity to collect numerous historical achievements. I have always been a supporter of Lewis and I think he will go on to be one of the most outstanding grand prix drivers of the future and make his mark in the history books. I have no doubt that if Lewis stays healthy and well and focused, then a hatful of World Championships will come his way. He will need to remain focused – the biggest challenge is not to lose your way when you are winning so well. You mustn't rest on your laurels; you must always keep pushing, improving, moving forward. That's when you need to have the right people around you and just stay focused on your job. If you don't, then before you know it, the opportunity will be gone.

I am pleased for Lewis that he had the opportunity to defend his world title – something that destiny ordained wasn't going to happen for me. To be able to defend it in a car as strong as that Mercedes is even better. Both Nico and Lewis have the most fantastic opportunities in the future and it will be fascinating to see how it all pans out.

In 2014, Lewis surpassed my record of the most wins by a British grand prix driver, which had stood since 1994 at 31. He kindly thanked me for my support over the years in press interviews at the time. A lot of people would be begrudging of him, but I thought it was wonderful. I was delighted for him! People asked me if I was a little sad, as the record had now gone, but how can you be sad that a brilliant young British driver has achieved something so wonderful?

I might rib him that it shouldn't have taken so long – he has 20 or so races per season and we once only had 14. I might mention the biggest factor, of course, that is the reliability of present-day cars which is massively improved – we nearly always had upwards of five DNFs per season, whereas now reliability is second to none. There are also far fewer accidents and injuries, obviously. I might even point out that there were 26 cars fighting for a win not just 18. But only with a cheeky smile on my face and a wink of my eye. I look forward to bumping into Lewis on the grid after he has won yet more world titles. He is some driver.

So let's move on to the future of Formula 1. This is a fascinating subject and one that I always enjoy reading or chatting about. As I have said, the FIA have done an incredible job keeping pace with the teams in so many ways and also with the changing demands of being a global sport. Their task is incredibly difficult because the guardianship of the sport, evolving and protecting the future of F1, is a constantly moving target.

At the time of writing the first edition of this book, the 2014 season ended with two teams struggling financially – Marussia and Caterham. The subject of finances in Formula 1, who gets what and how the lesser teams can afford to continue to go racing, is extremely topical. The FIA are aware of these issues, of course, and there are many opinions in the paddock about what should happen to remedy these concerns.

In my opinion, you need to have some context when you are thinking about these matters. From right back to when the sport was in its infancy through to the modern era, many teams have been spearheaded by individuals, mavericks, entrepreneurs, lone visionaries like Enzo Ferrari, Colin Chapman, Ron Dennis, Frank Williams, Ken Tyrrell, Jackie Oliver, Gérard Larrousse, Emerson Fittipaldi and many other great names. These were all characters and, like I said, entrepreneurs; they were all incredibly driven and immensely successful people.

What this meant for drivers was that if these individual team owners wanted to give you an opportunity, they could do so. If they saw raw talent, then a test could be arranged. As I witnessed at Lotus, they would often test four or five drivers in one day. Those personalities were able to do that.

That has changed massively now, as the really successful teams are principally owned by manufacturers. So you can't just come in and get a drive in the way we could back in the day. Mercedes, Renault, Honda, Ferrari – they are huge organisations and the path to a drive is not that straightforward, notwithstanding the enormous entry costs of the sport these days.

In theory, you can throw an infinite amount of money at F1 and yet still always have something to spend it on: how many engineers do you employ, how many back-up systems do you have, how many wind tunnels do you need, how much R&D can you do each season? Naturally, the teams that spend the most money often, but not always, perform better. That's why money does talk and also why the FIA have tried to put spending caps in place and keep the rules sensible, so that it doesn't matter how much money you throw at a certain rule, there will be a limit of success you can have with it. And not only that – if you keep the rules stabilised it gives the lesser teams time to catch up. So it is a very fine balance.

Without these manufacturers supporting F1, it's hard to see how individuals would be able to fund the teams in the modern era. I remember Colin saying that about £2–3 million was what he needed to fund a whole season in the early 1980s; by 2014 several of the big teams have admitted spending £350 million, with one manufacturer rumoured to have spent nearer to £500 million. The FIA are trying; there are new regulations to keep costs down, but there seems to be a constant upwards pressure. The whole sport has changed beyond recognition from that perspective. I still believe there are individuals who can have their say, who can give people a chance – Ron and Frank, for example – and that can only be a good thing to preserve in the sport.

This brings us to the issue of how many teams are on the grid. When I was racing, there would be 26 cars lining up on the grid – with sometimes as many as 36 trying to qualify – and many of those had a decent chance of winning (Keke secured his World Championship after winning only one race, that is how competitive the grid was in that season). It's logical that the more cars there are on the track, the more likely it is there will be an exciting spectacle, with multiple drivers vying for the lead or having to overtake backmarkers and so on. The challenge is to attract manufacturers into the sport who feel they have a chance of competing. Who wants to go racing and know the best you will finish is tenth or eleventh? That's not racing, that's making up the numbers. So I do think the sport has to be mindful of keeping the grid healthily busy. More cars on the grid would be more of a spectacle for the fans, too. There would always be more to see on track, more backmarkers, more competitiveness, more chance for incidents and interesting situations to arise, more cars in testing, in practice and so on. Therefore, it would also be better value for money. In my humble opinion, Formula 1 would be enriched by that depth and diversity. I am F1's most avid fan and in my view it is irrefutable that Formula 1 is the best motorsport, bar none, in the world. However, if some thought is given to hopefully attracting more teams and cars to the grid, that will enhance the sport in the most exciting and spectacular way.

An offshoot of the discussion about how many teams are competing in F1 is the concern that young drivers are not necessarily getting the same chances to race as perhaps my generation did. The simple maths of the situation states that if there are 18 cars on the grid instead of 26, then it will be harder to get a race seat. There are more complex problems behind that simplistic equation, though.

I believe there is a huge stagnation of emerging talent in motorsport, youngsters aching for a chance in F1 but unlikely ever to get a shot. In years gone by, if you completed, say, 180-plus F1 races, you'd had a great career, especially if you walked away with all your limbs intact and indeed if you were still alive. Then it was time to hand over and give someone else a chance. Michael Schumacher and Rubens Barrichello each competed in more than 300. This has been helped by the fantastic safety measures introduced over the years, which means drivers are far less likely to be badly injured or killed. Drivers are coming into the sport younger and staying longer. That creates a bottleneck at entry level so, for example, super-talented drivers in GP2 are no longer guaranteed the chance of winning a seat in F1. I actually think whoever wins the G2 championship should be offered an automatic opportunity in F1. If they win GP2, in my opinion, they have earned a ticket to at least a test, or even maybe a couple of guest appearances in a race, *an opportunity*.

However, for many brilliant young drivers, there is a ceiling on how far they can go. The money side of the sport is also well known to deter many young drivers; some come to the table with sponsorships that can help get them a seat above a racer who is widely considered to be superior but does not have the same financial backing.

I was very pleased that I was able to make it in Formula 1 despite the background I had – the lack of money and the underdog status, which at times was very draining, of course, but conversely made the achievement feel all the more special. Would I have been given the opportunity to race in Formula 1 if I was racing as a kid today? In my view, probably not.

People will point out that there are some fabulous driver programmes in F1, which is entirely true, of course. And, in fact, that is immensely impressive, but the reality is that there are only a very limited number of seats in F1. The young men coming through have got a tough road ahead and I really hope they can be given the chance to shine. Then some of these young drivers could win a seat in one of the lesser teams and that would be their apprenticeship, the learning years, their chance to put some hard yards in and learn their craft. If good enough, you would then graduate up the grid because better teams would want to employ you. That chance is still there but again, because of the smaller number of teams, to a much lesser degree. I am not playing down what it took to be an F1 driver in my era at all – it was very hard and demanding – but at least there were *more* doors that might open if you did have what it took. There are fantastic drivers out there at the moment who will never get a chance, the door will never open for them. I feel very disappointed and sad for these young drivers, who have spent their entire life dedicating themselves to their endeavours on track but will never get that shot. To keep the sport fresh and the new blood coming through can only be a healthy approach.

Although the volume of emerging talent is becoming restricted, one remarkable aspect of recent years is the way the drivers just keep getting younger and younger. In the modern era, you are now able to leapfrog into F1 at a remarkably young age. This means some of these very young drivers have not had as much race experience as in previous generations. The reason very young drivers are able to clock up 'hours' racing is because of the astonishing accuracy of the simulators. They really are incredible pieces of kit.

Moreover, I would suggest that there is no simulator as accurate as real-world laps, especially if you are in a race situation with other cars around you; but in terms of mirroring the car and the circuits, these simulators are astounding. They allow drivers still in their teens to rack up thousands of laps of experience. So, yes, they have these remarkable simulators but that is not the same as the white heat of a battle on track. Nonetheless, the debut drivers keep getting younger and younger. Case in point, pertinent to the start of the 2015 season as I am penning this book: Max Verstappen, who tested for Red Bull aged just 16 and made his full Formula 1 debut aged 17. Funnily enough, his father Jos debuted in F1 when he was also relatively young, albeit 22.

In yesteryear, there were a number of drivers who got seats at 19, but most were into their twenties before they had their chance. In my opinion, to have a 17-year-old debut in an F1 car in my era would simply not have been viable. Physically, they would not have been able to handle the car and, if they had managed to get around, they would be so far off the pace it would've been embarrassing.

Red Bull have brought Max through their young driver programme, which is fantastic for him. Of course, some people say if you are fast enough you are old enough. That is a fair point, I accept that. However, these young drivers will be up against seasoned racers who have got track presence and track craft, but they haven't had those years of training and experience. They might make some simple mistakes which could turn into a big problem. To be fair, judging by Max's performance in the 2015 season, he is obviously a very talented young man. It is all interesting stuff and many things can be debated, so I shall watch with great interest how his team develop this young driver.

As another example of the dramatic changes in the sport since I was racing, while I've been writing this book, Max was involved in a heavy accident at Monaco. In yesteryear, two things would've happened. In my opinion, there is no question that at the very best he would've broken his legs and feet. Seeing him get out of that car and walk away was very surprising and delightful to watch. It was amazing to see that he could hit the back of a car at such speed and then smash straight on into a barrier and just jump out of the car. Max will recover and learn from his mistakes.

However, in my era, there would've been a severe physical penalty for that incident. In my opinion, it was wholeheartedly Max's fault, as he didn't give enough room to pass the car – had he given enough room, he would've made the pass, made the corner first and it would've been a great manoeuvre. Secondly, again in terms of my era, there would've been young talent waiting in the wings for their opportunity to fill in for a few races while Max was recovering. Even these small opportunities don't exist anymore.

There are a great number of what I call really promising – and possibly great – drivers out there. The future of Formula 1 could well be incredibly exciting. I have really enjoyed thinking about these comparisons between my era and the modern generation of cars and drivers, and what is absolutely clear is that these young guys are hugely talented and need to be unleashed just to show how great they can be. If the sport of Formula 1 can get that right, then we have some fabulous, wonderful times ahead.

PART III

ISN'T LIFE WONDERFUL?

CHAPTER 19

ONWARDS TO WOODBURY

You might think that retired racing drivers find life out of the fast lane quite pedestrian and even mundane. Certainly, you never get to drive cars on the road that feel particularly fast, but in terms of my life since retiring from motorsport, I have had periods when I've never been busier.

After I stood down from McLaren in 1995, my involvement with motorsport did not stop completely just because I was no longer racing in F1. I enjoyed a brief spell with British touring cars in the 1990s. I had been back to race in the UK fleetingly on the last day of October 1993, making a one-off appearance at Donington in the TOCA Shootout in a Ford Mondeo, in front of 90,000 people. It was a painful day out. I was very disappointed with another driver who crashed into the back of me, pushing me into a concrete wall at very high speed, something in the region of 120mph. It was totally unnecessary, I hit the wall really hard, and had to be cut from the wreckage. The incident broke some ribs and concussed me. One commentator said it was 'one of the biggest saloon car accidents I have ever seen'. I was seriously lucky to not be more badly injured.

Touring car racing is very different to Formula 1, immeasurably so, to be honest. Touring cars back then were based on proper road cars, albeit with a souped-up suspension and engine (they are somewhat more sophisticated now, but still nowhere near the technology of an F1 car). It is a different way of racing altogether; you can't compare the two. For starters, you don't have any sizeable G-force in a saloon car; you might get a little bit but nothing too troubling. The acceleration and deceleration are good but not savage, unless, of course, you hit a wall. I call them Dodgem cars because the drivers are allowed to lean on other cars and push one another about, which can be a lot of fun if it's done in the right way. Racing saloon cars just made me realise how brutal and ferociously hostile driving an F1 car can be. It was a very sharp comparison.

I came back to the British Touring Car Championship in 1998 with Ford for three races. This time, my beloved Red 5 was taken so I raced under Red 55. Oh, and by the way, contrary to popular opinion, my car was not called Red 5 because that is the number of Luke Skywalker's X-wing (although I actually really like *Star Wars*). It was initially my racing number years ago; I had a kart bearing the number 5, for example. I have also been flying (and playing golf) with the Red Arrows (in Red 5), plus Red 1 was taken by another driver. Red 5 was different, available and it seemed to go down well. Anyway, my career in touring cars was relatively short-lived, but I did experience some great races. The Donington Park race that year is regarded by many people as one of the great touring car races ever, which is pleasing to hear.

Another very enjoyable experience came in 2005, when I raced in the Grand Prix Masters series, a fantastic opportunity for F1 drivers to race again, in places such as Kyalami and Qatar. It was brilliant fun but, sadly, after the Silverstone race the sponsorship dissipated, so it came to an end.

Around the time that we moved back to England from America in the mid-1990s, we became involved in a golf course in Devon called Woodbury Park. When we first bought the site, it was still in its infancy; so, for example, the clubhouse was pretty much a 60ft by 20ft Portakabin. We set out on an intensive 16-year development programme that ultimately transformed the fledgling club into what I would argue was the best golf complex in the southwest, if not one of the best in England. We built a complete clubhouse, a sports centre, a hotel, a driving range, tennis courts and a Premiership-standard soccer pitch (I will come to that later!), all from scratch.

It was an enormous amount of work but certainly in the early days I found it very calming to go to Woodbury, do the work and play some golf. We were lucky enough to have some amazing golfers help us tweak the course, players such as Greg Norman, Frank Nobilo and Gary Player. These fabulous players came in and gave their input, which was incredible. The course would eventually become one of the qualification schools for the PGA in Europe. It was very relaxing to go down to Woodbury and play a quiet round of golf, surrounded by the beautiful countryside, the deer wandering around, the nature. It is so beautiful down there. I found it had such a peacefulness about it.

Rosanne and I were excited and driven to make a success of the complex. It was very much a hands-on project; we weren't absentee landlords. We were intimately involved in the running of it, the operations, the building, management – we had to be but we also wanted to be.

277

When the famous Dutch footballer Ruud Gullit took over at Chelsea for a couple of years in the mid-1990s, the team stayed with us at Woodbury for one night when they came down to play a friendly against Exeter. Some of them played golf; obviously we entertained the squad and looked after them, and it was a really nice time.

We got chatting to some of the players, who said they enjoyed coming down this way for friendly matches, but it wasn't realistic to do so very often because there was no football pitch in the southwest up to the high standard that top players require. They were either too small or too bumpy, and what a Premiership side can't afford is to get a load of injuries in pre-season friendlies. These players are precious commodities. It wasn't just the pitches; the facilities elsewhere were not up to standard either. For example, after each game top footballers will want to have a physio session or sports massage straight away, or maybe take an ice bath. They are very particular about their training and fitness. At the time, the southwest just didn't have facilities that were up to scratch.

I listened to Ruud and his players chatting and later that night I had a brainwave. In a couple of weeks' time, we were due to have one of the biggest earth-moving companies in England bring some of their vehicles to a field we owned opposite the hotel, which we had agreed they could use to exhibit and demonstrate their state-of-the-art caterpillars and diggers. They were bringing 15 or so vehicles, so I thought about this and called them in for a chat. At the meeting I said, 'I have got an idea for you. How about if I let you dig the entire place up? Really dig it up with all your kit?'

They said, 'Well, that would be great, of course, but it would really mess the place up!'

'I understand that but if you build me a full international

soccer pitch, 120 yards by 80 yards wide, flatten it, prepare it, do everything, then we would have a deal.'

They loved the idea. So we had the land levelled and prepared, then laid with top-of-the-range turf and grass seed. It was situated in a natural amphitheatre, surrounded by woodland. Then I did a deal with a company to get a high-tech computer irrigation system installed throughout the whole pitch, so that you could manipulate the ground to be hard or soft, depending on what you wanted. There was a brick entrance built with gates right opposite the hotel. We even bought in international-standard soccer goals. The pitch was like a carpet; there wasn't a ripple on it.

Without further ado, three months later I rang Ruud up and asked him if he had any spare time to come down to the hotel to play a round of golf, as I had something to show him and wanted his opinion. As you approached the hotel, you couldn't see the pitch, so he was in for a surprise. When he turned and went through the gates to find this international-standard football pitch unveiled in front of his eyes, he was dumbfounded! He wanted to know how we had done it so well in such a short period of time. That was a proud moment.

We showed him all the facilities and he wandered around with his chief trainer and a couple of players for quite some time. They couldn't believe how wonderful it was and soon after they booked the facility to use for training purposes. From that moment, they used to come to Woodbury every year for a week or ten days, take over the hotel, use different rooms. The Colin Chapman Suite was their meeting room; they had their own breakfast room, everything they could possibly want. They loved it. Word soon got around the various top teams and so Woodbury has welcomed Manchester United, Liverpool, and many other Premiership clubs. From that, we then had various high-profile women's teams visit too; cricket teams, rugby teams – it became excellent business. The only downside was that Sir John Evans, the ex-chief constable of Devon and Cornwall and president of the Woodbury club, plus the head golf pro, Alan Richards, were massive Everton fans, so when the Toffees came to train you couldn't do anything with those two. Everything stopped!

Eventually, Woodbury became a rather large concern. At one point we were employing about 250 people. We had a way and a system of doing business: it was very important that we tried to treat everyone the same, with courtesy and professionalism. The team knew how ultra-professional I wanted them to be, especially courteous. It was a great culture for the business and it seemed to really work.

My memories of Woodbury are wonderful, although there was one horrible incident when we were in charge there. We weren't on site one day when we received a panic phone call from the club, which came straight through to me. 'Mr Mansell, we have a problem and we don't know what to do anymore.' This member of staff was really agitated, talking very fast; she was clearly in a bit of a bother.

She carried on, 'What shall I do? They've played golf, they've had some lunch, they've had quite a lot of food and drink … Now they want to help themselves to quite a lot of clothes out of the club shop … What shall I do?'

'I'm not a mind reader,' I said. 'Who are you talking about?'

'Your mother and her friends, Mr Mansell.'

I just went deathly silent.

My mother had been dead about 20 years. I was absolutely shocked to the core. To be told that was so upsetting; it caught me completely off-guard. To hear the words was shocking enough, but then the instant realisation that there was someone at the club pretending to be my mother was sickening.

'Try to act normal,' I said. 'Put the phone down, call the police from another room and try to keep them there until the police arrive.' Unfortunately, the people in question had obviously picked up on this staff member's nerves and made a swift exit. We never caught them. How sick is that? That was one of the worst moments of my life when I was told my mom was having a great time at my golf club ... I would like to think that the woman who was pretending to be my mom reads this and realises how upsetting and awful it was that someone could stoop so low.

Unrelated to Woodbury, but just to serve as an example of another unpleasant incident I had, in 2002 I confronted some youths who were on my property. I challenged them and suffered what was described in the press as 'superficial injuries' in the resulting altercation. We tried to play it down as much as we could, but it really knocked my confidence, I have to tell you. For some time I didn't sleep particularly well, either. Then a wonderful thing happened. I found myself being supported by some young men who were actually in the Feltham Young Offenders' Institution, where I had gone to do some support work with UK Youth. These individuals were in a terrible situation themselves, but they talked to me and reassured me and I found that very inspiring. There I was trying to help them and they completely turned the tables and actually helped me. Isn't that fantastic?

Anyway, getting back to that beautiful golf complex in Devon, Woodbury was very proud to host various business and academic events. One I am particularly proud of is the recognition of the hotel as an academy for degrees, master's and doctorates. This came about initially as a way to create business in the winter off season. We were brainstorming as a team and a family when the name of a certain Dr Knezevic came up. This man is a world authority on the subject of reliability, in terms of the engineering world, including within Formula 1. He is asked by many aerospace industries to examine and predict the reliability of planes, engines, all sorts of hugely complex projects. He is also a professor at Exeter University, so this is a very impressive man. We knew of each other and he'd asked me to give some lectures at the university, then we had become good friends, so around this time we got chatting and he said, 'Why don't you start an academy at Woodbury Park?' By academy, he meant hiring out the hotel so that he could organise lectures to high-powered individuals as well as various academic institutions.

So that's what we did. We set up an academy at Woodbury and hosted all manner of fascinating events and lectures. Woodbury Park became the first non-university in England where over a three-month winter period you could study towards a PhD, master's degree or bachelor of science degree. We had the most amazing people come to study there, including numerous captains of industry, an admiral of a nuclear submarine, all sorts. The academy is still running to this day and is a huge credit to both Dr Knezevic and Woodbury Park. Rosanne and I are both incredibly proud to have been a part of that amazing hotel and golf complex.

CHAPTER 20

LIFE ON A SIXPENCE

It's no secret that I love golf. I started playing in the early stages of my racing career when Rosanne bought me a lesson, and it has been a passion for me ever since. You might find this strange, given my racing career, but I really like individual sports. No F1 driver has ever won a World Championship in a bad car, with a bad engine or driving for a bad team. The whole package has to come together perfectly to win the title. Of course, the driver can show just how fantastic he is at his job when he has got all that in place, but no matter how talented he is, if his car is not up to scratch then it's end of story. Obviously, that's not a negative, it's a crucial part of F1 – it is a team sport.

Golf is the opposite, in my opinion. For a relatively modest amount of money you can buy a set of golf clubs and head out on to some of the world's top courses. If you think about it, in theory you could go and win the Open (if you were really something special!) and you don't need millions of pounds behind you, or a team that is perfectly aligned, or a set of clubs that is far better than the other clubs in everyone else's bag.

Indeed, if you have a handicap you can even play the world's number one golfer and give him a game! It's very blunt, brutal – you, the clubs, the course and a ball aiming for a hole that is just 4¼ inches in diameter hundreds of yards away. On paper, could it be any simpler?

I love the physical demands of golf, too. You have to be an incredible athlete to play well. Look at Tiger Woods in his heyday. I also love the fact that you are at one with nature, the tranquillity, which, when I was racing, was absolutely wonderful compared to the frenzy of a race weekend. When I retired, one of the elements of my future life that I was really looking forward to enjoying was my golf.

By 2004, I had managed to get my golf game to a really good standard. By that I mean I was a scratch golfer. One particular morning, Rosanne was due to accompany me on a trip to England, to watch me play in a tournament. She had been feeling under the weather for several weeks and had had various tests which proved inconclusive. I left that morning on my own, but only after much heated discussion, and an insistence from me that she stayed home, as she was feeling quite unwell. She finally agreed and I arranged for our GP to call round for a home visit.

When I finally arrived at the golf club, it was a beautiful day, the sun was out and the banter was fantastic. Then my phone rang. It was a surgeon at Jersey General Hospital who informed me he was about to perform an emergency operation on Rosanne. Little did I know just how severe the emergency was.

Unfortunately, when they did the operation they discovered that she had a tumour the size of a small grapefruit growing on the side of her appendix. Luckily, we were able to get Rosanne in straight away. Time was of the essence (this is where I feel so sorry for people who receive terrible news and then have to wait for weeks or even months sometimes).

Matters became even more serious during surgery when the appendix burst and, as if that wasn't enough, she developed septicaemia, itself acutely life-threatening. I didn't know what to do, where to turn, what to say … It was a total nightmare. Then, a number of weeks after the appendix was removed, they told us that there had been cancerous cells present. Cancer does not discriminate; it hits anyone at any time. You can plan for the eventuality, but illness has a way of catching you off-guard.

The appendix operation was just the start of a protracted sequence of events that lasted many years, including numerous operations with different specialists for various health challenges, in Jersey, London and Southampton. It was almost like working on a car. You fixed one part and then another part broke. What was needed was a complete overhaul. Unfortunately, with this really complex series of problems there was one calamity and complication after another.

I didn't feel equipped to deal with Rosanne being critically ill. I had no idea how to deal with this challenge. I think a large part of that helplessness was because I had always been on the receiving end of the medical emergencies in our house. I had the accidents; I had the operations, the recovery. I was at the centre of that and I knew the landscape, I knew what was involved, I knew the surgery needed and the recovery process to go through. Most of my injuries, apart from concussions, were physical in the sense that broken limbs heal, cuts are stitched up, torn muscles recover. I felt more in control. This was something altogether more insidious and unknown, not in my control at all.

Relatively speaking, when you are frequently injured like I was, you can almost carry on as normal. You can choose to drive with a broken limb. I drove with broken bones on many occasions. I knew that if I hadn't done that I would've been replaced in the car, a simple fact. So you have a choice: do you want to do it or don't you want to do it? However, serious ill health like Rosanne's does not give you choices. You *can't* just carry on as normal.

An illness is totally different to an accident. Okay, illness comes out of the blue just like an accident. One moment everything is rosy in the garden, then a severe health challenge or an accident hits you and poleaxes your family. However, that's where the similarity ends. There's nowhere to go with illnesses like Rosanne's in terms of analysing them. This has happened to you; all of a sudden your world and life are totally put on hold. It was no good me trying to find out what had caused the various problems, what could be done to prevent it happening again, as I did when I analysed all my on-track accidents. If my suspension broke and I crashed, we could analyse that suspension, find the cracks or faults, manufacture the part differently next time and prevent it from happening again. This was a completely different scenario and I was totally shellshocked by it. I wasn't equipped to be a witness to this type of carnage.

This feeling of helplessness was exacerbated by the fact that, up until that point, Rosanne had been blessed with very good health. In sharp contrast to me, she hadn't got a single broken bone in her body or even been particularly ill. Now we were looking at a series of very worrying developments that was going to take years to overcome. With me, when I was injured at work, it might be a month, two months, six months. Worst case, you might lose a season. Eventually, though, I'd be back to full fitness and crack on in a car and start being successful again, and then the racing would overwhelm the downside of the injury.

In Rosanne's journey, this would be very different. What I

found hard to get my head around was the fact I couldn't apply those time parameters. It wasn't possible to define the recovery in the way you can with a muscle strain. 'Oh, that hamstring pull will be four weeks and you will be back to normal.' We couldn't say anything like that. All we knew was that it would be a long time if she was going to beat this. And it was an 'if'. What we didn't realise at the time was just how many years – and how many more setbacks – it would actually take before she finally conquered these problems.

I don't wish to go into detail because it is Rosanne's private business, but she has very graciously agreed for me to write about elements of her health in this book. Without going into depth, what happened next was beyond anything any of us expected. Over the course of many procedures, and too many setbacks and recurring problems to recount, my lovely Rosanne endured multiple operations and eight years of fighting very serious ill health. Even the simplest operation can cause so many downsides. People don't realise that complications can be catastrophic and dangerous. On two separate occasions, she was critically ill. When you are a motor-racing driver, death is potentially around the corner every time you go out on the track for up to two hours. With Rosanne, we lived with the stresses of ill health for eight years.

I have to be honest, the aspect that impacted on me perhaps most of all in terms of processing what was happening was the indeterminate timeframe: was it going to last a month, two months, six months, a year, five years? Like I said, in the end it was eight years. Over that timescale, you run out of puff. I don't mind admitting I did. You are actually totally guilty of going braindead, not making decisions, not focusing. You are in pure survival mode.

Then, a couple of years into this period of ill health, she was put on certain drugs, the side-effects of which meant she gained two stone, a lot for a dainty lady such as Rosanne. This put an enormous strain on her heart (which in turn caused great concern, as her mother had died of heart disease). So another operation was looming, but this might prove to be too risky, due to these heart problems. However, it was explained to us that this procedure was essential.

I can't go into detail, again to protect Rosanne's privacy, but there was one particular day in theatre when I very nearly lost her. As I tell you about this now, I am filling up. It was just the most dreadful moment in my life, but I refused to let the circumstances take her away from me and, thank God, she somehow found the will to pull through. Life isn't always fair. It is an extraordinary realisation when you've had good health most of your life and then you suddenly hit a brick wall. Rosanne's brick wall came at 50 years of age. She has sadly had to face more obstacles than most women have in their entire two or three lifetimes. What a woman. Her iron will to beat this has just been a privilege to witness. She is an incredible lady.

I don't mind admitting that when I was racing, and indeed in life generally, I had a strong degree of self-esteem and confidence about most things. Certainly in terms of winning races, I had an incredible level of self-belief. I knew what I was trying to do and I knew how I wanted to do it. However, Rosanne's ill health and the very lengthy recovery absolutely rocked my self-belief to the core. I pretty much lost that overnight, through no fault of my own, but because someone I love immensely and care for dearly was fighting so hard for so long. This impacted on me hugely and I don't mind admitting that for a long time I was in the wilderness. I lived several years just numb from dawn to dusk. All of a sudden, my whole life came to an emergency stop.

I also noticed that when an illness like that suddenly smashes into your life, you quickly find out who your friends are. That applies to all of life's downturns – business, money, success, achievement and so on – people who are around when the good times are rolling are often nowhere to be seen when tougher times arrive. Thankfully, we did have a number of very good and dear friends and family who were wonderfully supportive.

Looking back now, at the time of writing it is 13 years since I had that phone call by the golf course that changed our lives forever. Only now, writing this, am I beginning to realise the magnitude of what Rosanne went through. What we all went through. It was a shocking, terrifying experience.

Due to Rosanne being so ill, I didn't play competitive golf for over three years. As I have explained, when I took that phone call and first found out about how very sick she was, my game was in the most spectacular place. However, because I had to give my full attention to Rosanne, I didn't hit another golf ball in anger for those three years. That is as it should have been, too. Here was someone who had helped me achieve so much, been there with me all the way, and had cared and nursed me back to full health all the times that I was ill or injured. Now it was my turn. I had to put Rosanne first and help her to get back on her feet again. I don't regret the decision for one second because it allowed me to give my attention to someone who needed it and absolutely deserved it. As much as I adore the game of golf, shooting a low score is of no consequence what-soever if Rosanne is ill and I'm not there to help.

I was poleaxed with what was going on, still functioning, but at 20 per cent for a long time. I can remember turning down jobs and opportunities because I was just terrified to go away in case the phone rang. Hence why I never played golf. It just felt pointless attempting to do anything because of the possibility of receiving a call, so the trepidation ruined anything you were trying to do.

I didn't speak to anybody professional about what I was feeling. I was so focused on Rosanne and making sure she was okay. Eventually, some specialists I know personally told me to be careful of becoming too insular and they advised me to speak with someone. I wasn't keen on counselling as such, but I knew I needed some really sound, solid advice about what to expect. This was not going to go away, for a long time.

I am being really honest with you here, but at this point in my life I was very lonely. When your partner is so ill, it is a very lonely place to be. You can't put any unnecessary worries on their shoulders because it is all they can do to battle their own ill health. You can't unburden the severity of the situation on your children because as a parent it is your job to protect them, too. So I took it all on my own shoulders, alone. I found this very, very hard to manage, I don't mind saying.

Part of not wanting to open up is that I noticed a lot of people (not close friends, obviously) ask you how you are but actually they don't really want to know the answer. They don't want to know the truth. When I did decide to open up a bit, I noticed that a lot of people were uncomfortable with that. 'How's the family, Nigel, how's Rosanne?' 'Well, actually, she's really quite poorly . . .' They didn't want to know. I have learned now that when people ask you how you are, the best thing is to just say, 'I am fine, thanks!'

To be fair, I wasn't my usual self. I love to have a laugh and a joke. I like to think I have a playful disposition, but that was being eroded all the time. Life had me utterly on the back foot.

Even when Rosanne started to beat this challenge, the changes it made to our life were enormous. As I mentioned, that first major operation was an emergency life-saving

Celebrating another trophy with Paul Newman and Carl Haas. It was the filmstar who persuaded me to drive for his IndyCar team in 1993.

Racing at Surfers Paradise, where I won my first IndyCar race, was so much fun.

The worst accident of my career at Phoenix when I crashed while going at 187mph, puncturing a three-foot hole in the concrete.

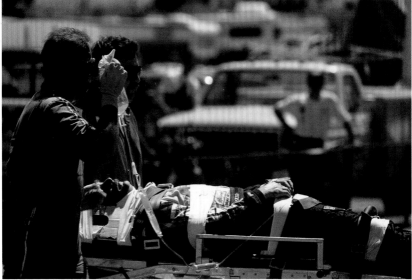

Stretchered away from the track, the pathologists told me they'd only seen injuries like mine on victims of plane crashes. Despite the damage – I had to have 148 stitches in my back – I returned to racing just two weeks later.

Talking to my team-mate Damon Hill in Adelaide soon after my return to Formula 1 following the death of Ayrton Senna. He was battling with Schumacher for the world title, but when they collided, it saddened me greatly to have a grandstand seat as I watched this unfold.

My brief spell at McLaren in 1995 lasted just two races before I decided to call time on my F1 career.

With James Hunt on the golf course. He was one of the greatest characters of motorsport.

Flying my Jet Star during the time I lived and worked in the US.

I've also had the chance to have plenty of fun in the water, as here at Surfers Paradise, perfecting the Rocket Ride, which was a new challenge.

Fishing is another passion of mine, whether out at sea or somewhere a little calmer.

The John O'Groats to Paris charity ride was a major undertaking and we all had to muck in to ensure we could complete the challenge.

The aim was to raise money for UK Youth and the trip was just about the hardest thing I've ever had to do, cycling 1320 miles in 11 days just nine days after breaking my collarbone. I was lucky to be supported throughout by some fantastic riders and crew too numerous to mention.

My last motorsport race: the 2010 Le Mans. After a crash during the race, I decided it was time to call it a day.

However, I am still involved in the sport as an FIA steward. Here I am back at Silverstone with Martin Sorrell, Bernie Ecclestone and Jean Todt.

With my family after receiving my CBE from Prince Charles at Buckingham Palace in February 2012.

We had to do a lot of work to restore the home of the Mansell Collection to its former glory.

The Mansell Collection we have on display in Jersey, above our Mitsubishi franchise, is packed with fond memories from my career.

procedure. It was touch-and-go for about six days. The aston-ishing thing for me was that, when she woke up and started her recovery from this operation, she was a different personality in some ways. Specifically with regard to our two boys going racing. Everything changed. All of a sudden, from being told for years and years the boys will never go racing, she completely flipped that upside down and said, 'We should support them in whatever they want to do. It is their lives and who are we to dictate what they should and shouldn't do?' The close escape she'd endured had altered the way she looked at certain things in life. At times, it's been like dealing with a totally different psyche in my wife. However, I totally understand and accept that; I think it is a normal and natural reaction. If you are not careful, and I include myself in this, being around serious illness ends up changing your psyche completely.

Of course, Rosanne's health impacted massively on the chil-dren, too. We tried to play down the full extent of her situation as much as we could. My youngest lad, Greg, couldn't handle it, not surprisingly at that age, so we shipped him back to Woodbury where he stayed in a lodge and we put him to work with the greenkeepers. We did a deal with him: we said, 'If you work really hard with the greenkeepers, you can start going racing.' He just couldn't handle seeing how poorly his mom was, day after day. The children had their own lives and we were very conscious of not overburdening them. You can choose to sit them down and explain what is going on, but it would have been a massive worry and also hard for them to understand. In that sense, I don't think you should reveal all to them about what you as a wife, husband and parent are going through.

Writing this book has been a very emotional experience in many ways for me. With regard to Rosanne, I have never really sat back and reflected on what happened, how it affected her, affected me, the family, the repercussions at the time and those we are still feeling to this day. Due to the process of working on this book, we have both talked about those events and we are very proud to feel that we have turned a negative into a positive.

We have bounced back. Again.

You have to. What I really want to come out of this book with regard to Rosanne's journey is that you *can* beat illness. You *can* come through the other side and move on. You *have* to bounce back. At times during that eight-year period it was very hard to imagine a light at the end of the tunnel. However, you have to bounce back. *Let me say that again: you have to bounce back*. Whatever challenges you face, whether it is a family member, a friend, someone close to you, you can get through it, and our family is no different from any other family in that sense. Just because I am well known for driving fast cars is totally irrelevant. Serious illnesses do not discriminate. My family has had its ups and downs like any other family. I am very proud to say that, although it's been a long and very tough battle, we have finally bounced back from this one. Rosanne is back to her best and I am very thankful for that. She is a blessing to me. We have made it. Rosanne has made it.

After 16 years of working and building up Woodbury, we decided to sell the hotel and golf complex. I don't mind saying now that if it wasn't for the ferocity of Rosanne's complex health issues, I don't think I would've wished ever to sell that wonderful place.

As I mentioned, the children never knew quite how seriously ill their mom was, for the reasons I have stated. They had school life to contend with, socialising, growing up; they had their own lives, so we were conscious of shielding them from the severity of Rosanne's state of health. The boys were reaching an age where they could contribute up at the club and the youngest one, Greg, was doing a fantastic job greenkeeping. After a short period of time working there, he came to me one day and said he felt that he could cut the fairways in probably two-thirds of the time it was normally taking. There was a big team and so there were some efficiencies that we were able to implement. Greg also told me a few other ideas to make the club run more smoothly, so I was very impressed with his instinct and application. We had something of a revolution down at the club and Greg was absolutely a part of that. He did a great job.

Anyway, out of the blue we received an offer to buy the club. At first we were totally not interested, it was not for sale. Apart from the fact that Woodbury was very dear to our hearts, I was completely focused on Rosanne getting better. Then another offer came in, higher this time. We both started to wonder if we should consider it. The problem was, I was so worried about Rosanne that it was very hard for me to focus on anything else and selling a golf club, hotel and resort like Woodbury is not exactly a simple transaction.

When yet another revised offer for the club came in, I was confused, upset, uncertain – it was just such a massive development at a time when we had so many other things going on that were, let's face it, far more important. Eventually, we decided that we would consider this offer and possibly sell Woodbury. However, I did not want ever to regret the decision so, with the legacy of the club in mind, I spoke to all my three children individually and said, 'Look, the business has really grown at Woodbury now, we have had this offer to buy it and we are considering it because your mother and I want to step back a little. So I want to ask, do you have any appetite to take over the business instead? Do you fancy coming in and putting some elbow grease into the business and one day taking over?'

Unilaterally, the answer was, 'Not on your life!' All three of them said, 'We have seen how hard you and Mom have worked and how many hours you have to put in, 24/7! And how much stress that can create.' People don't realise how hard those in the service industry work; it is literally non-stop. My children had seen it first-hand, to be fair, so they knew exactly what would be involved. They knew that we hadn't closed Woodbury for one single day in 16 years. So they politely said they did not wish to take it over. I went away for a week, then asked them again, 'Are you absolutely sure? I don't want you to come to me if I was to ever sell the place and say you wish I hadn't done that,' and, once more, they said, 'No, absolutely sure.'

While this conversation was going on, in the same week we had another offer. It was time to decide. Two weeks later I called a family meeting and said, 'Just so you know, I have sold the business.' The shock and horror on their faces was very surprising; they didn't believe me! I explained that because of their mom's health we had decided this was the right thing to do; that in fact it was quite a reluctant sale, but that I couldn't concentrate on the business and it was the right call to sell. The initial offer had, after all, come out of the blue and to me that felt like destiny was again changing the path of our lives.

I have to say now that, all these years later, Woodbury still has a very special place in my heart. The golf course especially perhaps, the memories, the people we had play there, Greg Norman, Gary Player, Frank Nobilo, Sandy Lyle, the senior PGA tour, the qualifying school there, running the events we did. It wasn't just the golf, though; there were such fabulous, wonderful people down there, all the golf unions, the associations, the members, the families of the members, the children of the members, Sir John the president, all the golf professionals we employed, all great people. We had mostly exemplary staff and some of them are still there now. We go back very occasionally and, of course, it is not the same, but we know we built every brick on that site. I am smiling as I write about the club, even now! I am so, *so* proud of Woodbury Park and in my mind it felt like winning a third World Championship. That is how very special that place is to me.

CHAPTER 21

THE POLICE

As a kid, I wanted to be an astronaut, a fighter pilot, a fire-man and a policeman. Oh, and a racing driver. Luckily for me, I have been able to do elements of quite a few of those jobs. I've not yet been into space and I'm not sure my back would pass the medicals, although I guess you could say I'm used to work-ing with G-force! I haven't been a fighter pilot, just to clear that up, but I have been blessed to fly jets for over 30 years, including my own planes, as well as helicopters. I've not put out any fires other than a few excitable barbecues, and some of you may recall I won a few events in a race car. So that only leaves the police and I am very proud indeed to say that since the early 1980s I served as a special constable. I just always wanted to help in the police; I liked the idea of working for the benefit of the commu-nity, the work seemed really exciting and challenging, and I was very drawn to it. After I retired from racing I was keen to carry on this work. I loved it. I was a special officer of the law in England for a considerable number of years, and in fact I am very proud to say I've got my long-service medal. I have worked with the police in England, America and Australia.

In the earlier years of my police work, I was already a racing driver, so, perhaps understandably, a few of the regular officers thought it was just some sort of gimmick. As a result, I was often put on the so-called 'graveyard shift', during turfing-out time at the pubs and clubs, the less glamorous side of police work, shall we say. I had to earn my stripes, which I eventually did chasing after someone over garden walls and fences early one morning. I was at the height of my racing training at the time, which was a blessing because I was able to catch up with this individual and tackle him, despite him trying to hit me with some four-by-two. In the end, I was able to disarm and apprehend him, which helped my colleagues take me more seriously. I would often go out on patrol on the shifts that no one else wanted, for example, Christmas Eve, Boxing Day or New Year's Eve. When the children were really young and used to go to bed early, I would do the night shift till two, three or four o'clock in the morning. It wasn't fun sometimes; it could get ugly. I have dealt with motor-vehicle deaths; I have carried dead bodies out of houses at midnight and had to put them in the back of ambulances. I've done my fair share. Knowing what I know, I have to say the police do the most incredible job under very difficult circumstances and must be applauded and commended unreservedly. They are amazing individuals.

I had a very serious incident one time when I wasn't actually on duty, but when I felt my training as a policeman helped me contribute to a very sad moment. It's also another example of that feeling I had the night before Elio was killed at Paul Ricard. One night, Rosanne and I were coming back from a function and there was quite a big hill approaching. I just looked up the incline and something caught my eye in the distance. I had a really eerie feeling and just knew something wasn't right. I was only doing about 50mph when a car came past me quite quickly from behind, so I just slowed down. I felt really uncomfortable. I sensed something very bad was going to happen. I didn't know what but there was just this overwhelming feeling of dread again, like that night at Paul Ricard.

We came over the brow of the hill to find absolute carnage in front of us on the road. A car that had been coming towards us down the hill was upside down on its roof, with the headlights still on. It looked like it had been in a head-on collision with the car that had overtaken us. As I was a serving police officer at the time, I got out and walked towards the upside-down car. As I passed the car that overtook us, I could see that the driver was dead. I walked over to the upturned car and found that the driver was trapped by his seatbelt; it was almost strangling him, he couldn't breathe. Other drivers had stopped to help, too. I managed to find a knife from somewhere, got inside the wreckage and slashed away at the trapped man's belt to free him. The cabin was cramped, smelt of petrol and there was glass everywhere. He was badly injured and clearly very shaken up. Eventually, I managed to help free him.

Then I heard footsteps on the road, so I just shouted into the darkness, 'Whoever is walking up the road, stop now! There has been an accident – there are petrol and fumes everywhere. If you have got steel tips or anything steel on the bottom of your shoes, stop, do not walk, one spark and we'll all go up!'

The police were on the scene very quickly and were brilliant; the fire brigade too. One of the firemen came over to me and said, 'Nigel, are you okay?' I said I was fine, but he pressed me, 'Are you sure? I think you'd better come with me . . .'

He walked me into the headlights of the fire engine and that's when I noticed I was completely covered in blood. There were lacerations all over me; bits of glass were stuck into my skin and clothing, I had petrol on me, I was a complete mess. They hosed me down and then explained that, because there was blood on site and I was cut, there was a risk of AIDS and other diseases. That was quite chilling but it shows you the kind of risks that these amazing police and firemen are exposed to every day. That was a terrible realisation. I was washed down in front of the fire engine and they helped me with bandages, antiseptic, and cleaned me up.

Eventually, we were allowed to go home and I was very glad to get through the front door. As you know, I don't drink, but that night I had a very stiff double brandy. The realisation of what had happened hit me really hard. There was a loss of life. I was numb for about a week.

Another time, in the USA, I had a similar feeling again at a set of traffic lights, so I moved my car out of instinct and I narrowly avoided being shunted from behind at high speed by a drunk driver. Now, some people would say that these three examples are all just coincidence. That is their point of view. Others might suggest that, given my years of experience with police drivers – I've been on courses where they train you to anticipate accidents, events, avoid situations, look ahead for danger – all I am actually doing is exercising this knowledge. That could also be true. Road awareness, anticipation, thinking ahead, yes, all of those things could be true. That's their opinion. My feeling is there could be something deeper than that. What do you think?

There are also many lighter moments from my police work – please don't think it's all sadness and problems. One night, we were on the late shift when we were called out to some trouble at this really rough local pub, which was turning out all the drunks and revellers. When we got there, we could see this one guy really being picked on – there were five men laying into him; he was totally outnumbered and getting a real pasting. There's an unwritten rule that 'you run to a fire, walk to a fight' – the theory being that, if you walk to a fight, by the time you get there the warring parties will hopefully have already worn themselves out. We watched this ruck going on for a couple of moments, to decide a plan of action, and were just about to wade in when this guy managed to break free and run off, towards our police car.

Just in front of our car there was a low-level chain-link fence, those old-school ones that were set between concrete posts. This guy ran up and jumped over it, but the five blokes who were chasing after him didn't see the fence. They sprinted after him and ran straight into the chain, which tripped all of them over at once, Laurel and Hardy style, right in front of our patrol car. We burst out laughing, I don't mind admitting; it was so comical, pure slapstick. The guy who'd been on the receiving end of the beating saw this happen and, to our amazement, turned back and started to lay into them on the floor. Now we were really stuck, because in theory we were supposed to get out and stop him, even though it was one against five! That was such a funny night.

It's interesting, working with the police, how you view incidents when you are on the other side of a situation. Shortly after winning the World Championship in IndyCar, I was flying late at night, ahead of shooting a safety commercial for the US police the next morning, aimed at improving road safety. I've done loads of seatbelt infomercials; we did anti-drink-driving campaigns, anti-drug-driving ones, all for free. I knew it was a really positive way to use my profile as a racing driver to try to help the community and make the roads safer. Although it often placed a lot of extra time demands on my already hectic schedule, I always really enjoyed it.

Anyway, this one particular time I was driving myself up from the airport with one of the TV team, and he was briefing me on the next day's shoot as we went along. It was very early in the morning; there were no cars on the road, four lanes empty of traffic, and we were catching every green light. Anyway, because I was listening intently to the briefing and maybe wasn't paying enough attention to the road, I ended up going far too quickly, I'm afraid to admit. By way of a feeble defence, I had just been testing for three days at over 230mph, so although I was doing about 100mph, it felt more like 20mph to me (I said it was feeble).

I was concentrating so hard on the briefing that at first I didn't even notice a sheriff car chasing behind me. Eventually, the sheriff put his lights on and I pulled over. He wasn't very happy with me. Not at all. He got out of his car with his gun out, the whole nine yards.

'Hands on the steering wheel!'

Oh, great! I'm going to get arrested for speeding a few hours before I am supposed to be filming an advert about road safety ... This is so embarrassing!

He really went ballistic at me, castigating me for my excessive speed, for not stopping straight away, not paying enough attention – he really tore a few strips off me. Then he asked me for ID, which I didn't have on me, itself an offence in America.

'I am genuinely sorry, officer, I wasn't concentrating enough. I apologise for my speed. Ironically, this is actually kind of funny ...'

He wasn't laughing ...

'... but I am filming an advert tomorrow about road safety and I was being briefed in the car and that's why I wasn't paying enough attention.'

'That is just about the most ridiculous thing I've ever heard,' the officer snapped. 'Do you really expect me to believe that?' He was getting visibly more and more irate. 'Who the hell are you to make up an effing story like that?! So, if you are so clever, who is it that can validate your story? Go on, who?'

I had no choice.

'Er, your chief of police.'

He looked shocked, went back to his car, made a phone call and then came back. Although he obviously wasn't going to be my best friend anytime soon, he gave me a ticking-off again and then sent me on my way.

I didn't mention this incident in the road safety film.

Another time, not long before I started writing this book, in fact, I was driving too quickly from a golf game with my good friend Jimmy Slattery, who is the pro at the Belleair Country Club, near to where I live in Clearwater. We were on our way home on a highway that was completely empty. There was no one in front of us at all and on the other side there was a car in the distance heading in the opposite direction. I admit I was maybe going very slightly faster than allowed (I sound like a speeding driver – I'm not, honest! Just twice in 45 years, if you don't include doing 200mph chasing after the likes of Ayrton Senna, of course).

Anyway, when this car got near to us, it suddenly made a sharp turn, headed across the central reservation, joined the carriageway we were on and started following us. I thought at first he'd had a blow-out, such was the suddenness of his turn. Then, a moment later, he put his sirens and flashing lights on and that's when I realised it was a police car. I thought, *Wow, he's obviously just had an emergency call in the opposite direction. That was some manoeuvre – he's going to fly by in a second, better keep out of the way . . .*

Only he didn't fly by, he just sat there behind us. I was

puzzled and drove along a bit further, for about two miles. Eventually, Jimmy said, 'Er, Nigel . . .'

'Yes, Jimmy?'

'You don't think that maybe the police car is still behind us for a reason, do you, Nigel?'

'Why?'

'Because he's been following us with his lights on for two friggin' miles!'

I pulled over and the patrolman was not happy. He asked for ID, which again I didn't have, and, like his colleague before, he was most displeased. I think I am right in saying that in America they can, in theory, lock you up and impound the car until you prove who you are (note to self: put ID in your wallet next time you go out in the car). He really did a number on us, shouting at me and Jimmy about this. Jimmy did have ID so the policeman said he should have been driving instead. Then he went back to his car to check out our vehicle details and get some paperwork.

While he was rooting around in his car, I got out of mine, walked around to the passenger seat and swapped places with Jimmy. Then the officer came back, didn't look at Jimmy who was now in the driver's seat and just continued to talk. Then he peered out from under his hat and the look on his face was a picture. 'Who the hell are you?' he said to Jimmy.

'We just took your advice, officer,' I said really politely and in my best English accent. 'You said I shouldn't be driving, so now I'm not.'

He didn't know what to do. He'd checked up on me and found out that not only was I the former IndyCar world champion, but I was also volunteering a lot of my time to his police force, helping out where I could and so on. He was still not happy but he did let me off with a warning, as I had been only very slightly over the speed limit. In fact, in the end he was pretty polite (he even shook our hands), but he did remind me of the speed limits in no uncertain terms. He was a great officer of the law; it was nice to meet him but just a shame about the circumstances!

I served as a special constable from the early 1980s, so that includes the times when I was fighting it out on the track with Senna, Prost et al. That might seem a bit odd to some people, but I have always found the work hugely rewarding. That said, can you imagine Lewis or Sebastian out on the beat anytime soon?

CHAPTER 22

LE MANS

As I alluded to earlier, when Rosanne was very ill, Greg opened up to us and said he really wanted to go racing. He was so intent and said all he ever thought about was racing. We were taken aback. We had never heard this from him before; he had kept it all to himself. That's when Rosanne said, 'Who are we to stop him having a go?'

I arranged with an old friend of ours who was still in the karting business for Greg to have a test in a kart. We thought he would hate it and that would be the end of that (just like my parents had!). However, of course he didn't; he absolutely loved it. So then he started working his way through the karting circuit, as did Leo, and we obviously supported them as much as we could.

They progressed through the karting races and moved into single-seater racing around 2006. It was a wonderful experience for them both but, looking back, it was perhaps doomed to failure before it started, because they were seen by many people as just having a big budget. So really, neither of them, in my opinion, were given what I would call a proper fair chance.

We had an interesting year with the Formula BMW UK series and it was an enjoyable experience, but then the intricacies of racing, even at the lower levels, were always in play. Some teams were able to manipulate the regulations better than others and that could be very frustrating. In motorsport, you always have to know your way around a rule book. After their time with BMW, they progressed to Formula 3 and had a little bit of success there. But it was a very steep learning curve by then; plus it cost an extraordinary amount of money. They also went into Formula Renault and Leo also went on to enjoy success in sports cars.

Leo is 30 now and he recently confided in me that, if he had been as mature then as he is today, he understands things might have turned out differently, as he was an outstanding young golfer. I think that is fantastically rounded of him to realise that and then to be brave enough to admit it to me. I admire him for that. You can't turn the clock back, of course, but it is brilliant that he is able to see it, and he will learn and become a better person because of it. In hindsight, I think perhaps we made elements of the racing too easy for them. We were just trying to help them out. We spent too many years and far too much money chasing other people's dreams for them when they themselves weren't chasing them as hard as they should've been. Every single parent in the world can be guilty of that.

It is very hard to watch your children go racing. As a former racer, you are acutely aware of the risks. What I do know is that when they decided to retire from motorsport I was hugely relieved. My younger son Greg had done some serious professional cycling these days and he has been in races where people have actually been killed, so I am not altogether comfortable with that either, but each to their own.

*

In June 2010 I had a high-speed crash at Le Mans that finished me with motorsport. I was there racing with Leo and Greg for Beechdean Motorsport. I was flat out down the straight after Mulsanne Corner when a tyre blew on the rear of the car. I vividly remember the explosion and the sensation of the car lifting up at the back before turning completely sideways. I looked down the straight then I looked where the nose of the car was pointing – perpendicular to the straight – and for the very first time in my life I thought, *I am dead. This is it.*

If you have ever had an accident in a car, you will know that, even at 30mph or so, they are over in a split second. So you might imagine that, at over 235mph, everything is even faster and in theory that is true. Yet on that day at Le Mans, it was all played out in very surreal slow motion; it took quite a while for the accident to complete. I distinctly recall having the time to think where the car was, what might happen next, what my chances of survival were – it was all very deliberate, almost pedestrian. It was also in total, eerie silence. The overwhelming sensation was, *Oh my word, this is it.*

What actually happened was the tyre blew, the first impact on the right-hand barrier was at around 200mph, then the car pinged off that and went backwards across the road and had a second impact into the barriers on the other side of the track. When I was pointing sideways the car had dug in, and then started to grip, and I was thinking – I actually had time to calculate – *If this car takes off, are those barriers high enough to contain me?* I was looking at all the trees in the forest and thinking, almost calmly, *If I jump these barriers and cartwheel into there, then I am dead.* I had all those thoughts, but there was no fear involved at that point in time; it was just a realisation that my life was highly likely to be over.

In that window of warped time, which was a matter of a few

seconds but felt like a lifetime, all that I had done, my achievements, my career, my family, my friends, everything did flash before me and I thought, again quite calmly, *So, it's all come down to this, a stupid effing tyre blowing out, throwing me off the circuit and that's it, I'm gone.* I distinctly remember momentarily chastising myself, thinking, *Where's the skill in that? This is just stupid.* I even had the time to rationalise and say to myself, *Well, at least it's happened to me and not to one of my lads. So if I die, I die hugely proud of them and I know they will go on to be even more amazing individuals.* I felt this strange acceptance that this was my end game.

I remember the first impacts vividly, but the final impact, when the car slammed laterally into the barrier, just switched my lights off. The sheer force of the car whipping around twisted my neck and just switched me off. Then the car slid along the barrier and came to a standstill.

When I started to come around, I didn't have a clue where I was. I had some vision, albeit blurred, but I recall the sensation of not being able to move my legs or arms. Apart from that, I barely remember anything at all.

And I didn't know who I was.

When I saw Rosanne and the boys, I didn't know who they were, either.

It was like a complete out-of-body experience. I was there but I didn't know what I was doing or what was going on; it was really bad news. The emergency teams were there quickly to help me, but I don't have any recall of the specific events of the rest of that day, or indeed for several days afterwards. It's just a vague, random selection of hazy moments. I was 57 years old when I crashed at Le Mans. One thing was for certain: my racing career was finished. I was just very lucky that my life wasn't over too.

Although the aftermath was very unpleasant, it is a fact that I was exceptionally lucky on a number of levels. Other cars didn't smash into me, for example. Most obviously, because I pinged across the track it wasn't one massive impact; if it had been, at the 200mph mark, I am pretty sure it would have killed me.

A part of me was angry that I had put myself in harm's way. I'd found out first-hand why Colin Chapman paid me *not* to race Le Mans during my time at Lotus. The diversity in the pit lane from the fast cars to the slow cars can be just enormous, so you can have closing speeds with a difference well in excess of 100mph. You can have semi-pro drivers who make a very small mistake that ends up being a monumental life-threatening mistake. It can be a very dangerous race indeed. Colin, you knew what you were talking about all those years ago.

At Le Mans, the risk was considerable. I have to say, I was very disappointed that the tyre blew but you are often wise after the event. I was older, obviously not as robust as I used to be. Further, to try to compete at the level we were – LMP1, which is a seven-figure race – was totally unsustainable. It cost a fortune to do that one Le Mans. I like to compete but the truth is in reality, in my opinion, in 2010, that was unlikely and we paid very dearly, in more ways than one.

I must speak in defence of Le Mans, though, because although I had a traumatic time there, it really is a great event. Endurance racing is very special. The car has to sustain the hours and hours going round the circuit without things breaking; pit stops can cost you a lap or so; strategy is enormous; the drivers are supremely talented – it is really quite something. Reliability becomes almost the single most important element of the car. The gearbox, the engine, all the electronics have to be heavily tested and reliable; if you are running for 24 hours, the demands that places on the car over and above a Formula 1 car, which only has to last two hours, are ridiculous. Endurance car technology is fascinating, because the vehicles are built to be quick to repair, so have quick-release wings, easy-to-change wheel arches and so on. There are other issues that come with operating a high-performance car for hours. For example, they have vanes on top for cooling purposes, because the car is under such strain for so long that if your cooling isn't spot on then your race is run before it's started. It's extremely complex. This all makes for a unique racing experience. I believe there is a magic at Le Mans; it is an incredible race and not to be pooh-poohed, not to be understated. For me, despite the crash, the short time I had there was wonderful.

After Le Mans, my two boys carried on racing for a while and, in fact, during that same year they won a prestigious six-hour endurance race together in Hungary, which was a fantastic achievement and I was thrilled for them. Although they are now retired from motor racing, they are both members of the BRDC, which is a fine achievement. They should be very proud of that. I hope their experiences on and around the tracks have made them better individuals, as well as given them memories that money can't buy and that not many people in the world will ever have.

In the aftermath of the Le Mans crash, I reproached myself for doing the race. I also realised that I thought I had been doing it for the benefit of my two boys but in fact I wasn't benefiting them at all. Other than the experience of racing at Le Mans it was a pretty fruitless exercise. And how would it have benefited my two boys, Chloe, Rosanne, and my beautiful grandchildren if I'd come home in a box? In my opinion, going to race there was a very bad error of judgement. One that very nearly cost me my life. I am still here but it was a very close call.

To be fair, we were very unlucky that day. I was very unlucky that the tyre blew at the fastest point in the straight; I was unlucky that the blow-out turned the car sideways and caused me to have a massive accident. If the car had stayed in a straight line then I could've come into the pits, changed the tyres and carried on. However, destiny and Lady Luck were definitely not on my side that time.

I have been told now a number of times by different specialists that, if I have another major bang on the head, that's the end of me. I know that anyway, I have a sixth sense; it is a case of admitting it and knowing my own limitations. If nothing else, Le Mans taught me it was time to hang up the helmet and overalls once and for all.

CHAPTER 23

SAVED BY MAGIC

After the big Le Mans crash, I flew home the next day. It appeared that I had concussion, so they only reluctantly released me and on the condition that I flew home low level and with an accompanying doctor, my good friend Mike. There was very little the hospital could do after they'd checked me over. The paralysis had been temporary, possibly an instant shock after the impact, so it was really just the concussion. I was told to go home and spend as much time as possible recuperating in a quiet, dark room. After suffering a concussion, you have to be very careful because although much, if not all, of your body seems to be working absolutely fine, the reality is your brain has had a trauma and, if you aren't very cautious, this can cause big problems. Fernando Alonso missed the first race of the 2015 season because he was recovering from concussion, and it is very sensible that the team were protective of him in that way.

I think, in the aftermath of my Le Mans crash, it didn't help that I'd had so many previous accidents and several big concussions. I didn't realise until relatively recently the extent to which bruising on the brain can cause damage, or the length of time it takes for the brain to recover properly.

Unfortunately, although I felt reasonably okay the week following Le Mans, it soon became apparent that all was not well. When I tried to speak, my words came out as gobbledegook. At first, I put this down to the shock and thought it would quickly pass. But it didn't. We later found out that I'd had severe bruising on the brain, and this had a devastating effect on my ability to communicate, my ability to speak. The first time I ventured out of the house after Le Mans was acutely embarrassing: I bumped into a few people I knew, but when I spoke to them the words were just garbage. As I said, I was talking gobbledegook. I was mortified, it was really embarrassing. We actually kept it quiet for obvious reasons; you don't want people to think you have turned into a vegetable. Only our very dearest friends knew; we didn't tell most of our wider social circle. If people said they hadn't seen me for a while, Rosanne simply told them I'd been busy working or made other excuses.

After that first humiliating time when I'd ventured out and had difficulty speaking, I decided to stay in the house because that way I couldn't embarrass myself. It's one thing when you are with your family in private and you have the confidence to try to engage and speak correctly, but another altogether when you are out and people talk to you – you are hearing them, but when you reply and your words are slurred, they look at you strangely because they can't understand what you are saying. You just crash and burn. Plus the concentration needed to speak clearly was exhausting. So you just go home and think, *I am not doing that again.*

So I stayed in my room in the dark for some weeks and effectively became housebound. Over the weeks, the speech improved only slightly and certainly not enough for me to work up the courage to venture out again. I had a lengthy phase during which I wouldn't go out; and even if people were in the house visiting I wouldn't engage with them because I knew my words wouldn't come out properly. It was a horrible time. The headaches were vicious, too, really painful. In the immediate term, I didn't go out of the front door for some time.

Very gradually my speech started to improve, but remained far from back to normal. Rosanne was concerned that I was essentially becoming a recluse, so she was keen to try to coax me out of the house. At first I kicked against this; I was very self-conscious and still felt fragile. I knew she was right and that I couldn't stay indoors for the rest of my life, but it was a very intimidating thought, going out. In my moments of clarity, though, I knew I had to challenge my brain to start operating properly again. Agreeing to go out with Rosanne one night, to be with a few friends over dinner, is one of the most intimidating things I have ever done. But thank goodness I did, because that is how I found magic and it changed my life.

Magic has literally been my saviour. You might wonder what on earth card tricks and magic have got to do with brain injury, but bear with me on this. Like I said, Rosanne urged, 'Nigel, you have got to try to go out – you have just got to have a go . . .' She pushed and pushed and eventually I gave in and agreed to go to a very good friend's house for a small celebration party they were having. I was incredibly nervous on the night of the party, but we went. When we got there, they had a magician going round entertaining the guests, and this immediately put me at ease because it meant I could watch the magic and not have to make lots of conversation with people.

The magician was a very flamboyant individual called Maximilian Somerset, complete with a pristine black top hat, and he was doing the most amazing tricks. I am very inquisitive by nature, so I was trying to work out how he was doing these tricks. He then performed some really close-up card tricks that were just fantastic. I tried to talk to him slowly and it was a little jumbled, but fortunately Max was extremely patient and made me feel very comfortable.

I said, 'Will you show me how you did that?'

Obviously, as all professional magicians should, he declined and politely explained that, as a member of the Magic Circle, it was forbidden for him to reveal the secrets of his trade. 'I can tell you if you are a member of the Magic Circle,' he said.

'Well, how do I become a member of that, then?'

'By being invited.'

'And why would I be invited if I don't know any tricks?'

'You won't be!'

It was a catch-22. I was very frustrated because something about the magic tricks really struck a chord within me, not least because it made me temporarily forget my fears of being out of the house. So I took a gamble and decided to tell Max what had happened to me and what I had been going through. I took him to one side and explained about the crash, about my speech problems, and I said I needed something to focus on to help my recovery and was wondering if magic might give me that purpose. 'I need help to function as a normal human being – will you please help me?'

Max is a fabulous magician and a fantastic man, so he listened carefully and I could see he was beginning to understand my difficulty. To my delight, he then agreed to help me. 'Magic will help you recover, Nigel, because to be a great magician you have to work your brain at times in completely the opposite way to a normal person. It is often counterintuitive. Plus the motor skills you will need for card tricks and other magic will really stretch your brain and make you relearn how to think. You will definitely use different parts of the brain. I would like to help.'

First, Max had to go to the president of the Magic Circle and explain my medical difficulty, hoping to get permission to show me some tricks to aid my recovery. Fantastically, the Magic Circle understood my plight and granted that permission, which meant I was able to start working with Max. He was brilliant. He would come to the house and show me tricks, teach me things and set me challenges that I had to practise. For much of the time, he would show me a trick and then leave me to practise. This suited me perfectly because I was still not confident about going out, so here was a recovery strategy that didn't involve me having to leave the front door.

I absolutely threw myself into learning magic. I spent hours and hours learning to shuffle cards in particular ways, counting cards while they were in my hand, dealing them in certain ways. I practised non-stop; I was pretty much obsessed. I've since been told I did three years of practice in 12 months. The regenerative effect it had on my speech was remarkable. Each time I felt better, I would try to go out and, if my speech was okay in public, that would reinforce my confidence, and thus a self-perpetuating cycle of recovery had begun. All because of magic.

The icing on the cake came when I was invited to join the Magic Circle. At first, I was a little apprehensive because I wasn't sure I was good enough, but they reassured me I was and so I accepted the great honour of becoming a member. I had some incredible mentors within the Magic Circle, who befriended me and got me to a level of proficiency where I was good enough to be invited, which was obviously fantastic. I am very proud of that achievement indeed, but above all I am grateful to magic and the people within that world who have helped me out of a very dark place.

I have since done my own magic shows and now have material that could last two hours, but I limit the performance to 30 minutes or so. I've really enjoyed these performances and have had some great shows in America. When I do a magic show, if there are motorsport fans in the room who recognise me, I enjoy the look on their faces very much. They obviously know me as a racing driver so it's fun to see them watch me as a magician.

I still adore magic and practise it all the time. Once my recovery from the Le Mans injuries was complete, I also found a phenomenal new benefit of magic. In my work with UK Youth, I obviously meet some young people who have had very challenging lives. Very often, they will sit round a table and simply not engage at all with any adults, or indeed with the other young people. My profile is irrelevant to them. They don't really want to know who I am; they don't actually care that I've won this race or done that or whatever; they have got their own challenges and problems to face. So it can be really hard to make a breakthrough.

However, I found that when I was having a hard time chatting with a particular group of young people, if I got out a deck of cards and did a few tricks, they would suddenly engage. They'd pick a card, then laugh or look shocked when I showed them their card out of nowhere. *They engaged.* Then they'd quite often start to talk and the ice would be broken. At that point the most important thing to do is *listen* and sometimes that young person, who hasn't said a word all day, will suddenly talk about their lives for 20, 30 minutes. In those cases, the tricks and little stunts *literally* are magic.

As a deliberate recuperative plan, learning magic was exceptional for me. It led to a total transformation from being housebound and unable to talk, to putting on my own magic shows within 24 months in front of random members of the public. I would love to tell you all about the specific tricks that really helped me get better ... but I'm not allowed.

CHAPTER 24

ON YOUR BIKE

Being a racing driver is a dangerous job. Even with today's fabulous safety standards there is still enormous risk on any racetrack. Yet I've nearly killed myself twice on bikes! A major part of my life since retirement from Formula 1 has been my involvement in two epic bike rides and a professional cycling team. Over many years, this has provided me with a lot of fun, a lot of work and the single most difficult sporting challenge I have ever faced, including my entire motor-racing career.

Initially, the impetus to get involved in cycling on an elite level came through my involvement with UK Youth. I am extremely proud to be president of UK Youth, a fantastic charity that I hold very dear to my heart. UK Youth supports and helps disadvantaged young people with the largest network of youth clubs and projects. UK Youth actually started way back in 1911; in the 1980s it was spearheaded by Princess Anne, who is an absolutely wonderful person and an incredible representative of the royal family.

I first became involved when I was a racing driver and then, after I retired, I began to donate more and more of my time, such that by 2000 I was asked to become president. What an honour! I was so privileged to be asked, although I have to admit that following the Duke of Westminster in the role made me feel somewhat intimidated. How do you follow someone like that?! (For the record, I am also president of the IAM (Institute of Advanced Motorists) and co-patron of the Road Safety Awards of Great Britain and the Commonwealth with His Royal Highness Prince Michael, which are roles that are also very dear to my heart.)

At the time I took over the presidency, the charity did an amazing job of reaching around half a million children who needed help and support. That has now risen to upwards of one million in some years. This has been achieved through an enormous amount of incredible hard work on the part of upwards of 45,000 volunteers each year, as well as the staff at the charity. It is a tremendous honour to be part of such an incredibly profound charity and to help so many young people. I am hugely proud to hold that role.

One day we were all brainstorming ideas and thinking of ways we could get the message out. My two lads were very much into cycling so we decided to start our own cycling team, beginning in 2009. That professional cycling team was simply called UK Youth, designed to raise awareness of the charity. I was the major sponsor personally and it was a very good outfit. We won a lot of races across the country and enjoyed great success for four years.

I am very proud of all the riders in that pro cycling team and it was a magnificent achievement when they won the highly coveted Tour Series Championship. In terms of putting UK Youth on the map, it was a great exercise; it definitely helped raise the profile. It was a lot of work – that sport is incredibly complex and people have no idea how hard the riders train and how demanding the competitions are. In fact, I will say this: I consider professional cycling to be *the* most brutal sport in the world. It really is. What those guys put themselves through for six, seven, eight hours a day, day after day, at the very highest level, is just astounding. Brutal, there's no other word. Greg was involved as a rider and I was very proud of his part in the team.

To run a professional bike team is not a cheap option; it costs a seven-figure sum each year. Sponsors can help but we were let down by some companies who promised a lot but delivered very little. So we were left holding the baby to a certain extent, and for a number of years we personally contributed very substantial sums of money to that team's subsistence. Relatively, if you put the same amount of money into motorsport it would be insignificant, of course, but in terms of the charity it was a very sizeable amount. I think having a well-known name can sometimes work against you, because a few potential sponsors definitely implied that we were comfortable enough financially and therefore didn't need their money. Of course that is nonsense – the charity and team needed a lot of funding. We really wanted to make the charity more visible and it cost a lot of money to do that. It was tough trying to get money out of sponsors and we did become rather disillusioned at times. It could be very disheartening.

When it came to the centenary of the charity in 2011, as a professional cycling team we decided that it would be amazing to stage an epic bike ride. Basically, we were all still on a mission to put UK Youth on the map, get more visibility for the charity. The idea was put forward to stage a charity ride around the country, the notion being that along the way we could call in at a large number of the 5500 or so youth clubs that the charity supports around the UK. The plan was to start in London, go around Wales, up the coast to Glasgow, then all down the east coast and finally drop back into London and finish at Number 10. It was in excess of 1300 miles in just 13 days. To give you some context, the pinnacle of cycling, the Tour de France, is 2200 miles in 21 day-long segments over a 23-day period. So this was a serious challenge.

Being a public charity, the idea wasn't something you could do easily. It wasn't simply a case of throwing yourself on a bike one morning and setting off. There was the team of riders, a physio, two motorbike outriders, the motorhome driver, representatives from the charity – all in all, it was quite a team. There were lots of expensive supplies too – special recovery drinks, pre-ride drinks, muscle recovery drinks, breakfast drinks, sleep drinks, you name it! Plus all the physio supplies, spare bike parts, fuel for the back-up crew, their lodgings, food, and so on and so on.

All of this back-up and logistics costs money. Obviously, the charity can't be seen to be spending many thousands of pounds on that rather than the main focus of its work, so the costs of an event like this have to be underwritten. To complete such a ride as this costs hundreds of thousands of pounds. It was a Mansell family decision to underwrite this whole amount and support the programme in its entirety.

I just felt very strongly that this was a great opportunity not only to raise the profile of the charity, but also to drop in at the youth clubs and centres and really try to inspire young people and give them a well-deserved lift. Some of our meeting points were my old stomping grounds at McLaren and the Williams F1 headquarters! At the end of a day's riding, it was wonderful to arrive at the youth clubs and see all these young people there, welcoming you and cheering you in. As tired as we were some days, we often wouldn't go to the hotel or get changed. We'd just roll up at the end of the ride after hours on the road; we'd be dirty, shattered, cold, wet, but we'd just put some coats on, go and meet the youngsters and play games, talk to them, sometimes do a presentation. It was absolutely fantastic, every single night we did that was brilliant.

We had a bit of a false start behind the scenes. However, when we took over total responsibility things started to run smoother, and this stuttering start just made me even more determined to push ahead and make the bike ride a huge success. We set off from Kensington Palace in London and were privileged that Prince Michael was there to drop the flag and send us on our merry way, with his best wishes. He is an unbelievable supporter of the charity. It was the most wonderfully exciting feeling, and when Prince Michael started us off no one jumped the flag and there were no start penalties incurred!

Have you ever been shot by a gun? Well, I was asleep in the motorhome after the first day's ride when I woke up absolutely screaming in agony. My leg felt like someone had come in and shot me with a gun. This was due to having the most severe cramp I've ever experienced in my life, and because of this something just snapped in my leg, which we later found out was the hamstring. At the time I just felt something totally rip and explode in my leg, it was actually a terrifying experience. The team physio examined me and confirmed I had torn my hamstring. On that second morning of the ride, my leg was black and blue from the internal bleeding caused by this hamstring tear. Everybody just looked at me and you could see they were thinking, *What on earth are you doing?* The physio told me it was a bad tear and that I should not start the ride. Needless to say, I carried on.

I didn't captain the ride and, in my opinion, there were a few things that didn't really go to plan. This one day, we were pushing very hard and going quickly and so I said, 'What the hell is going on, guys?' It turned out a mistake had been made in the logistics and we were going to arrive at our destination that night over two hours late. In that circumstance, I'd rather people say they have made a mistake and provide the information, and then resolve it all together as a team.

On the eighth day, my youngest lad came up to me and said, 'Dad, you look really terrible, you are gonna kill yourself. Get in the car and knock it on the head now. Follow us and we will carry on the riding.' All along the way, people had obviously been checking that I was okay, but this time there was more urgency to it than just being cared for and I said, 'Look, you indifferent person. I've gone through what I've gone through. I am gonna finish this!' And then Greg started to chuckle and said, 'Well, we've all lost then!'

'What are you talking about?'

'Well, we had a sweepstake on how many days you would last and because I know what you are like, I was the longest. I said you'd get to eight days ...'

Cheeky buggers!

When I found out about that sweepstake on the first ride, after all the laughs had died down, I was actually quite surprised – I felt that my team did not know how dogged my determination could be, because people had made plans for the day when I crashed and burned and couldn't continue. However, you do what has to be done. Little did I know, I was starting to kill myself.

We finally finished at Number 10 Downing Street, which was really special, and, to top it all off, shortly afterwards I was awarded the CBE and the Queen even acknowledged the bike ride we had done, which was a real honour. (The great thing about being awarded the CBE is that the Queen ordains that your family can have its own coat of arms. Wonderful.) I was really nervous on the day I went to get the award. Even with all the work I have done over the years with different members of the royal family and the high-powered government people I have met, those two days were the most nervous of my life because the honour meant so much to me. I was just so proud. I was very emotional too; I had to stop myself welling up. When I accepted the award, the investiture was with Prince Charles and I was elated because I think he is a wonderful royal. Prince Charles was absolutely marvellous! The royals are briefed on everybody who goes up, but it must be a huge undertaking to research all that detail and remember so much. He was wonderful; he clearly had done his research and was really kind to me. It was absolutely one of the proudest moments of my entire life.

That first epic bike ride was a fantastic achievement and we had created a lot of great publicity for the charity. Despite the gruelling nature of the event, in my mind I was already planning the next epic two-wheeled adventure.

Two years later, it was time to get back in the saddle as we decided to set out on an even more gruelling bike ride. I just felt like I really wanted to push the limits of what we could do. Lots of people ride from John O'Groats to Land's End and that is an amazing achievement, but the cycling team and everyone involved with the charity wanted to push past that and do something really special. So we decided to cycle from John O' Groats to Paris, a distance of 1320 miles, this time in just 11 days. The plan was set for three of us to start in the Highlands, head down to Blackpool and join up with some friends, make it to London and then join in with the pre-organised London–Paris event, which about 475 riders embark upon annually. By that point, we would already have covered about 1000 miles, so the hope was that the influx of cyclists and the excitement of joining that ride would re-energise us for the last section of the trip. So that's what we did.

I have to say this now: it would prove to be the hardest thing I have ever done in my life. By some way. That includes all of my most gruelling races. It includes my worst crashes and the recovery from my worst injuries. That bike ride to Paris was the single toughest endurance challenge I have ever faced in my life. Period.

The reality was that we had to cover 120 miles a day. That is an elite distance and, looking back, it is ludicrous that we even tried. When we were planning the event, I talked to a pro cyclist about what we were thinking of doing and he said, 'If you do a ride, it's got to be meaningful – you have got to step up to a totally different level, maybe even an elite level. You should be looking at over 100 miles a day, maybe 120.' We really wanted everyone to look at what we had done and think, *Wow, that is really impressive.*

For those of you who don't know cycling, 120 miles a day is a long way on a bike, a *very* long way. As you now know, I am a big one for preparation, so in the six months leading up to the ride I trained as hard as I ever did in Formula 1 – in fact, I would say even harder. I was extremely focused and also conscious of my injuries. People were saying it was a big ask, perhaps too big, to do 120 miles a day with the amount of broken bones and residual injuries I was carrying, but, of course, that just made me even more determined to complete the ride. For months, I went out on my bike for four or five hours a day, in all weather. I ate correctly, watched my diet, kept going over the route in minute detail and was constantly planning. It was months and months of training and preparation.

The training really did take over. I had a great friend called

Peter, who asked me to be his best man at his London wedding, which I was very proud to agree to. Then, quite late in the planning, his future wife's father became rather ill and couldn't travel. The problem was, the dad lived in New Zealand, so the wedding was moved to there! Having to fly to the other side of the world turned out to be the most wonderful trip and adventure, down in New Zealand and Australia. We said that, as we were flying to the other side of the world, we might as well extend our break and have a great holiday afterwards, so that's what we did.

I'd already started training, so I couldn't afford to take a three-week break. When we got to Christchurch, therefore, I went to a bike shop and bought one so that I could continue training every day. Then for the rest of the holiday I was doing four or five hours a day in the saddle while Rosanne followed me in the car. I'd do upwards of 100 miles a day. That took a long time and Rosanne was very patient; she'd have to go ten miles up the road then wait for me. She did this for three weeks.

During another training session, this time in La Manga, a friend of ours, who was due to come on the ride with us, had a horrific crash on his bike. One of my best friends in the world – who I have known for 50 years from way back in my karting days – almost killed himself. We were going down a hill when he had a puncture and hit a pylon, which then launched him almost over a cliff. He then somersaulted and landed at speed in a culvert. He badly damaged his hip and was in hospital, so that put paid to his chances of making the ride. That was really unlucky and ended his career in biking straight away.

Typically for me, though, I even made the training a health risk! Going out cycling on the roads in Jersey (or anywhere) can be dangerous. In the dark, especially so. When you are training and minding your own business, a lorry or car driver who is not paying attention can so easily maim or kill you in a flash, just a fleeting moment of recklessness or lack of concentration. A split second of being absent-minded can take someone's life.

There is an esplanade near where we live which is lit up, so going up and down there with no traffic, backwards and forwards on my bike, was very good. Ten days before heading off to start the ride at John O'Groats, I went on one last long training ride and during the final hour of all these months and months of training, it started to rain heavily. The traffic was bad; I felt quite exposed on the bike and I was very tired. So I decided to come off the roads because everyone was rushing to work and I felt a little vulnerable.

I decided to play it safe and went to a local cycle track. It was really pouring down with rain by now and I was having a conversation with myself about whether I needed to push the training right to the end of that last hour. I was determined to finish the programme, though. However, as I was going around the track I was saying to myself, *You've done enough – don't do anymore, just slow down.*

Then I went around this one corner and BANG! I lost the front wheel; it just went straight from under me and I slammed into the tarmac, smashing down on my side, with my shoulder taking the brunt of the impact. I was unconscious in the middle of the track for several minutes.

When I came round, there was a lovely woman standing over me asking, 'Are you all right? You came off your bike . . .' I was groaning and mumbling and as I came back to my senses I started to feel a searing pain in my shoulder. The woman told me to stay at the side of the track while she phoned an ambulance, but I said, 'Please don't phone an ambulance, I am fine . . .' She said, 'You are not fine! You've just had an accident and have been lying here unconscious!'

I noticed I had a big chunk out of my elbow, my clothing was ripped and torn, there were deep grazes and blood on numerous parts of my body, and my shoulder was absolutely killing me. I was so disappointed, angry, annoyed.

I repeated that I was okay, got up and picked up my bike. It was fine, hardly damaged, because when the front wheel slipped it just whipped out from under me and my shoulder hit the tarmac first, so that took all the impact. I wearily lifted my leg to get back on the bike and the woman said, 'What on earth are you doing?'

'I'm going home. I need to get back . . .'

'You are not going home – you are going to the doctor's.' She was really concerned for me, this complete stranger, what a lovely lady. I never did find out who she was and I'd like to know, because it was such a generous act of kindness.

I said I knew the doctor locally, who was a friend, and I could ride to his surgery. I got back on my bike and, unbeknown to me, she followed me there. I do recall starting off really slowly but, I have to be honest, I don't remember any of the rest of that journey.

It was only a short distance to the doctor's surgery. I don't even know what I did with my bike, but I do remember there was a surgery full of people. I felt really groggy by now, so I sat in the corner and it was all a bit of a blur. But I could hear my Good Samaritan saying, 'This guy's been knocked out. He's bleeding all over the place. You need to see him urgently, he is not well!' There I was, blood dripping down the chair, my legs and arms all ripped and my clothing torn – I looked a real state! Then I passed out.

Next thing I knew a doctor was with me. He took me into his surgery and spent a good deal of time dressing my wounds. Let me tell you, tarmac and skin don't go together! They put gauze on the cuts and bruising, but it was the shoulder that was of most concern so I was booked in for an X-ray. I don't know who collected me from the surgery to take me home, and I don't know how my bike got back home either.

With just nine days left now till the start of this 1320-mile charity bike ride that I had been training for over months and that we'd been planning for the longest time, the doctors told me I had broken my collarbone. Great! They couldn't operate because the break was too close to the shoulder, so they just put me in a sling and sent me home. Everyone in the camp was seriously concerned as to whether or not I'd be able to continue with the challenge. Actually, nothing could have been further from my mind; as long as I was breathing I was going to complete that ride.

The day finally came when we set off to the airfield to take the plane to John O'Groats. Bizarrely, on the day before, I stubbed my toe and it was agony. It turned black really quickly and a physio looked at it and confirmed it was broken. And this was all before I'd even got on a bike and done one mile! They just taped it up and I got on with it.

We lucked out because we had a light tailwind for the first day of the bike ride, so our average speed was over 20mph – we were flying, helped along by gallons of adrenaline and excitement. My shoulder was very painful, but adrenaline is a marvellous thing and the pain quickly numbed. The agony comes when you stop, so I didn't sleep very well that night and I was on loads of painkillers. You have to be very careful not to take too many of those pills, though, because not knowing exactly where you are on a bike going 30mph downhill can be very dangerous.

This time, I took full charge of the planning and logistics, which were far more controlled. Race-car drivers learn always to be honest with themselves, which is incredibly helpful when doing special planning and logistics. A lot of people kid themselves.

We built in fudge factors. If we did more miles one day then we had a cushion the next. We were so mindful of our safety that we had two ex-police outriders on motorbikes with us at all times, David and Roger, who were fantastic; patient, kind, funny. We had some laughs with them because they'd occasionally take us down the wrong road, which we'd rib them for, but they are splendid men who kept us safe and I am eternally grateful to them.

With just the three of us on those early stages we rode in single file, but crosswinds were a big problem. Once we had more riders later in the trip you could peel off the back and go to the front, slipstreaming, which really helped. The maximum we would ride without stopping was an hour and a half to two hours, then, regardless of whether or not we felt fresh, we stopped. We'd vary it from day to day depending on the terrain.

We had a great time during the first few days and then the weather hit, really cold temperatures, snow, black clouds, freezing rain and wind. One day, riding through Aviemore in the Cairngorms, even though it was the middle of summer it was snowing and freezing cold! Nobody wanted to get out of their lovely, warm motorhomes.

The great thing about endurance riding is you can have as much chocolate and as many iced buns as you want. I am not built to be a cyclist; I am too big, too heavy, too meaty. The serious cyclists are all flipping emaciated. Rosanne always looks at them and says, 'They need a good meal!' You are burning so many calories all the time, although, of course, it's important to eat the right stuff to get the correct nutrients in. However, every now and then you can eat what you want as a treat. You can have a few naughties and who the hell cares! I remember stopping during the run through Aviemore and we had some sticky buns. Oh, my goodness me, what a taste – the greatest taste that's ever passed my lips! Iced buns, woo-hoo!

Rosanne did the cooking and she was brilliant. She would be in the motorhome with the driver and they would go on ahead and find a place to stop safely. Then she'd set out some chairs and a table, go back in the motorhome and cook up mountains of pasta – it was like some kind of mobile *Ready, Steady, Cook*! Before long we'd come around the corner because we were riding so fast and relentlessly that we'd catch up pretty quickly. Then she'd feed us all and we'd get back in the saddle, while she'd be left behind to clear up all the mess, pack up the motorhome, zoom off ahead to the next stop-off point and do it all again. What a star. She was exhausted too!

One strange part of the ride was that while everybody else lost about a stone or more in weight, I was the only rider to put weight on! My whole body was in crisis all the time, so it was hanging on to everything, and it wasn't until two weeks after the ride that I finally started losing weight. My body was in such turmoil that it hoarded every bit of energy that I put into it. As soon as the ride was over and I went home to relative normality, my body quietened down and the weight dropped off me.

When we were dragging ourselves up Shap Fell in Cumbria, the rain was lashing into our faces; it was horizontal and cold. It cut into my skin; it felt so harsh. The side winds were over 50mph and as we came down the other side of the hill it felt genuinely dangerous. Quite hair-raising.

Some days I got on my bike early in the morning and my legs could barely turn the pedals. Until my body recovered and the lactic acid subsided, it was very gruelling. One day, I was so exhausted that I said to the group, 'We have got to have a rest,' so we pulled over on the kerb. I lay on the grass verge by the road with all these cars whizzing past and within less than a minute I was fast asleep, in the middle of the day, completely passed out on the side of the road! Obviously, the toll on your muscles and body is massive, but there are specifics to bike riding too; you get all sorts of bumps, boils and rashes in places that we won't talk about . . .

There were many times on that ride when the will to keep going had to be so strong, so resolute. We finally got down to London, which was 1000 miles or so into the route, leaving us with another 300-plus miles to go to Paris. On the penultimate day, there was a logistical cock-up that had a terrible effect on my already exhausted body. For a bike ride of that length, with that daily mileage, the team has to have a complex support system: there are physios around you all the time, people logging your performance and physical reaction; very particular dietary requirements that are planned to exact number of calories (apart from sticky buns); you get to your destination at the end of each day and have to have sports massages, etc. One of the most important techniques for recovery each night is a combination of hot and cold baths to both revitalise and soothe your muscles. The whole enterprise is very disciplined and precise; it's not just a case of jumping on a bike and heading off.

Well, this particular day we had joined up with the London–Paris ride and therefore our team were no longer in charge of the accommodation. Unfortunately, because of an error with the hotel booking my room only had a shower. That sounds relatively trivial but it meant I could not have the required hot and cold baths. I was completely exhausted when I got to my room and really just wanted to lie on the bed and fall asleep, but I figured the shower would suffice and I didn't want to make a fuss, so I had a hot shower. My legs didn't feel right, I could tell that, but I got out of the shower and on to the bed and fell asleep pretty much instantly. I'd also missed eating any food because I was so tired.

The next morning I had a hearty breakfast as I was very hungry, but when I got on the bike my body wouldn't function, it just wouldn't work properly. All of a sudden my body went, *I am going to pay you back!* The experience was like being a passenger in my own body. My will wanted to do something so much, but my body just would not allow it. I couldn't even walk properly; it was the most amazingly weird feeling. It felt like pedalling lumps of lead; it was one of the most horrible experiences of my life. My legs were just useless.

It wasn't until we had covered 90km that the leaden feeling went away and I could finally spin my legs to ride more freely and with less pain. I am aware that the physical difficulties I experienced were not helped – in fact, they were sorely exacerbated – by my numerous racing injuries. However, this was another level – this was complete exhaustion and I got really quite deflated on that day. I was very down. I couldn't see how I could get up and do another 180 miles or so to the finish line. In fact, I became so tired, so exhausted, so demoralised that I decided to make it to the next food break just after lunchtime then quit. I was done; I was toast. I was almost crying inside on the bike, I just felt so sick and ill. It was dreadful.

We stopped for a bite to eat and, as soon as I had a little bit of sustenance, a trickle of resolve started to come back into my head. As my legs rested and I had some fluids and more food, my competitor's brain began to think, *I am going to finish this ride even if it kills me!* The body and the mind in sport are an amazing thing, aren't they? If there'd been a film crew doing a fly-on-the-wall documentary at that point, it would've made an epic programme seeing someone totally seize up and age 20 years overnight, but actually still go through all the pain barriers and get the job done.

When we restarted I dropped down into a slightly slower group just to make sure that I got to the end of that day, which I am proud to say I did. However, in terms of sport, I think that particular day on the Paris ride was *the* single hardest thing I have ever done in my entire life. At times, I really thought I was going to keel over and die. I made it to the end of that awful day and I'm not reluctant to say that I made it known that unless I had a decent hotel with a bath the following night I'd pull out of the ride and go on with my own team to Paris. They were full of apologies because it was simply an oversight, but that could have derailed our incredible effort. We'd already spent ten days on the road doing the most fantastic event and that simple error could have proved catastrophic.

But we also had some fantastically funny moments. We got pulled over for infringements on the road by police several times. Another time, we pulled up at a set of traffic lights and, because we were all so tired, one of the team couldn't get the cleats out of his bike's pedals so he tipped over, bumping into the bike next to him, who then fell on to the next and so on like some comical Lycra-clad row of dominoes! The cars behind us must have been crying with laughter looking at that. We had a few crashes, but fortunately nothing really serious. One time, someone knocked into me, then I smashed into the bike in front and we all went down in a heap, but the great thing was that I fell on them, so it was a really soft landing!

One lovely moment happened when we were going through a small village and we stopped off for a break in the local church car park. This little old dear came up to us and said, 'I was going to go and get my hair done, but I am not now. I am going to donate the money to UK Youth instead.' Marvellous.

We finally made it to Paris and the sense of achievement and relief was overwhelming. Against all the odds, we had done it, and completing that second epic bike ride is something I will always be exceptionally proud of. I am also proud that I didn't let the charity down. For around four years, my whole life revolved totally around supporting the charity and these epic bike rides, the publicising of the centenary and trying to make sure that UK Youth was kept as prominent as it should be. I am very proud of that.

Without doubt it is one of my proudest personal achievements to get on that bike every day for 11 days straight. To anyone who hasn't done that, try cycling 120 miles in one day, then try it for two days, maybe five days, maybe even seven or eight days. But for 11 days? That was something else.

CHAPTER 25

THE CONSEQUENCES OF EPIC RIDES

Unfortunately, there was a more sinister side to the fluctuating weight issues I had after the second epic bike ride. What I have never admitted to the world is that those two epic rides affected my immune system and my health to such a degree that it threatened my life.

In the aftermath of the second epic bike ride, I was of course immensely proud of myself and the entire team. I was also absolutely wrecked, shattered, exhausted in a way that I had never been before. It was this all-consuming exhaustion that didn't seem to go away.

The broken collarbone took a long time to heal. The fracture became what is called a 'non-union', which happens when the ends of the bone rub together where the break is, to the extent that it never fully heals. It would take about two years for my collarbone to feel right again.

What I didn't know at the time was that the broken collarbone, the previous hamstring injury, the exhaustion, these were all relatively minor challenges compared to the most serious consequence of that huge bike ride. Lurking in my body was something far more menacing.

For some time after the epic Paris bike ride, I still wasn't feeling right. In fact, in some ways I was beginning to feel worse. At first, I put it down to the sheer scale of what we had done, the intensity of the ride and the fact that I pushed myself through too many pain barriers, which I shouldn't really have done. An event like that just takes everything out of you. Great bike athletes are on the edge of being ill all the time; they push it right to the edge, but they know exactly how to pull back. As an amateur, you don't have that same finesse; you just push and push and push out of sheer determination to complete your challenge. After the ride, I got every single cold, sniffle, flu bug, everything, for months. The simple fact is that I had lowered my immune system to such a degree that my body was open to attack.

This niggling sense of feeling not right, in a worrying way, just got worse. Now, please forgive me for sharing a little too much detail here, but it's important for you to know what happened.

As you get older, it is a known fact that – men especially – need to go to the bathroom more often. There, I've said it – I bet that's not something you thought you'd read in a Nigel Mansell book! Well, as much as we like to think of ourselves as invincible, Old Father Time has a habit of laying traps and, for men, one of these traps is this issue. Sometimes it is nothing more than an inconvenience; sometimes it can develop into something much more dangerous.

Well, while I was still recovering from the ride, I noticed this was happening to me more and more. I might play a round of golf and end up going in the bushes. Before you say it, no, it wasn't to find my stray left hook off the tee; it was for a pee. This often led to much merriment and sarcasm from my playing partners, which was taken in good spirits, but in private I was a little concerned. I knew something wasn't right, but I didn't want to worry Rosanne so I didn't say anything.

The situation continued to worsen, however, and I really began to feel ... it's hard to say exactly, but *I just didn't feel right*. I knew something was wrong. So I booked myself in to see a top specialist in Harley Street.

Now, your men's kit is very personal, so this was all rather awkward and embarrassing, but I felt I needed to know what was going on. So I took a deep breath and went in to see him. He did extensive tests and asked a lot of questions. He wasn't particularly chatty but I thought nothing of it. Then, after getting all the results back he rather sternly said, 'Sit down, Mr Mansell ...'

'Okay, so what's going on with all this then, please?' I asked.

'I need to operate, Mr Mansell.'

I was completely taken aback but in a way I was also very pleased I had found an expert who was so forthright; he knew what needed to be done and he was on it straight away. I had a busy schedule, so I wasn't sure when I could fit this operation in, but I said I could do it in a few months and then I'd be fully recuperated by the autumn, which then wouldn't affect my forthcoming heavy workload. So in my head I quickly rejigged my diary.

'Okay ... the problem is I have all this work going on for a little while, but maybe we could look at a couple of months ...'

'No, Mr Mansell,' he interrupted. 'I need to be perfectly clear here.' He explained that there was a severe obstruction internally, complicated by the historic injuries I carried, which had obviously damaged my body in a number of ways in those internal areas, not helped by the years of having heavy-duty seatbelts strapping me in so tightly to the cockpits, crushing my insides. Specifically, the epic bike ride – with the length of time spent on the hard saddle – had exacerbated the problem and created a major challenge.

'So, Mr Mansell, you need to decide. Your kidneys and liver are already being affected. In three more days you could be completely blocked and that could potentially lead to septicae-mia. If we don't sort this out and you do contract septicaemia, then there is a distinct possibility that you won't have to worry about anything.'

I almost didn't compute what he said.

'Pardon? What did you just say?'

'Mr Mansell,' he continued, 'the test results are very clear. You are at risk of contracting septicaemia. Given your medical history and the current status of this problem, if that takes hold you will be in a very serious and potentially irrecoverable situation.'

I took all this in and said, 'Right, this operation ... first thing tomorrow then!'

I walked out of that consultation in a state of shock, extremely upset, so I immediately went and phoned Rosanne. Before this appointment, I hadn't told her how ill I'd been feeling, so of course she was taken aback when I broke the news that I was being operated on immediately. I had some more tests and then was taken in for surgery. Despite the shock of the day before, I felt quite positive going into surgery and I had confidence in the experts around me. By way of reassurance, I did ask one of them about how routine this procedure was and kind of led him towards confirming it was all pretty straightforward – right?

'Yes, in theory. Although there are a number of complica-tions that can happen.'

Right, okay! Thanks for sweetening the pill.

Luckily, the operation was a success, although they weren't especially impressed by what they found – thanks! – given how mangled much of my body is, and some elements of the surgery were trickier than normal. However, these guys were complete experts so I was cleaned out, stitched up and sent back to the ward. I was told I'd have to stay in hospital for about four days before being allowed home.

Sadly, some complications did set in, which started to put a strain on my heart. Thankfully, the medical staff were on the ball and had some very powerful drugs to combat the problem, so I was doped up on those. Sadly for me, I had to take them for six weeks. Now, bearing in mind I am the world's cheapest date – I don't drink and if I ever have a tipple, I am drunk after about half a whisky – these powerful drugs played absolute havoc with me (but were entirely necessary).

Eventually, I was given the all-clear to go home and headed to Gatwick with Rosanne. As I walked through the airport I felt really strange; my head was swimming and my eyesight seemed peculiar. I said to Rosanne, 'Please hold my hand, don't let go of me ...' I looked out of the window where there was a 747 being boarded and, to my amazement, I could swear that the plane's wings were flapping like a bird. The hallucinations were horrendous, really unsettling.

After two weeks on these strong drugs I felt like I didn't want to live anymore. The medication was so powerful, the side effects were so distressing at times, that it just sucked the life out of me. Just horrible. I actually thought to myself, *If this is what life is going to be like, I don't want to live anymore.*

I had to stay on this medication for six weeks and thankfully the team managed to get matters under control, so in retrospect hitting the bug hard with those extreme drugs had worked.

I did suffer a relapse a year later when the infection reappeared, but luckily it was quickly dealt with. Obviously, they monitored me for a while after, but I was, in theory, out of the woods. Both in medical terms and the next time I'd go on the golf course.

CHAPTER 26

EXCITING TIMES AHEAD

As well as the wonderful Woodbury Park, we have had other business interests since my retirement from motorsport. One is a karting track in Honiton, Devon, known as Mansell Raceway. The site came up for sale and it was a lovely spot which needed preserving for the benefit of karting going forward. The track is in a rural location right next to the airfield at Dunkeswell. It is 1000 metres long and has been designed and evolved so that it offers a very exciting and safe place to race karts. We have made it one of the safest tracks in England: the surface is very rewarding in that it is not bumpy, so it doesn't damage the expensive karts or promote people-banging; and we have a strict regime down there that encourages very fast but clean racing.

The clerk of the course and the RAC have a very good view of that etiquette and we stamp down on reckless driving straight away. In my opinion, over the years karting has got out of hand, so we pride ourselves on stopping racers being too aggressive. Not only is there the danger of someone getting hurt, but it's also a question of the amount of damage they can do to very costly machinery, which is prohibitively expensive for most of the parents trying to encourage their children. They rightly don't want to go racing and see their children exposed to unnecessary risk and, secondly, nobody wants to have hundreds if not thousands of pounds of crash damage when it is avoidable.

I have to say it hasn't been the easiest of businesses at times, though, because we have encountered opposition locally to some of our plans and ideas. We have had many difficulties over the years with planning and restrictions on noise and noise abatement orders. For me that is rather bizarre considering we are located on the side of an airport! We have worked in collaboration with the planners and hope to ensure it is a business that provides employment and gives people a lot of pleasure. I think it is a great facility and I am very proud of what we have done there. The business is holding its own and will hopefully continue to move forward.

Over the years I have collected some fabulous mementoes of my career – helmets, overalls, trophies, my awards, medals, even cars. There is also a photograph dedicated to me by Juan Manuel Fangio, which is something that I cherish very much. Originally, we kept everything at Woodbury and it was very popular with guests and also fans who travelled to see it. Obviously, when we sold Woodbury we needed to find a new home for this collection of memorabilia, although for some time they kept it at the hotel because it was bringing in some business. There were interested parties we talked to about housing the memorabilia, but the investment and security around the collection wasn't right so we decided to go it alone.

Eventually, the plan was to house the collection in our own permanent location. It was actually Leo who came up with the idea when he found a building in Jersey that would be perfect. He'd discovered this old art-deco building that was in need of some TLC and it was clear that, with the right restoration, it could be perfect. Better still, there was room downstairs for a sizeable car showroom. In the past, I have run a Ferrari dealership and suchlike, so this was already a business model we were comfortable with.

So we bought the building and the plan was to have a dealership downstairs and the Mansell Collection exhibited above. We spent a lot of time and a huge amount of money restoring the listed building to its former glory and now it looks wonderful. Then we were approached by Mitsubishi about opening a franchise dealership and I was really intrigued. The obvious angle given my background would have been to open a Ferrari or Aston Martin dealership, something high-end, but we wanted to buy and sell cars that pretty much anybody could afford. Mitsubishi have a great reputation and their products are fantastic, so we were delighted.

Part of the franchise dictates that we have to have our own workshops, so we joined forces with a local full-service centre. We have a pristine workshop, state of the art, where we can service and repair cars. We also acquired a petrol station just across the road, that needed extensive modernising. However, despite all the delays and growing pains, we now have an excellent site down there; all the different elements are up and running. Over these past few years, Leo has grown in business acumen and matured into a first-class businessman, something I am extremely proud of. He has really come into his own and done a brilliant job. I have total trust in him with the business, which is marvellous.

These days, I like to have more leisure time every now and then. One part of my life that I couldn't have written about when I wrote my first book over two decades ago was the notion of getting older. Of course, back then I was in my forties so I wasn't exactly in the first flush of youth, but I was extremely fit from racing and, although I was carrying injuries, I was as strong as a bull.

As I write this, my next birthday will see me turn 64 years young. Let me offer you some advice: getting old is not for weenies! Getting old can be one of the most frightening things in the world. I made my name in a supremely alpha-male job; being a racing driver is a very physical, male-orientated, adrenaline- and testosterone-filled world to inhabit. There is a paddock full of men absolutely obsessed with winning – drivers who will do anything to be champion, and team owners who want to smash the competition into the tarmac.

When you retire from a career like that, the transition from chasing pole position all around the world to not racing anymore can be a shock. I was playing competitive golf and running various business interests, so for a lot of the time I was too busy to feel any void. As you have seen, I raced touring cars, sports cars and, of course, Le Mans, so it wasn't that I stopped racing overnight, but after the biggie at Le Mans in 2010, that was me done, all over. It's a strange feeling. I don't miss the danger, or the politics or the travel. I do miss the excitement, and the feeling of stepping up on top of the podium, of course.

I am relatively comfortable with that part of getting older, if I am honest. What does unsettle me is the physical change. As race drivers, we were all proud to be very fit, training most days, eating well, working hard in the gym. We felt almost invincible at times; not just me, we all were very fit indeed. However, you cannot fight Mother Nature. You will get older and your body will not work as well as it did when you were 20, 30 or 40. We are all fighting this constant dynamic of realising that the mind might be young but the body is inexorably getting older.

Sometimes it catches you off-guard: you might do something as simple as jumping over a fence to retrieve the dog's ball, thinking nothing of it, but when you land your knees or ankles crunch under the impact. You might feel your joints ache more if it is wet or cold. So you adapt and become more careful, and constantly remind yourself how easy it is now to get hurt. I broke my neck in '77 at Brands Hatch and even to this day, when I move my head and neck in a certain way, I am very wary of a recurrence of that injury. When you have broken your neck in a serious place you can become very fretful and worried that something is going to go wrong again.

More recently, I have also had some problems with my teeth. When you suffer big accidents in a racing car and maybe hit a wall, your teeth and gums come together and it damages the nerves and kills them off so they have to be drilled out. A few years ago, I had to have a tremendous amount of work done on the root canals of many teeth. Like the Mansell Lesion, the doctors and dentists raised more than a few eyebrows because at first they said they would all have to come out, the damage was irreparable. I found a dentist doing very experimental work, who was able to operate and save the teeth, which has been noted anonymously as another test case. It's that Mansell guinea pig again!

Not long before I started work on this book, I had a very scary episode when I fell down the stairs in the middle of the night. I was suffering sleep deprivation through pain from some of my old injuries and so the doctor recommended I take sleeping pills. We still don't know exactly how it happened, but I was evidently trying to come downstairs when I just fell headfirst down the staircase. I sustained severe bruising and carpet burns on the way down; I was a right mess. The funny thing is, I can remember the whole thing as though I was dreaming. I felt as if I was in a dream and I remember gambolling down the stairs and shouting in pain. It was really weird. How I didn't break my neck or end up killing myself, I don't know. I was very lucky. The bruising and cuts healed, of course, but it really unsettled me because I realised how vulnerable I felt. I am paying a very high price for the world I worked and lived in, and the way I used to drive cars, because when I was on track, I didn't have any reserves left – I gave it everything, all the time, every race.

What I have learned is that you just have to reprogramme your mind and accept your limitations, then work out how to get through your daily business with these new parameters. It's no use moaning about it; some of your ailments will be there for good, so get on with it. You have to manage your body because your mind wants to do all sorts of things, as it can still remember when you were 20. Each morning I get up (slowly!) and take a concoction of pills and potions for my various war wounds. Spending several winter months in Florida helps, as the cold won't bite into my joints there. Everything is relative. Recently they cancelled a golf tournament over in Belleair because the temperature was only going to reach 50 degrees Fahrenheit and it was considered too cold! The warm Florida sun and easy lifestyle really help with the aches and pains.

The doctors sometimes revisit my old injuries and suggest new plans of action. I can't bend my big toe and I have to have implants in every single shoe I possess because of how my foot was all busted up in 1991. At one point recently they wanted to put 16 screws, two plates and a steel bar in my foot to work around the damage that still troubles me. I asked them what the percentages of success for this type of operation were, and in my opinion they weren't that good, so I decided to leave that one.

Some of my ailments are peculiar to an ex-racing driver. When you are pulling high Gs for years, as well as the consequences of specific accidents, your body has an unusual amount of wear and tear for its age. I am not alone in this; it is common for all ex-racing drivers to suffer in a variety of ways and it can put us at an increased risk of problems such as arthritis and osteoporosis, all sorts of complications. As I've mentioned, back in my early days, we didn't have proper seats to support us, so that didn't help. Both my shoulders dislocate very easily because I was squashed into steel cockpits for so many years that the joints have too much wear and tear in them. Same goes for my knees. I have had to have many operations since I retired for complications arising from racing injuries and wear and tear – hence the bolt and titanium anchor in my shoulder for life (my left shoulder is far worse then my right because we predominantly went round right-hand corners on clockwise tracks). It is maintenance, a consequence of the profession.

I lost a friend recently who was only 59. It's tough when that happens; it really makes you question yourself. I try to find a positive in everything and in this case you have to say you need to live each day to the full – it's a cliché but it's true. Plan your next trip, your next idea, your next business, *your next adventure*. Make the most of the fact that it wasn't you whose time was up.

The thing that frightens me most about getting older is not dying – it is *not being able to live*. I dread the possibility of no longer being mobile, of not being physically capable of enjoying life. I don't expect to race cars at 200mph anymore, but I just want to be able to do simple stuff, like playing with the grandkids, a round of golf, walking the dog, strolling on the beach with Rosanne.

I think all of us can be guilty of not making the most of the good times. Every day that you are healthy is a blessing. I know that sounds like a platitude but I truly believe it. We are all guilty of taking things for granted, especially our health. If you have that taken away from you, you realise you need to embrace life. When you have your mortality touched in the most incredible, intense way, such as when Rosanne was so ill for so long, it is ultimately a good lesson, because it makes you realise what goes on in life. It fascinates me that a near-death experience can make you appreciate *life* so much more. Never take your health for granted and enjoy every moment when you are well, because it is a blessing.

As you know, I like to have fun. So I try to find humour in getting old as much as I can. It's not always possible when my body is creaking under the strain of a particularly cold or wet day and yet my mind tells me I am still the same as that driver taking the world title in 1992. However, you can find some very funny moments if you have the right mental attitude. I played in a fourball the other day and on the first tee the conversation kicked off when someone said, 'Right, well, how old are you guys?' They went round and one was 78, one was 76, another just 50 and then me, 62. Then the 50-year-old turned to the 78-year-old and said, 'Can you still get it up?' I've never had such a laugh and the old boy was giggling away as well. What can you say to that?

Apart from good humour, another obvious way to fight the ageing process is to keep fit. Sounds self-evident, of course, but it is important. If you can keep your body in good shape through your twenties, thirties and forties, then you will have a much better life expectancy and better quality of life in your fifties, sixties, seventies and beyond.

There is one massive benefit of getting older and it is by far the most joyful: becoming a grandparent. In 2008, Rosanne and I became grandparents when our daughter Chloe gave birth to a wonderful little boy. Becoming a grandparent is just the most fantastic feeling in the world. I am incredibly proud of Chloe and her son is just a joy. In my opinion, the mother is the key to the grandchildren, because she knows what the daughter or son is going through having a child. The bond that Chloe has with Rosanne is truly fantastic now.

In principle, the responsibility is supposed to be less when you look after a grandchild rather than your own child, but as Chloe and her son lived with us for a period of time, we felt like we were more than just grandparents to him. It is a very special relationship. I would say this little lad is probably my soulmate, because he confides in me and he tells me things that are so enlightening and wonderful. At the time of writing, he is still only eight, but he is a wise young man who listens intently and learns voraciously.

We play a lot of golf together! We have started playing tournaments and, in late 2014, I am very proud to say that we won the 'Best Gross Score' at the adult/junior stroke-play competition at Belleair Country Club in Florida. He is a very special little boy. He told me that when he is older and is a golf pro, he wants me to be his caddy. What a joy that would be! I am now proud to say I have two other grandchildren as well, one each for Greg and Leo. Greg has a dear little son, so he is very happy, and Leo gave us our first granddaughter and she is delightful.

I am also really enjoying watching how people change when they become a parent; it's wonderful to see. What is also pleasing is noticing how your children start to acknowledge that maybe their parents did know a few things after all. You try to instil in them advice and ideas, but often you don't think any of it is going in, especially as they're growing up, when they don't always want to hear: 'Oh yeah, we know Dad, you cycled uphill to work and uphill back home as well.' Family joke. However, Chloe has recently said to me that she's been thinking about quite a few things we've said to her over the years and it's really starting to make sense. She was praising us for our advice, which was just lovely.

In case you think that you might feel sorry for this ex-Formula 1 driver, don't panic! My competitive spirit is as strong as ever. Since retiring from motorsport I have just channelled that will to win into the game of golf. I started playing golf during my racing career and it was always a brilliant escape, such a tranquil and yet competitive way to relax. Once I started to improve, it wasn't long before I became completely fascinated with the game, the techniques, the tournaments. I'm pretty much obsessed.

Golf has also given me many wonderful friendships and I've been privileged to play alongside some of the greatest names in the game. I took part in a few pro-celebrity tournaments, which were invariably great fun. One of the greatest honours was to play with the legendary Seve Ballesteros. It was fascinating and wonderful to be around him on the course. He used to carry photos of all his major wins around with him, and whichever hotel he was staying at would therefore have pictures of all these amazing triumphs, so the whole ambience of success travelled with him. Very clever. He was a fabulous person, a wonderful human being, incredibly softly spoken, charismatic and one of the greatest talents the world of golf has ever seen. A beautiful man.

To play with these people and learn from them has been a joy. Of course, developing Woodbury was also a great experience and, as I've said, some of the professionals I've just mentioned helped me improve that course.

I've had some incredibly fun times on the golf course, too. In the mid-1980s, I was in South Africa for a race and I spent some time with Mark McNulty and Tony Johnstone, both great golfers and friends of ours. One of their friends had a private jet so they said, 'How about we fly down to the Kruger Park, play some golf down there, have a barbecue, maybe see some of the animals and then come back?' That sounded fantastic so off we went. Things seemed to be so much easier to do in the 1980s!

We each had the tallest caddies I've ever seen, they must have been about seven foot tall! Anyway, we played a few holes and the heat was incredible, it was over 40 degrees. Then we came to a beautiful water-hole par 3, which I could see had some hippos in a nearby river, which was not fenced off.

We were having a good laugh so I said, 'Let's have a picture together.' I was standing in the middle of Mark and Tony when we all heard some strange grunting noises from behind, then the next thing I know my two friends were shouting, 'Run! Run! Run!' I thought they were pulling my leg until I saw them and the caddies running off down the fairway. I looked behind to find a number of massive, angry hippos charging us (they'd been startled by the camera's flash). Ignorance is bliss and, to be fair, I've never had a problem with hippos on a golf course before. It was a good job I was fit because I ran like the wind!

Happily, we managed to get away safely and were able to have a good laugh about it, but in fact it was pretty dangerous. Anyway, we carried on playing in this searing heat and my left foot, which I'd injured in karting years before, started to swell up and became very uncomfortable in my shoe. Mark asked me what size I was and it turned out we were all within half a size of each other. So I put his left shoe on, but then Tony asked if his shoe might help. We ended up swapping shoes and, to cut a long story short, walked off down the fairway each with an odd pair of shoes on. We looked so strange.

A few holes later, we played by what I thought was a lake. My ball landed about 30 feet away from the water's edge so, as I was hot and my feet hurt, I decided to dip my toes in the water to cool them down. I'd done this for only a few seconds when my huge caddy rugby tackled me and pulled me away from the water's edge, just as a crocodile lunged out to try to grab me. What was I thinking? I had no idea of the danger I was in. After that I just thought, *What on earth is going to happen next!*

A few holes later, Mark was on the tee and we were standing nearby when the sprinklers went off, completely soaking all three of us. By now we were just laughing so much, it was just the most funny and bizarre round of golf you could ever wish to play.

We ended up getting a little late after all our adventures, so Mark was driving really fast to get out of the park before it was closed for the night and we'd be locked in. What do you know, we then got pulled over by the park police. You couldn't make this up! This huge policeman was really laying into Mark for speeding, telling him off and starting to write out a ticket.

Mark said, 'Oh, come on, give us a break please,' but this guy wasn't interested. Then Mark said, 'Do you know who this guy is?' and pointed to Tony.

'I'm not interested in who he is,' the policeman snapped back.

'That's Tony Johnstone, professional golfer, and I'm Mark McNulty . . .'

'Not interested.'

Mark tried again. 'Okay, well, we've also got our friend who is a Formula 1 racing driver, he's won all sorts of races . . .'

The policeman immediately looked up.

'What's his name?'

'Nigel Mansell.'

This guy's whole demeanour changed instantly, much to the astonishment and delight of Mark and Tony. This massive policeman, a Dutch Afrikaner, just melted and became the friendliest guy you could wish to meet. It turned out he was a huge F1 fan and he was so chuffed to chat to me and ask a few questions. He ended up just giving us a verbal warning, so that was yet another lucky escape.

That day was one of the most extraordinary times of my life. I tell you what, we laughed and had so much fun. Great guys, great friends and thank you for all the fabulous memories.

I don't just play golf to get some fresh air, however. I like to win. I love to compete. Of the thousands of rounds of golf I've played over the years, I am extremely proud of a few achievements in particular. The first was when I managed to play in the Australian Open alongside my good friend Greg Norman in 1988 at the Royal Sydney Club. At the time, my handicap was 1.9 and I was given a wildcard entry by the Australian Golf Union. Some people criticised that and virtually everyone suggested it could be a very embarrassing day on the greens for me, given that I was playing in one of the world's top professional tournaments. Most suggested I would be lucky to break 90.

They'd obviously never met me. I admit to taking a double brandy the night before and, of course, I was nervous on the first tee. My first tee shot wasn't great but I controlled my nerves and started to improve, saving par on that opening hole. When I birdied the fourth, my name climbed up on to the leaderboard. I was so proud! A challenging front nine saw me take 39, which was a great score. I worked really hard for the rest of the round and, at the eighteenth, I managed a fantastic approach shot to the green that finished inches from the hole, giving me a birdie and a final score of 77, only five over par. Ian Woosnam, who was top 50 that year and soon to be world number 1, shot a 75.

On the second day my old racing injuries bit back and my left arm in particular was extremely painful and inflexible. Worse still, on the seventh I choked. I swung but I was so tense that I duck-hooked it straight into a bush. I made a double bogey but after that I calmed down and ended up playing okay. That was the biggest choke I have ever suffered, including all my time in motorsport. It was because I felt naked; I didn't have a helmet on, I wasn't in my overalls and I wasn't hiding in a car going past everyone at 200mph. I was incredibly visible, exposed. So it is the first time I felt what a professional golfer really experiences when they choke. My second round came in at 86 but that first score of 77 was something I was hugely proud of. What was that they said about not breaking 90? Hopefully this vindicated my sponsors' exemption, but either way it is one of the most fantastic memories I have in the game of golf.

I also played in other pro tournaments, such as the Balearic Open and the South Australian Open, and I've played at the qualifying for the Senior PGA Tour. However, the second highlight of my golf career was in 2004 at Harlech in north Wales. On my third round, among 80 other golfers and professionals, I shot a 66, the third lowest score of the day, putting me in the top half of the field. I was also super-proud of the support of my caddy Leo, and also that of Greg.

Another golfing achievement is the World Senior Championships I won in Albuquerque in 2014. A further highlight of my golfing career came just as I was writing the first edition of this book when I won the Strokeplay Open at Belleair

Country Club, again in 2014. I've also recently bagged two aces, as well as an albatross on a par five. And how can I ever forget winning that tournament with my beautiful grandson? Wow. I am also hugely proud to be a member of Royal & Ancient Golf Club of St Andrews, the best golfing organisation in the world, custodians of the game and a wonderful body of men.

It's not all glorious wins on a golf course, obviously. I haven't escaped the two most dreadful diseases in golf. The first is the flippin' shanks, where you shank a ball from nowhere and hit it sideways when you are playing quite well; the other one is the yips on the putter. I have, very sadly, in competition had a seven on one green where I got close to the pin and then yipped it round the hole for three or four putts. The people playing with me thought I was taking the mickey, but I'd lost my head. These totally involuntary twitches come from the brain to the elbow to the wrist, and every time you go to stroke the ball into the hole, just as you are about to hit it, your wrist twitches and opens or closes the face of the putter and you miss the hole from six inches. It is the most involuntary sabotage.

Golf for me has saved my life. Through my whole career, it has been a grounding influence, and my set of clubs has travelled with me all over the globe. I have had so much pleasure playing some of the greatest courses in the world with some of the game's great names. It's a complete contrast to a racetrack, which is full of noise, full of hustle and bustle and cameras – when you are playing a private game of golf, it is very tranquil, you are at one with Mother Nature. But the strong competitive element is very exciting; it keeps me sharp.

I'm actually more fired up to play golf than ever. I've had little snippets of the skill level I used to have years ago and I want more of it. The only trouble is I am older and more fragile now, so naturally I haven't got the same physical attributes, but mentally I am there, the appetite has come back. Golf challenges me, gives me great laughs, introduces me to some wonderful people and tests me with more than a few moments of panic and frustration, of course, but that is all part of the game. Golf fascinates me. For example, during a round of 18 holes, you are only actually 'playing' – as in swinging the club – for around seven minutes. Yet the round might take you three or four hours. That is an astonishing statistic.

I am lucky to live very near to two fabulous golf clubs. Belleair Country Club in Clearwater is a home from home. It has two championship courses, the people are really nice and friendly and supportive, and we have a wonderful time there. I enjoy my time playing at La Moye Golf Club when I am back home in Jersey.

Golf is also now my main way of staying fit. It keeps you young in so many ways. The stress on my wrists isn't ideal but the competitive atmosphere, the flexibility you need, the long walks – it's fantastic. I need to wear strong strapping on my left wrist to play a round but that's okay. I don't let any worries about getting older plague me for too long. I live life to the full if I can; I find humour in as much as possible and I am blessed that, although I might ache and creak a bit, I am still here.

Besides, getting older has its advantages. I enjoy being wiser, more mature, more mellow. Certain things in life don't bother me like they used to. Certain decisions come easily because I have seen what to do in the past and learned from my mistakes. It is an unavoidable part of life that we all make mistakes. That is understandable and forgiveable. What is not okay is repeating those mistakes. Age gives you wisdom, the knowledge gleaned from yours and other people's mistakes, and I find that wiser knowledge invigorating.

Let me finish up with another anecdote that starts on the golf course. I was playing with some guys and the age question came up again. When I told them I was in my early sixties, they were genuinely surprised. They said, 'No way, you look about early fifties!' They were really shocked and I was, of course, extremely flattered. Made my day, that did. So with this recently in my mind, I had to go to the specialist to get some X-rays to check over the various bits and pieces of my body that have been mashed up over the years. Sometimes they see X-rays and go, 'Oh my word, your neck is broken!' and I have to reassure them, 'Oh, that's just an old injury.' Anyway, this one particular time they did the tests and the specialist pulled up the X-rays on screen. And then he said, 'How old did you say you were again?'

I puffed out my chest, anticipating that the recent compliment on the golf course was about to be repeated.

Crikey, it's happening again. I must be looking good for my age.

'Thank you for asking, doctor. You may be surprised to know I am 62, as it happens . . .'

'Blimey, yes I am. Looking at these X-rays, the wear and tear in your joints looks like you are about 162!'

Chapter 27

Honest, Sporting Competition

I love winning. I love competing. I always have and, no doubt, I always will. Whether that is winning a race in the lower formulas, becoming a world champion, playing snooker with a friend or leaving a golf course knowing that I've played a cracking round, I just enjoy the feeling of competing and doing well. During my racing career, I think it's fair to say that I developed a reputation for being very competitive, for never giving up, for trying to squeeze the very last ounce out of my car and my body in trying to win, even if a victory seemed completely against the odds. That was how I loved to race and I was blessed that fans of the sport seemed to enjoy watching me do that.

I first felt competitive as young as five or six, participating in school sports such as running and soccer. Even then, I noticed that I wanted to be as good as, and eventually perhaps even better than, everyone else. I didn't realise at that young age that my competitive spirit brings out the best in me, but that is something that I came to recognise and revel in at a later age.

Of course, choosing to pursue a career as a professional

sportsman has meant that I surrounded myself with other individuals who were also intensely competitive. I've never met a world champion or, indeed, a world-class athlete who isn't fiercely competitive. I have never had a problem with that, in fact it fuelled my desire to win and be the best.

As long as I have been involved in sport, I have enjoyed competing. My golf game is doing very well and that is something I am proud of. One aspect of golf that I love is that I can play a round on my own, with no one to compete against other than the 18 holes and the game known as Old Man Par, and yet I still feel very competitive, all alone on the course, with just Mother Nature and the scorecard to battle against.

Recently I was runner-up in a high-profile tournament to a very accomplished golfer, albeit someone that I felt I should've beaten. A friend later asked me if I was pleased with second place and, I have to be honest, I wasn't really, no. As long as I can do my absolute best then I will be satisfied; I prefer to win, that's a given, but I always endeavour to do my best, first and foremost. It's when you don't do your best that it is hard to accept, when you think to yourself, *I should have left nothing out there and I could've made a difference.* As a competitor that is hard to accept.

Sometimes, of course, you do have to acknowledge that there is someone out there who is better than you; when that happens you just have to go away and practise and hope that one day you will be better than them. That takes an enormous amount of dedication, particularly at a world level, but that sense of competition was always something I found completely compelling.

Competitiveness doesn't just apply to world champions or high-profile athletes, of course. You can compete at an amateur level and still enjoy that dynamic. Just a few weeks ago I was playing backgammon against a gentleman who was very seasoned and skilled at the game (which I had never played before). I found myself playing into the early hours, not just because I enjoyed his company very much but also because I didn't like losing and so I kept on playing, learning the game and *competing* until I eventually was able to beat him (well, a few times anyway!).

Not long after the first edition of this book was published, Lewis Hamilton secured his third world championship – his second consecutive title. As the Formula 1 world prepares itself for the first race of the 2016 season, Mercedes have announced that they will let their two drivers, Lewis and Nico Rosberg, compete against each other for the title, and that team position will only bring out the best in their respective competitive spirits. Fans of F1 like to see competition, they like to see drivers battling against each other – that's how I raced and that's how I like to see other drivers race.

As I write, the pre-season testing for the 2016 season suggests that Mercedes will again be the team to beat. I can only congratulate Lewis on a job very well done in 2015 and also compliment Mercedes on producing such an incredible race car for him and Nico to drive. The reliability they enjoy, indeed the performance consistency that all modern F1 drivers enjoy, compared to yesteryear is remarkable and Mercedes are certainly breaking all sorts of records in that area.

Cynics sometimes argue that if a car is relatively easy to drive and never breaks down then that somehow diminishes the achievement of modern drivers. How competitive do you need to be in those circumstances? There is no doubt, as I touched on earlier in this book, that reliability in the modern era is a world apart from in my day, that's undeniable. However, you can only race what you are given and Lewis has done a very fine job of that. That maxim applies not only to him, but also for any past world champion. Jenson Button is perhaps the best example, he did the most superb job in the car he had in 2009, he maximised that opportunity and then the moment was gone, he didn't have the opportunity again. Whatever car you have got and no matter how much tech you have at your disposal, you have still got to drive the car well and – crucially – *compete*.

Of course, this applies to all racing drivers, not just those at the front of the grid, but what differentiates the world champions from those who win a few races or maybe never win a race at all is the ability to know what it takes to compete and win *consistently*, to produce competitive drives over the course of a whole season, to stay dedicated, to remain competitive mentally and physically, no matter how difficult the circumstances are. These drivers' degree of understanding of what it takes to become a world champion sets them apart. Lewis has shown that ability; all world champions do. If you can't do that, then you will not be world champion and if you haven't got the competitive edge to try, then you shouldn't be there at all.

Any driver needs to be given the credit for making the opportunity work for them and any world champion can demonstrate in a great car how well they can win the championship – the fact is that Lewis has done that very, very well. He is at the top of his game, success breeds success, he has the confidence, with three world titles under his belt now and I don't see any issue or problem preventing him from getting a fourth title. Both Lewis and Nico are in a wonderful environment, with a fabulous car, a great team and the opportunity to make history. To their credit, they both obviously recognise this and know that this is a very important moment in their careers and I have no doubt they will both fight hard to maximise that opportunity. It is up to the other drivers and teams to compete with Mercedes, and I am pleased to see that Ferrari in particular seem to be closing the gap. More drivers having a chance of winning races can only be a good thing for the sport.

True competitors stay hungry. They win world titles and then want to come back and win again and again and again. That fire in them never subsides. Some drivers are fortunate enough to have the opportunity to defend a title, others not so fortunate. But what I can say is that to win two world titles consecutively takes an enormous amount of competitive spirit, dedication, determination, will to win . . . It is a huge effort.

Perhaps the ultimate symbol of success for any competitor – certainly in motorsport and definitely in my experience – is standing on the top step of the podium. Any podium place is a great achievement, but I'm not going to pretend that being the winner on the top step isn't far better. You've battled in the race, there are so many things that could go wrong, but somehow you've brought your car over the finish line first for victory. Then you head, quite quickly, to the podium, your body is still full of adrenalin from the effort of the race and yet at the same time you are physically absolutely exhausted. When you get up on to the top step, it means everything, you hold your breath and hope that the moment is real, the fans are in front of you cheering and shouting their support, other drivers shake your hand and you are given the trophy.

But yet, even in that moment of glory, a small part of you is still worrying that the car might not pass scrutiny, because certainly in my era there were times when the complex rules and regulations did see cars excluded, even after the race was completed. So that is in the back of your mind to some degree. However, the overwhelming sensation is one of pure, unadulterated elation. You've won, you've done the best job in the world, you are top dog that day – maybe you've accumulated valuable points towards the dream of the world title – it's fabulous. Then they start to play your national anthem and if you are a staunch royalist and proud countryman like myself, the elation goes up another notch. It is a feeling like no other. The hairs stand up on end all over your body, it is like an electric flash. You almost feel as if a vacuum has sucked every little bit of energy out of your body and then in a split second this mass of adrenalin and emotion is injected back into you. After the anthem, you still have to do your press conference and chat to sponsors and fans – it is incredibly tiring, but such a wonderful feeling. I feel very blessed to have had that experience on many occasions. For me, as a competitor, those are very, very happy memories indeed.

So yes, I was innately competitive and strongly so, but a very significant part of that feeling inside me also came from the fans. The fans were everything, I didn't need to be told that, they were just as important, if not more so, than the race itself. The fans support you whether you win, lose or crash. What the fans want is an honest competitor who they can watch and enjoy and go on this crazy rollercoaster with. If they like who you are and what you stand for, and the energy that you put into each drive, then the fans are just incredible. I was very blessed with the most remarkable fanbase, perhaps even greater than Lewis has now, and I am delighted that we were able to have achieved what we did.

I often use the so-called 'Royal We' when I talk and that is because throughout my career I have always seen my achievements and triumphs as a team effort. So when I say 'we are very pleased to have been able to win today', then I am referring to the many people who have made that possible: my family, the engineers, the team, sponsors – it is such a team sport. And one of *the* single biggest factors – if not the biggest – in that is the fans.

Silverstone 1987 is a case in point. Coming back from 29

seconds behind to beat Piquet is one of my greatest wins and I am very blessed that many observers regard that as one of the great F1 wins of all time. And do you know what? The fans won me that race. I knew I was up against it, but I felt their support, heard those cheers, that surge of energy and I just thought, *What the hell!* Then I saw that Mexican wave going around the circuit faster than I was driving and I had to keep up with that, didn't I! How can you not be competitive in a situation like that? I simply had to win that race. The fans made that happen. They are absolutely a crucial part of any team. They were certainly an integral and cherished part of *my* team and I cannot thank them enough.

AFTERWORD

I 've had the most wonderful time sharing these stories with you. When I sat down and started work on this book, I really had to think long and hard about how much of myself to put into these pages. I wanted people to feel as if they had spoken with me about my life, chatted about the racing but also got to know the real me away from the track. It's been a very emotional experience which has brought back many fabulous memories, a few unpleasant ones, admittedly, but mostly I have been completely overwhelmed by the process of revisiting these special moments in time.

During the course of writing this book, I have occasionally popped over to the Mansell museum before opening time, just to have a wander round and look at all the fabulous memories captured in that room. As each chapter has evolved, I've found those memories coming back to life. Just yesterday I stood next to the Williams FW14 that took me to the world title, and I have to say, to this day, it still looks like an absolutely fabulous car to drive. I can almost smell the pit lane and hear those wonderful engines roaring past when I stand next to my old car. Sometimes, I can hear the buzz of the garage or the chaotic noises from across the pit lanes. Maybe an old rival will flash across my mind, or perhaps I will suddenly find myself in the middle of a certain overtaking manoeuvre at 180mph in some far-flung country. At times, I almost check my fingernails for oil. I was lucky enough to have had a very exhilarating career flying around the world and racing very fast cars, but I can see now that I was often too busy rushing around with my hair on fire to enjoy the journey. Standing in the museum, I can now finally pause for breath and soak it all in.

I am extremely proud of my career in motorsport, proud of winning two world titles back-to-back and of all the amazing races and triumphs that I was able to secure. Wonderful. I've also noticed how, with the passage of time, the moments that stand out are not the intrigue, the politics and the complexities of the sport, but the people, the races, the cars, the fans.

I know that F1 has changed beyond measure to become what it is today and I am proud to say that it is still the greatest motorsport in the world. I remain an absolutely avid fan. As for my part in that history – well, I believe records are just set as a benchmark, and I was fortunate enough to post some good examples of those. Although, as time ticks by, I am dropping down the order, I am still there in the history books in a number of ways. Even when all my records are finally overtaken, hopefully people will still remember me winning two consecutive World Championships, my five wins on British soil, the outrageous overtaking manoeuvres, my passion for the sport and my will to win. I also hope that my life outside of racing – which has been just wonderful – has been similarly fascinating to you.

I know I am one of the luckiest people to be alive, not just because of the accidents but also because of my more recent health problems. I have been close to death a number of times, on and off the track. I have sustained terrible injuries and been hit by extremely challenging illnesses, but I've always come back from them, I've always – eventually – walked away, at least from hospital; many of my fellow drivers, and also friends outside of motorsport, have not been so fortunate.

People often chat to me and ask me what was my biggest success. That one is easy: still being alive and surviving the journey. I have been very lucky in that there are not many people around who have broken their back more than once, broken their neck, both wrists, feet and various other bones, so I count my blessings to have had the career I've had and enjoyed the success I've had and still be here today. I feel very lucky that I have survived. For large parts of my career, I didn't honestly believe I would see my 60th birthday. I just didn't think I'd live that long, so I am really thrilled to have achieved that milestone.

Rosanne and I have each had our challenges, as you now know, both professionally and personally. We've had to bounce back many times, but that is what we are like as a couple and as a family. I am proud of the way that we have done that (even if at times it felt like we were on some kind of emotional rollercoaster). We are like any other family in that respect. Whatever challenges life throws in your way, you have to just keep going. You have to bounce back, whether that is from the loss of a loved one, not winning a World Championship, being seriously injured in an accident, a friend letting you down ... all these challenges come our way and it is vitally important that you bounce back. You can do it. *Bounce back.*

Sometimes, I look at all the memorabilia in the museum – the trophies, the posters, the racing suits, helmets and cars – and I have to pinch myself. Some of those events were a long time ago and recounting them for this book has brought them vividly back to the front of my mind. Sometimes I stand in that room, looking around at all that history, and think, *Wow, did that really happen?*

So, if you find yourself in Jersey one day and fancy an afternoon reminiscing about the days when racing drivers sat in bare metal cockpits and drove with broken backs, come along to the museum and have a look. You never know, you might even bump into a crazy ex-racing driver ...

INDEX

Index

Index